HISPANIC CHILDREN AND YOUTH
IN THE UNITED STATES

REFERENCE BOOKS
ON FAMILY ISSUES
(VOL. 20)

GARLAND REFERENCE LIBRARY
OF SOCIAL SCIENCE
(VOL. 608)

Reference Books
On Family Issues

1. Resources for Early Childhood: *An Annotated Bibliography and Guide for Educators, Librarians, Health Care Professionals, and Parents*, Hannah Nuba Scheffler, General Editor

2. Problems of Early Childhood: *An Annotated Bibliography and Guide*, by Elisabeth S. Hirsch

3. Children and Divorce: *An Annotated Bibliography and Guide*, by Evelyn B. Hausslein

4. Stepfamilies: *A Guide to the Sources and Resources*, by Ellen J. Gruber

5. Experiencing Adolescents: *A Sourcebook for Parents, Teachers, and Teens*, by Richard M. Lerner and Nancy L. Galambos

6. Sex Guides: *Books and Films About Sexuality for Young Adults*, by Patty Campbell

7. Infancy: *A Guide to Research and Resources*, by Hannah Nuba-Scheffler, Deborah Lovitky Sheiman, and Kathleen Pullan Watkins

8. Postpartum Depression: *A Research Guide and International Bibliography*, by Laurence Kruckman and Chris Asmann-Finch

9. Childbirth: *An Annotated Bibliography and Guide*, by Rosemary Cline Diulio

10. Adoption: *An Annotated Bibliography and Guide*, by Lois Ruskai Melina

11. Parent-Child Attachment: *A Guide to Research*, by Kathleen Pullan Watkins

12. Resources for Middle Childhood: *A Source Book*, by Deborah Lovitky Sheiman and Maureen Slonim

13. Children and Adjustment to Divorce: *An Annotated Bibliography*, by Mary M. Nofsinger

14. One-Parent Children, The Growing Minority: *A Research Guide*, by Mary Noel Gouke and Arline McClarty Rollins

15. Child Abuse and Neglect: *An Information and Reference Guide*, by Timothy J. Iverson and Marilyn Segal

16. Adolescent Pregnancy and Parenthood: *An Annotated Guide*, by Ann Creighton-Zollar

17. Employed Mothers and Their Children, by Jacqueline V. Lerner and Nancy L. Galambos

18. Children, Culture, and Ethnicity: *Evaluating and Understanding the Impact*, by Maureen B. Slonim

19. Prosocial Development: Caring, Helping, and Cooperating: *A Resource Guide for Parents and Professionals*, by Alice Sterling Honig and Donna Sasse Wittmer

20. Hispanic Children and Youth in the United States: *A Resource Guide*, by Angela L. Carrasquillo

HISPANIC CHILDREN AND YOUTH IN THE UNITED STATES
A Resource Guide

Angela L. Carrasquillo

GARLAND PUBLISHING, INC. • NEW YORK & LONDON
1991

Library of Congress Cataloging-in-Publication Data

Carrasquillo, Angela.
   Hispanic children and youth in the United States : a resource
guide / Angela L. Carrasquillo.
      p.   cm. — (Reference books on family issues ; vol. 20)
   (Garland reference library of social science ; vol. 608)
   Includes bibliographical references and indexes.
   ISBN 0–8240–3337–X; ISBN 0–8153–0467–6 (pbk.)
   1. Hispanic American children. 2. Hispanic American youth.
3. Hispanic American children—Bibliography. 4. Hispanic American
youth—Bibliography. I. Title. II. Series: Reference books on
family issues ; v. 20. III. Series: Garland reference library of
social science ; v. 608.
E184.S75C37   1991
305.23'08968—dc20   91–6
                                                              CIP

Printed on acid-free, 250-year-life paper
Manufactured in the United States of America

CONTENTS

PREFACE

This book discusses the characteristics, status and future developments of Hispanic children and youth in United States. It presents a holistic picture of the unique demographic, cultural, linguistic, socioeconomic and educational characteristics of Hispanic children and youth, describing how these conditions are reflected in their health, labor force participation, higher education and criminal justice status. These children and youth share historical, cultural and linguistic experiences that make them a unique group with similarities and differences among themselves. Among the similarities shared are socioeconomic deprivation, cultural isolation and prejudice. Society plays an important role in the children's and youth's collective and individual development; and their psychological, physical, social, educational and linguistic development are affected, in part, by the services provided by the society they live in.

There exist many misconceptions in society about Hispanic children and youth, stemming from a lack of knowledge and understanding of their history, culture and language. There is a need to see Hispanic children and youth as a group that enriches the United States. And Hispanics themselves need to be more aware of the status of their community, especially of their children and youth, in order to cooperate among themselves to improve their conditions. Other ethnic groups need to understand the ethnic, cultural, linguistic and socioeconomic status of Hispanic children and youth in the United States in order to cooperate in improving these conditions for the benefit of the United States as a whole. These children need understanding and resources for their development and nourishment.

The content and focus of this book are based on statistical information and the work of many researchers and theorists from a variety of disciplines: history, social sciences, education, linguistics, health, criminal justice, labor and higher education. This information is carefully analyzed using recent data to objectively describe the present status of Hispanics in the United States. The terms *children* and *youths* are used throughout this book to include individuals from childhood to adolescence. For many individuals, the term *children* is used through puberty. This book goes beyond puberty to include adolescents up to 21 years of age. Issues such as drug prevention, teenage pregnancy and participation in institutions of higher education of Hispanic adolescents are addressed in this resource guide.

I would like to express my gratitude to those persons who contributed to the completion of this investigation. My special thanks go to all those government agencies and advocacy groups who provided me with pertinent information; to my students and colleagues at Fordham University who encouraged me to complete this work, Lourdes Nuñez and Ben Willems who patiently typed and re-typed the manuscript, to Philip Segan, a dear friend and colleague, who read and gave me advice and directions on every chapter.

I also would like to express profound gratitude to my family. I have been far more than blessed to have such a wonderful and beautiful husband and children. My husband put up with the long hours that I spent away from home or in front of the word processor. I especially have to thank my children who contributed by believing in what I was writing, for the hours we spent together talking about their own personal experiences as Hispanic children and youth themselves. My son Olveen deserves special attention; he provided me with invaluable information on the topic of Hispanic health.

To all, my sincere thanks.

INTRODUCTION

Mírate en la mirada
de un niño,
Mírate en la esperanza.

The course of United States history has been motivated largely by the search for a social system that would allow all individuals to advance as their abilities and efforts permit—with no barriers based on race, religion, sex or socioeconomic status. However, this is not a realistic fact for many Hispanic children and youth in the United States. In 1988, Hispanics were the fastest-growing segment of the population on the United States mainland, making up an estimated 8.1 percent of the total population. Hispanic children and youth represent a group of significant size that soon will become the largest minority in the United States, outnumbering even African American children. The impact of Hispanic youth on the history, politics, economy and social life of the United States needs to be taken seriously. From this group will come the leaders of the United States; and this country's well-being as a nation will depend, to some extent, on how the American society nurtures these children. Very little is known however about the status of Hispanic children and youth as a group in the United States. Most of what is known about is their previous conditions, usually presented in isolated pieces.

Research on the status of Hispanic children lacks a holistic perspective. Much of the literature presents isolated facts about Hispanic children and youth in such areas as education, the work force, or in criminal justice without presenting the whole picture of these children and youth. Discussing, valuing, and nurturing these children as a whole may signal an acceptance of the value of cultural and racial diversity in the United States; and it may well contribute to the recognition of the interrelationship between the growth of the United States and the resources its people represent. Far too often minority children, especially if they are poor, are characterized as entering the educational arena poorly prepared to perform the tasks required and valued by the society and the school. If the mainstream United States society is serious about promoting academic success for minority students, it must first recognize the complexity of the Hispanic community in the United States and the importance of improving the conditions of their children and youth.

Programs need to be developed to help these children move out of the vicious cycle of failure which damages their self-image. We get some sense of powerlessness of these children when we realize that 26 percent of the Hispanics in the nation live below the poverty level (Bureau of the Census, 1988d). Effective measures require building a positive self-image; likewise they require some optimism in diminishing failure—the belief that effort makes a real difference.

This book has been developed as a reference guide. It contains essays about those factors that have affected—positively or negatively—the development of Hispanic children. The following chart presents a summary of the content of the book.

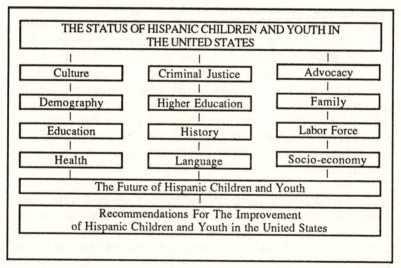

THE STATUS OF HISPANIC CHILDREN AND YOUTH IN THE UNITED STATES

Culture	Criminal Justice	Advocacy
Demography	Higher Education	Family
Education	History	Labor Force
Health	Language	Socio-economy

The Future of Hispanic Children and Youth

Recommendations For The Improvement of Hispanic Children and Youth in the United States

This book is divided into twelve chapters followed by references and an annotated bibliography to assist the reader in further investigations of the topics presented. Chapter one presents an overview of the historical and demographic characteristics of Hispanic children and youth in the United States with the purpose of presenting a historical and statistical demographic perspective of these children. Chapter two describes the diversity among Hispanic children and youth pointing out the differences related to different immigration and settlement histories. Chapter three discusses unique Hispanic cultural and linguistic characteristics emphasizing those areas of homogeneity among the different groups. Although there are unique linguistic features among Spanish speakers, there are more linguistic similarities than differences among them. The chapter describes these linguistic similarities and differences as well as the cultural and acculturation factors that have contributed to the language and culture of Hispanic children and youth in the United States. Chapter four identifies the challenges confronted by Hispanic children in terms of family structure and organization, family education, income, housing, and social and economic dependence. The educational status and the role of schools are discussed in chapters five and six. Health status is the focus of chapter seven, providing some insights into the parental factors affecting childbearing, physical health and mental health characteristics of Hispanic children and youth. The use of chemical substances and their consequences are also discussed. Chapter eight briefly describes the United States criminal justice system and the involvement of Hispanic youth in illegal activities. An effort has been made to discuss the causes of Hispanic youth's illegal behavior as well as the implications for Hispanic youth development. Labor force participation is the focus of chapter nine, especially employment and unemployment and recommendations to prevent Hispanic juvenile delinquency. Chapter ten goes beyond childhood to look at the involvement of Hispanic youth in institutions of higher education, especially in terms of their representation, retention and graduation rates. Chapter eleven includes a set of recommendations for government and community action which may improve the future of Hispanic children. Chapter twelve has two parts. The first part includes a selected profile of organizations that have been nationally recognized as advocates for the well-being of Hispanic children and youth. The second part lists a directory of agencies or organizations created with the main purpose of helping Hispanics in the United States.

Finally, this book provides informative knowledge about Hispanics as contributors to a pluralistic American society including mutual understanding and appreciation of all cultures; cooperation of the various cultures in a society's civic and economic institutions; peaceful co-existence of diverse lifestyles, folkways, language patterns and cultural values and beliefs.

ABBREVIATIONS

AFDC	Aid to Families with Dependent Children
AIDS	Acquired Immune Deficiency Syndrome
CDC	Center for Disease Control
EEOA	Equal Educational Opportunity Act of 1974
ESEA	Elementary and Secondary Education Act of 1965
ESL	English as a Second Language
FAIR	Federation of American Immigration Reform
GAO	Government Accounting Office
GED	General Educational Development
HHANES	Hispanic Health and Nutrition Examination Survey
INS	The Immigration and Naturalization Service
IRCA	The Immigration Reform and Control Act
NABE	The National Association for Bilingual Education
NAEP	National Assessment of Educational Progress
NCHS	National Center for Health Statistics
NDEA	National Defense Education Act
NHIS	National Health Interview Survey
OBEMLA	Office of Bilingual Education and Minority Language Affairs
OCR	Office of Civil Rights of 1965
SAT	Scholastic Aptitude Test
TESOL	Teaching English to Speakers of Other Languages

Hispanic Children and Youth
in the United States of America

CHAPTER 1

A Historical and Demographic Overview of
Hispanic Children and Youth
in the United States

Hispanic children in the United Sates represent an amalgamation of cultures, religions and races fragmented by various histories. The word *Hispanics* covers a wide spectrum of these ethnic and cultural groups. The word *Hispanic* is derived from the name of the Iberian peninsula, Hispania. The term is used mostly in the United States to identify the Spanish-speaking people of Latin America, the Caribbean and Spain. The United States Bureau of the Census identifies as Hispanics persons of Spanish origin or descent who designate themselves as being Mexican American, Chicano, Puerto Rican, Cuban or of other Spanish/Hispanic origin. By *other Hispanic origin* is meant those whose origins are from the Dominican Republic, South and Central America or Spain. These are Hispanic persons identifying themselves generally as Hispanic, Spanish American, *hispano* or *latino* (Bureau of the Census, 1988d). Not everyone accepts the adjective Hispanic favorably. Objection comes mostly from individuals who indicate that the word makes reference only to Spanish ancestry, specifically that of Spain, ignoring the African American and Indian ancestry of Spanish surnames in the United States. Those who oppose the term prefer to be called *latinos*. In this book, the word Hispanic is used mainly for convenience. The word Hispanic is used in most of the extant literature, especially in statistical data and government reports. It is also the term known best by non-Hispanic groups.

This chapter presents an overview of the historical and demographic characteristics of the Hispanic groups in the United States

3

with the purpose of presenting a profile of the Hispanic presence in the mainland United States. The chapter is divided into five general sections: (a) the historical significance of the Hispanic presence in the United States; (b) characteristics of Hispanic migration and special cultural patterns in the United States; (c) size, growth and distribution of the Hispanic population; (d) socioeconomic status of the parents of Hispanic children and youth and (e) status of Hispanic children and youth.

The Historical Significance of the Hispanic Presence in the United States

The influx of Hispanics into the United States has by no means been a homogeneous process. Different groups of Hispanics arrived in America at different times and for different reasons. Each group typically settled in a different region of the country (Jenkins, Sauber & Friedlander, 1985; Natural Hispanic Center for Advanced Studies & Policy Analysis, 1982; Sutton & Chaney, 1987; Weyer, 1988). In general, Mexicans settled in the southwest, the Puerto Ricans and Dominicans in the northeast, the Cubans in the southeast and northeast, the South and Central Americans have spread out in the United States, with large numbers found in the west and south (Nicaraguans) and in the northeast (Colombians, Peruvians and Ecuadoreans) of the United States.

Although Hispanics' presence in United States has been accounted only for since the second part of the nineteenth century, and their number in this country has grown noticeably since 1920, Hispanics have been living in North America even before the formation of what is today the United States of America. The first Hispanic presence in the United States is that of Mexicans. The roots of many Hispanics in the United States are as old as those of the Native Americans. When the Mayflower landed at Plymouth Rock, many regions in the southwest had already been established by Mexicans. However, historically the Mexican's presence is greatly noticed by 1846, when the United States invaded what is today Texas (which at that time was part of Mexico) resulting in the acquisition of the modern day states of Texas, New Mexico and California. The Mexicans who were already living in these territories remained in this newly acquired American land. Other

Mexicans also migrated and suddenly Mexicans were found in what is today Texas, California, New Mexico, Arizona and part of Colorado. Immigration from Mexico increased tremendously since 1920 when a socially disruptive revolution in Mexico and the agricultural development of the southwest United States caused the immediate and subsequent need for labor.

Puerto Ricans, the second largest Hispanic group in the United States, came later than Mexicans. By the end of the nineteenth century their presence was evident, especially in the northeast part of the country. In 1898, Puerto Rico became part of the United States. For the first time, Puerto Ricans were able to travel freely to the United States. At the beginning, few Puerto Ricans moved to the mainland . However, during the economic depression of 1920–1930 Puerto Ricans began moving to the United States in search of a better life. Puerto Rican presence in the United States increased greatly during the 1940's and 1950's, making them the largest Hispanic group in the Northeast, which they remain until today.

Cuban presence in the United States has been felt since the beginning of the twentieth century. Cuba was part of the United States for three years, after the Hispano-American War brought a small group of Cubans to the United States. After three years, Cuba became independent, but Cubans continued to move to the United States, especially to work for the cigar manufacturing companies. The largest influx of Cubans came in the 1960's when a significant group of Cubans left Cuba fleeing from the Castro regime and the communists. The *Mariel* group that came to the United States led the way for the millions of Cubans now living in this country.

In addition to the Mexican, Puerto Rican and Cuban presence in the United States other Hispanic groups have immigrated here in large numbers, especially from the Dominican Republic and South and Central America. Dominicans began migrating to the United States in large numbers after the 1965 change in the immigration laws. The change also coincided with the American invasion of the island and the establishment of the Balaguer government. During this period of economic difficulty, many Dominicans migrated to New York City looking for a better way of life. Still in 1990, Dominicans were immigrating in large numbers to the United States.

A large number of Hispanic immigrants are from Central and South America. From Central America, three countries are noticeable for the large number of emigres to the United States: El Salvador,

Guatemala and Honduras. Central American immigrants include a refugee group (a professional class and a large majority of children sent alone by their parents), professionals in search of a better economic way of life and mainly poor, undocumented individuals (Chaney, 1985; Suarez-Orozco, 1989). The experience of recent Central American immigrants appears to be related to their fears and dissatisfactions with their homeland in the context of increasing political violence and economic crisis. Immigrants from South America come from all countries, with the largest groups coming from Colombia, Ecuador and Peru. The unique historical, social and demographic characteristics of each of these groups are further discussed in Chapter Two.

The Hispanic population represents a significant group in the United States. The most recent data from the Bureau of the Census (1988d) indicate that:

1. The Hispanic population in the United States totaled 19.4 million and represented 8.1 percent of the total United States population. Additionally, there are three million persons who reside in Puerto Rico. Since the 1980 Census, the Hispanic population has increased by 34 percent or about 4.8 million persons.
2. The Hispanic population in the United States is represented by the following groups:
   • Mexican origin, 12.1 million (62.3 percent).
   • Puerto Rican origin, 2.5 million (12.7 percent)
   • Cuban origin, 1.0 million (5.3 percent)
   • Central and South American origin, 2.2 million (11.5 percent)
   • Other Hispanic origin, 1.6 million (8.1 percent)
3. The United States is currently one of the countries with the largest Hispanic concentration in the world. Hispanic growth resulted from net migration and natural increase (births minus deaths).
4. Hispanics are a youthful population with a median age of 25.5 years. Because of their younger age, Hispanics constitute a great share of American school children.
5. By the year 2000, one in three American residents of all ages will be African American, Asian American or Hispanic, with the number of Hispanics approaching the number of African Americans (Oxford-Carpenter, Pol, Lopez, Stupp & Gendell, 1984; Sanderfur & Tienda, 1988; United States Bureau of the Census, 1986).

The following sections of this chapter describe the historical and demographic factors that explain the above facts.

Geographical Distribution of Hispanic Children and Youth

Children of Hispanic parents reside in every state of the union. However, they are concentrated in the greatest numbers in nine states: California (33.9 percent), Texas (21.3 percent), New York (10.9 percent), Florida (7.6 percent), Illinois (4.1 percent), Arizona (3.3 percent), New Jersey (3.3 percent), New Mexico (2.8 percent) and Colorado (1.9 percent) (Bureau of the Census, 1988d). A large percentage of the Hispanic population is concentrated in five southwestern states (California, Texas, Arizona, New Mexico and Colorado) representing about 63 percent of the total Hispanic population in the United States. Fifty-five percent of all Hispanics in the nation reside in California and Texas. Four states outside the southwest accounted for 26 percent of the Hispanic population: New York, Florida, Illinois and New Jersey. The remainder of the country accounted for only 11 percent of the Hispanic population (Bureau of the Census, 1988d). These states contain almost three-quarters of all Hispanics in the United States. In 1988, Hispanics of Mexican ancestry represented the largest Hispanic group in United States, 62 percent of the Hispanic population. These are interesting geographic characteristics that need to be mentioned since they have had an impact on the development of Hispanic children and youth in terms of family structure, employment, education, health and social services provided in these nine states.

The port of entry for each Hispanic group has largely determined its current geographical distribution. Mexican Americans are concentrated in the southwest, particularly in California and Texas; Puerto Ricans are clustered in the northeastern section, especially in the New York metropolitan area. The Cuban migration stream has flowed primarily into Florida, the point of entry for Cuban refugees. Remarkably, Dade Country, Florida, still contains about one-half of the 1.2 million Cuban Americans (Bureau of the Census, 1988d; Valdivieso & Davis, 1988).

Geographical characteristics indicate that:

1. Hispanic children and youth concentrate in particular areas, especially in large urban centers. In California, most Hispanics live in the southern part of the state; in Texas, they are concentrated in the south (Rio Grande, El Paso); in New York they are concentrated in New York City; in Illinois they reside in Chicago; in Florida, their greatest numbers are in Miami; in New Jersey, they are concentrated in Newark and Jersey City (Bureau of the Census, 1988d; Moore & Pachon, 1985).
2. Hispanic children and youth are highly urbanized and contrary to widespread belief Hispanics are not all farm workers. In 1980, one-half of all Hispanics resided in the central cities of metropolitan areas compared with slightly less than one-third of non-Hispanics (Bureau of the Census, 1988d; Moore & Pachon, 1985). This pattern is in contrast with whites who are moving out of the cities to rural and suburban communities.
3. In general, Hispanics are mainly segregated in their own communities or *barrios*. In New York City, Dominicans are concentrated in Washington Heights; Puerto Ricans in Spanish Harlem, the South Bronx or the Lower East Side; in Los Angeles, Mexicans are concentrated in the eastern part of the city. Linguistically and culturally these *barrios* give cohesion and security to Hispanic immigrants who keep residing in the *barrio* mainly for economic and psychological reasons.
4. In states such as California and Texas, Hispanic children and youth are the largest minority population and Hispanics outnumber African Americans, traditionally the largest minority group in the United States. In California, for example, Hispanics (mostly Mexican Americans) constitute about 19 percent of the population, while African Americans make up about 12 percent of the population. In Texas, African Americans are about 12 percent while Hispanics are about 21 percent. These population patterns are a reflection of the history of these states where Mexicans were the first settlers and have emigrated in large numbers.
5. Larger proportions of Hispanics are leaving their traditional areas of settlement. Mexican Americans are making changes in residential preferences; there is a shift from Texas and Arizona to California and the Middle West, especially Illinois. A recent phenomenon is the move of Mexican Americans to small towns in the northeast,

especially in New York State. Puerto Ricans are showing shifts from New York to New Jersey, Illinois, Pennsylvania, and Florida. Orlando, Florida, for example is receiving a significant group of young professionals from Puerto Rico. Cubans, however, have remained concentrated primarily in Florida, although there is a noticeable small concentration in New Jersey and New York.

Size, Growth and Distribution of the Hispanic Population

Estimates of the number of Hispanics in the United States vary. Difficulties arise from the failure of earlier censuses to make a full count of Spanish-surnamed residents and the impossibility of knowing how many undocumented people of Hispanic origin are in the United States at any given time. However, in spite of this problem, there exists a fairly accurate count of legal Hispanics in the United States conducted by the United States Bureau of the Census of the Department of Commerce. Census information indicates that the legal Hispanic population grew from 4 million in 1950, when they were 2.7 percent of the total population, to 14.6 million in 1980 when they were 6.4 percent of the total population, to 19.4 million in 1988 accounting for 8.1 percent of the total population (Bureau of the Census, 1988d). Since the 1980 census, the Hispanic population has increased by 34 percent or about five million persons while the comparable increase for the total United States population has been only eight percent (Bureau of the Census, 1988d).

The above data are conservative figures: there are more Hispanics in the United States than are counted in the census. Other sources estimate that there may be as many as 3 million additional Hispanics not counted by the census. This estimate is based on some approximations of the number of uncounted, undocumented persons and the number of legal residents missed by the census (Moore & Pachon, 1985). Total undocumented immigration to the United States is estimated to account for an annual inflow of half a million aliens, the majority of whom are from Mexico, the Caribbean and Central America. When these estimates are added, the total number of persons of Hispanic background on the mainland is probably around 21 million. The 1990 census results will reveal the demographic changes that occurred during the 1980's. Recent projections show a Hispanic population of 23 million in the early 1990's and nearly 29 million by the year 2000 (Oxford-Carpenter et al., 1984; Sandefur & Tienda, 1988; Valdivieso & Davis, 1988). By the end of the century, Hispanics will comprise over 10 percent of the projected United States population, and about 16 percent of both school-aged children and persons 18 to 24 years old (Valdivieso & Davis, 1988).

The two key factors responsible for the increase of the Hispanic population in the United States are heavy migration to the United States and relative high birth rates among United States Hispanic residents. These two factors contributed equally to the 4.6 percent increase in the United States Hispanic population between 1980 and 1988 (Bureau of the Census, 1988d). Hispanic women tend to have more children than other Americans. This is particularly true of recent immigrants who may be reflecting the large size family norms of their native countries. The total fertility rate (average life time births per woman) for foreign-born Hispanics in 1980 was 2.9, one child greater than the 1.8 rate for non-Hispanics. Throughout the 1980's, Hispanic birth rates have been about 50 percent higher than those of other Americans (Bureau of the Census, 1988a; Valdivieso & Davis, 1988). The Census Bureau indicated that over 400,000 births to Hispanics occurred in 1987, accounting for 11 percent of all United States births (Bureau of the Census, 1988d).

Immigration and fertility, the two main factors responsible for the rapid increase of the Hispanic population, do not show any sign of levelling off in the near future. Immigrants will continue to arrive in the United States, in ever greater numbers, due to the escalating violence in South and Central America, the economic instability in Mexico and the Dominican Republic, and high unemployment in Puerto Rico (United States Bureau of the Census, 1988a). Hispanic families will continue to experience their high fertility, especially when many of them are Catholic and comply with the recent emphasis of the Catholic church against birth control and abortion. Immigration of Hispanics to the United States will remain high due to the high international debt and economic disarray in many Latin American countries in addition to unstable political trends in countries such as El Salvador and Peru.

The high growth rate of the nation's Hispanic population has led some to suggest that it may surpass African Americans and become the country's largest minority group in the decade from 1990–2000. If the population continues its growth, it is estimated that the population of

Hispanic children and youth will grow at a very high rate, perhaps 16 percent by the year 2000. The 1988 Census Bureau data indicated that of all Hispanics in the United States: (a) Children under five represent 10.7 percent of the Hispanic population, (b) Children between five and nine represent 10. 2 percent, (c) Children 10–14 represent 9.1 percent, and (d) Children between the ages of 15 and 19 represent 8.7 percent. Thirty-nine percent of the Hispanic population in the United States is under nineteen years old. This is a very conservative figure since it does not include many of the illegal children living in the United States. These data indicate that there will continue to be growth of the Hispanic school-age population in places where Hispanics are geographically concentrated.

Hispanics are a young population. The high fertility rate keeps the population young because of the continuously increasing numbers of births. Immigrants tend to keep the average age low because migrants are likely to be young adults, just at the age for starting a family (Valdivieso & Davis, 1988). In 1988, almost one-third of the Hispanic population (30.3 percent) was under the age of fifteen. In 1988, the median age in the United States was 32.2 years compared to only 25.5 years of age among Hispanics. Only 4.7 percent of Hispanics are 65 or older (Bureau for the Census, 1988d). Puerto Ricans (23.9 percent) and Mexican Americans (24.9 percent), with a median age of about 24.4 years, constitute the youngest Hispanic groups. Because many Hispanic women are now entering their childbearing years, and because Hispanic women tend to bear more children at younger ages than other women in the United States, the Hispanic population will remain young for some time. The Hispanic population still contains a high percentage of youth yet to reach child-bearing age. Valdivieso & Davis (1988), posing the question of the significance of a young age structure, answered by saying:

> . . . [the] young population will require day care, education, and jobs, for example, rather than pensions, retirement, planning and geriatric health care.
>
> From a strictly demographic perspective, the Hispanic's young age structure means that Latino youth form a greater proportion of the United States young people. Latinos accounted for 8 percent of the total United States population in 1988, but 11 percent of these were under age 15. Society's effort to educate and nurture the next generation will be directed increasingly at a Hispanic audience (p. 3).

Hispanic Migration and
Social and Cultural Patterns

Hispanics share a broad sense of ethnic identity based on allegiance to a shared mother language and culture. This sense of Hispanic identity is constantly being reinvigorated with persistent high rates of immigration and by the continual circular migration of Hispanics. The United States is the destination of about half the world's immigrants who seek permanent resettlement and has been so continuously year after year. Family reunification accounts for 90 percent of new admissions since legal immigrants living in the United States can apply to bring other family members to the United States. Hispanic groups became United States citizens or residents in different ways and at different times. Those immigrants who are already in the United States inform families living in their native country of their socioeconomic advancement in the United States. Most of the immigrants come for economic reasons, although there is another group coming for political reasons. When these immigrants arrive, they first live in their relatives' homes. This pattern has reinforced the tendency for immigrants to cluster in high concentrations in a limited number of areas.

The decade of the 1980's was one with the highest levels of immigration. In 1989, about 2,000 Central Americans arrived in south Texas each week, especially Nicaraguans, claiming to be refugees. They almost automatically received permission to work in the United States while their applications for asylum were being considered, a process which could last a year or more. Most of these asylum applicants entered through Texas and went to Los Angeles, Florida or New York to settle.

Premigration and religious patterns also have had an impact on Hispanics in maintaining their ethnic and cultural patterns of origin after they move to the United States. Family and religion contributed to the tendency of Hispanic immigrants to feel new needs and acquire new meanings and significance in their living styles due to: (a) a constant circulation of Hispanics to and from their not-too-distant homelands; (b) continuous high rates of new immigrants and visitors from home who help to maintain ties to the original customs; (c) Hispanics living in concentrated areas, helping to preserve their native culture. New immigrants bring their beliefs and social institutions, which, in general, stay with them, although they undergo changes in living patterns and adopt new customs. These premigration values, attitudes and customs do not simply fade away; rather they shape, often in a complex fashion, the way individuals in each group adjust to and develop new cultural and social patterns (Foner, 1987). For example, it is a yearly tradition in New York City to present musical shows composed of primarily famous Puerto Rican singers from the 1940's and 1960's: These performers can relate to old Puerto Rican immigrants and can help them to remember the Puerto Rico that they left many years ago. Traditional beliefs such as *bautismos* (baptisms), *bodas* (weddings), *confirmaciónes* (confirmations) are opportunities to revitalize cultural and ethnic customs and beliefs.

The cultural and social values new immigrants bring serve as a generating force for those that have been living in United States. Thus, all immigrants continue making use of these cultural and social patterns which they pass on to new generations. Both groups merge helping to maintain these values and ideas. Perhaps, this is a unique characteristic among Hispanic immigrants and since immigrants are constantly arriving, these cause those already living in the United States to remember and practice their unique customs and traditions.

The United States government, aware of this major immigration flow, has taken measures to control massive immigration to the United States through a new immigration law, the Immigration Reform and Control Act (IRCA). It is not clear yet what—if any—will be the repercussions of the new immigration law for Hispanics. The Immigration Reform and Control Act (IRCA), the Simpson-Rodino bill, became law in 1986 after five years of debate and compromise. The law has two phases: amnesty programs for the legalization of illegal residents and farm workers, and an employer sanctions program which makes it illegal for employers to hire illegal immigrants. The bill provides amnesty or legalization for a large group of persons. Undocumented individuals who have resided in the United States by January 2, 1982, may be eligible for the legalization program if they can demonstrate, among other things, continuous residence and the ability to support themselves. The employer's sanctions apply only to persons hired after November 6, 1986, the date on which the IRCA legislation was signed into law. Persons who were already employed as of that date are *grandfathered* under the bill and need not produce proof of legal immigration status.

Hispanics in the United States keep their original identities and cultural patterns of living, making Hispanics a distinctive and unique ethnic group in the United States and, although they may adopt other cultural and linguistic characteristics, in their homes or *barrios* they keep practicing those patterns that identify them as Dominicans, Colombians, Mexicans, or Peruvians, and not merely as Hispanics.

Socioeconomic Status of the Parents of Hispanic Children and Youth

In general, Hispanics in the United States are characterized by the following socioeconomic characteristics: poverty, unemployment and lack of educational opportunities. The only group that does not fit these characteristics is the Cubans who immigrated during the decade of the 1960's.

Economic Status

The low-status occupations and high unemployment rates among Hispanics translate into low incomes and high levels of poverty. In 1988, the Bureau of the Census reported that in 1987 the median income of Hispanic families was $20, 310 , not significantly different from the 1986 figure. The median for non-Hispanic families, however, grew by about 1 percent to $31, 610. Since the last economic recession in 1982, the real median family income of Hispanic families has risen by 6.9 percent compared with 12.3 percent for non-Hispanic families. Within the Hispanic community, income levels reveal marked differences. By sub-groups, the lowest median income was found among Puerto Rican families at $15,190, and the highest income was found among Cuban families at $27,290. In general, the income of Hispanics was only 66 percent of the income of non-Hispanics. One of the key reasons is that Hispanic males and females were less likely than non-Hispanics to hold professional or management jobs in which salaries are commensurate with their job positions. The mothers of Hispanic children, who were employed full time, had the lowest income of any of the major population groups (see Chapter 9). Another significant factor is that Hispanic families are relatively large, and their incomes support more household members than those of non-Hispanic families.

In 1987, about 26 percent or 1.2 million Hispanic families were living below the poverty level compared with 10 percent of non-Hispanic families (Census Bureau, 1988c; 1988d). The Hispanic poverty level was two and a half times as high as that of non-Hispanics families. Among Hispanic subgroups, Puerto Rican families had the highest poverty rate at 38 percent. Cubans, Central and South American families had the lowest poverty rates at 13.8 percent and 18.9 percent. A disturbing fact is that there has been no significant change in the poverty rate of Hispanic families between 1982 and 1987, although between 1985 and 1987, the poverty rate of non-Hispanic families dropped from 10.4 percent to 9.7 percent (Bureau of the Census, 1988d). A significant number of children and youth live with single parents. In single-parent families headed by a Hispanic female, over half (52 percent) were below the poverty level (Bureau of the Census, 1988c; 1988d).

Hispanics are a population in need of financial resources. They suffer from a variety of economic and social problems such as unemployment, underemployment, poor housing and inadequate health care, among others. However, in March 1988 when analyzing Hispanics as a whole, the Bureau of the Census found one positive socioeconomic development: the March 1988 unemployment rates for Hispanics was 8.5 percent (compared to 5.8 percent for non-Hispanics, age 16 and over) representing their lowest levels for both groups since March 1983. These economic data need to be analyzed carefully since they give the impression that Hispanics are improving their economic status. Divided by Hispanic sub-groups, one notices that while Cuban unemployment was only 3.1 percent, Puerto Rican unemployment was 10.5 percent. Parents of Hispanic children and youth were not able to improve their relative economic standing between 1980 and 1988—the Mexican Americans lost slightly, Puerto Ricans lost considerably, and even the Cubans dropped. These statistics highlight the handicaps faced by many Hispanic children. With large families, low incomes, and a high proportion of single-parent families, the success of a significant proportion of Hispanic children and youth is at risk (Valdivieso & Davis, 1988).

Educational Attainment

It is in education that the gap in achievement between Hispanics and other groups, extending from preschool through college, is the widest and most serious. Low educational achievement is a major barrier to the advancement of Hispanics in the United States, including children and their parents (Arias, 1986, Bureau of the Census, 1988b). The Hispanic adults most likely to have school-age children are in the 25 to 34 age bracket. In 1988, this group was more than three times as likely not to have completed high school as other Americans. Only 12 percent of Hispanics in the 25 to 34 age bracket had completed four or more years of college, less than half the percentage of non-Hispanics (Bureau of the Census, 1988b; Valdivieso & Davis, 1988).

The educational attainment level of Hispanic children and youth has improved, but remains below the level of their non-Hispanic counterparts (Bureau of the Census, 1988d). Improvement for Hispanic children was evident at lower grade levels, where 6 percent of the younger Hispanics had completed fewer than 5 years of school compared with 16 percent of their older counterparts (Census Bureau, 1988b). There have also been improvements in the educational attainment of Hispanic children at the secondary level. Although the proportion of Hispanics 25 years and over with four or more years of high school did not change between 1987 and 1988 (51 percent), this was the highest percentage ever recorded since the Census Bureau began to collect data on Hispanics in 1970, but is below that for non-Hispanics. The proportion of Hispanics 25 years old and over who had completed 4 or more years of college in 1988 (10 percent) was higher than the 5 percent recorded in 1970 (Census Bureau, 1988b). Despite this improvement, the proportion of Hispanic children who had completed 4 or more years of high school remained lower than that of non-Hispanics (51 percent and 78 percent respectively).

Differences exist among Hispanic sub-groups. Mexican Americans had the lowest median number of school years completed with 10.8 (57 percent), followed by 12.0 (67 percent) for Puerto Ricans and 12.4 (83 percent) for other Hispanics including Cubans, South and Central Americans (Bureau of the Census, 1988b).

A disproportionately high percentage of Hispanic youth leave high school without a diploma. It is more than double the national figure. The Hispanics who do remain in school may fall behind because of language difficulties and the lack of school reinforcement. For certain groups of Hispanics such as women, dropout rates are even higher.

The problems faced in elementary and secondary schools follow Hispanics into college. The proportion of college graduates among Hispanics is significantly lower than for non-Hispanics and their dropout rate is higher. This topic is further discussed in chapter 10. Among Hispanic groups, Mexican Americans have the lowest percentage of college graduates and the South and Central Americans have the highest.

The Status of Hispanic Children and Youth

When the demographic characteristics of the Hispanic population are analyzed, an important factor is revealed: Hispanic children and youth constitute about 38 percent of that growing Hispanic population and they constitute about 11 percent of all the children in the population of the United States. It is estimated that there are more than 1.7 million school-aged children in the United States who come from a Spanish-language background. Projections indicate that by the year 2000 Hispanics will comprise over 10 percent of the projected United States population, and about 16 percent of the school-aged children (Valdivieso & Davis, 1988). How well Hispanic children and youth fare in the socioeconomic and educational strata of the United States will influence the socioeconomic future of this country. Now, the future for Hispanic children and youth is not bright. The following list provides a summary of the social, economic and educational status of Hispanic children and youth in the United States. This summary serves as a foundation of the discussion throughout this book.

1. Hispanic children and youth represent a growing population estimated by the year 2000 to become the largest group of minority children in the United States.
   a. This high growth rate is due to immigration and fertility factors.
   b. The Hispanic population includes a high percentage of women of childbearing age.
   c. Mexican Americans are the largest Hispanic group in the United States.
   d. A significant number of Central American children are refugees.

2. Hispanic children and youth are not a homogeneous socioeconomic and educational group.
   a. Mexican Americans have the lowest educational attainment.
   b. Puerto Rican children are the poorest.
   c. Cuban children and some immigrants from South and Central America tend to have the highest educational attainment.
3. Hispanic children and youth suffer economic deprivation.
   a. About 26 percent of Hispanic families are living below the poverty level.
   b. The poverty rate among Hispanics is more than double the rates for non-Hispanic groups.
   c. The poverty rate for white children decreased in the 1980's but increased among Hispanics.
4. Socioeconomic conditions have negatively affected the family of Hispanic children and youth.
   a. Hispanic children live in poor housing conditions.
   b. Hispanic housing is likely to be overcrowded.
   c. A significant group of single-parent Hispanic families is welfare dependent.
5. A significant percentage of Hispanic children and youth shares the Spanish language and Hispanic culture.
   a. Language, religious beliefs, family structures and general customs are enhanced among Hispanics.
   b. There is a common denominator of Hispanic culture, especially in the same Hispanic socioeconomic class.
   c. Hispanic children have a broad range of language characteristics and needs that impact upon their development.
6. Parents of Hispanic children and youth are marginally employed, underemployed or unemployed.
   a. Hispanics tend to enter poorly paid, semi-skilled jobs with little chance of advancement.
   b. In 1988, unemployment for Hispanics was 8.5 percent, compared to 5.8 percent for non-Hispanics.
   c. Hispanic women, especially Puerto Ricans, are less likely to be working than other women.
   d. Low status occupations and high unemployment among Hispanics translate into low incomes and high poverty rates.
   e. The income gap between Hispanics and other Americans grew between 1978 and 1990.

7. Hispanic children and youth lag far behind the majority population in any array of standard educational measurements.
   a. Hispanic children and youth enroll in schools at rates lower than those for non-Hispanic groups.
   b. Hispanic children and youth fall behind their classmates in progressing through school.
   c. Attrition rates of Hispanic children and youth are higher than those of non-Hispanic students.
   d. The gap between Hispanic children and youth and their white counterparts tends to increase with age.
   e. Hispanic youth are twice as likely as whites not to have completed high school.
8. Hispanic youth represent a significant percentage of the inmate/offender population.
   a. Hispanic youth represent a high percent of juvenile criminals.
   b. Hispanic youth are overrepresented in clinical centers.
   c. Hispanic youth are also victims of crimes.
9. Hispanic children and youth suffer from poor health and limited prevention and health related services.
   a. Parents of Hispanic children are much less likely than whites to have health insurance and are less aware of preventive health practices.
   b. Poverty and poor pre-natal care lead to disproportionate numbers of Hispanic children who are sick or undernourished from birth.
   c. Hispanic children and youth are at greater risk for predictable problems such as substance abuse and AIDS.
10. Hispanic youth are not well represented in institutions of higher education.
    a. Although Hispanics have increased their participation in higher education, few Hispanics are entering and graduating from college.
    b. Hispanics are not entering the same kinds of colleges as whites.
    c. The majority of Hispanic youth attend two-year colleges.

Conclusion

The data presented in this chapter indicate that, in general, Hispanic children and youth have less education, lower incomes, and higher rates of unemployment and poverty than the general population. They share many characteristics that set them apart from other American children and youth, but which are also common to other low socioeconomic minorities and to earlier immigrant groups. Hispanic parents have not made significant progress in their socioeconomic and educational development.

The history of immigrant groups to the United States shows that Hispanics, in a way, are following the trend of many other immigrant groups in the United States. Minority groups have always been seen as responsible for the problems of the city where they settled. A significant proportion of immigrant children never enrolled in school. Many schools enrolling immigrant children had higher truancy and dropout rates, lower achievement levels and greater instances of grade repetition than schools with non-immigrant populations. The abundance of manual labor jobs which required no reading or writing skills in any language absorbed many dropouts. Efforts have been made to try to *melt* Hispanic immigrants into the American society by having them acquire American values and customs and teaching them English at the expense of their own culture and language. Since Hispanics are presently a young immigrant group, and their population shows many of the normal characteristics of immigrant populations, in many instances they reflect abnormal socio-demographic characteristics.

Presently, the presence of large numbers of new immigrants, many of whom are undocumented and thus highly vulnerable to employer manipulation, represents yet another arena of conflict and competition in which Hispanics in the United States must function. Indeed, American society has been enriched by immigration, although society in general has looked negatively at cultural differences and placed an emphasis on assimilation, causing ethnic groups to compete among themselves. This situation will not change until the United States society recognizes that cultural pluralism is and should be a fundamentally positive element in which every citizen works together to establish reciprocal relationships and trust.

The Hispanic community is a young, diverse and dynamic population that is experiencing rapid growth. During the last decade, the Hispanic population saw progress in only some social and economic areas. A profile of Hispanic youth revealed the similarities and differences they share among themselves and with the youth of other races. Most youth were raised in households where Spanish was spoken; their socioeconomic level was generally between that of African Americans and whites and their educational level is generally below that of the average white population. The challenges and opportunities that such a youthful, growing and diverse population pose to the United States are profound. Hispanic children will play an important role in the country's future economic social, political and educational life. Every social, political and educational institution should contribute to create constructive and positive changes in the lives of Hispanic children and youth. These changes are urgently needed.

CHAPTER 2

Diversity within Hispanic Children and Youth

American society needs to learn to value diversity. The right of children and youth to be different imposes many obligations on American society. The population of the United States is composed of people with a great variety of ethnic backgrounds; nearly all members of society can trace their ancestry back to some country across the seas or outside the United States (United States Department of Justice, 1988). These ethnic groups have enriched United States culture with their own particular beliefs, values, languages and customs.

The Hispanic community is a young, diverse and dynamic population that is experiencing rapid growth. The word Hispanic describes a heterogeneous group of people composed of clusters of ethnic groups whose priorities and concerns frequently differ from other minorities, such as African Americans, and often differ among the Spanish heritage groups themselves. This diversity is seen in the distinct communities of Mexicans, Puerto Ricans, Cubans, Dominicans, Central and South Americans and other Spanish-origin groups. Each group is a separately identifiable group, but, at the same time, these groups share many similarities. These groups show a juxtaposition of differences and similarities that makes the term Hispanic as a single group difficult to identify and measure. As mentioned in Chapter 1, the two characteristics Hispanics have in common are the heritage of Spanish conquest and culture and the utilization of the Spanish language (Melville, 1988). But there is no question that there are several differences among the different Hispanic ethnic groups.

The most important differences among Hispanics derive from raw demographic facts: absolute numbers, concentration in a given area, and settlement in their home areas. A second set of differences is essentially socio-cultural. It concerns generally the way the members of the Hispanic group relate to each other, to their own linguistic and cultural tradition, and to the majority society. In some respects, Hispanic children represent a diverse group within a group in a country that does not appear to value diversity but rather seeks to melt the diversity into a uniform group of people. Hispanics in the United States recognize their diversity within the commonalties of a common language, culture and race. They reflect different immigration and settlement history, demographic and economic status, perceptions of themselves and their place in United States history.

Contrary to public perception, the majority of Hispanics are not immigrants. Three-fourths of the Hispanic population were born in the United States. However, when asked, Hispanics identified themselves with their ethnic origin group. Also, the extended Hispanic family typically includes some relatives who are new immigrants.

Hispanic children and youth in the United States are mostly Mexican Americans, Puerto Ricans, Cubans, Dominicans, and of Central and South American origin (especially Colombia, Ecuador, El Salvador, Guatemala, Nicaragua, and Peru). This chapter presents a summary of the demographic characteristics of most of these ethnic groups, giving particular emphasis to their children and youth.

Mexican American Children and Youth

Hispanics of Mexican ancestry have long been the largest Hispanic group in the United States. In 1988, Mexican Americans accounted for 62.3 percent of all Hispanic Americans (Bureau of the Census, 1988d). In 1980, only about one quarter of them were foreign-born, underscoring the fact that they are among the oldest Hispanic groups residing in the United States (Barrera, 1979, Valdivieso & Davis, 1988). The Mexican origin population is multigenerational, legal and undocumented, is made up of recent newcomers as well as families with a long history in the United States. Mexican Americans became part of the United States not by emigration, but by conquest. More than 250 years before the 1848 Treaty of Guadalupe-Hidalgo, Spaniards and, later, Mexicans settled the area that is today the states of Texas, New Mexico, Arizona, Colorado, and California. In 1846, the United

States invaded this territory and embarked on a long war with Mexico (Barrera, 1979). The United States acquired half of Mexico's territory at the close of the Mexican-American War. In 1848, through the Guadalupe-Hidalgo Treaty, Mexico ceded the northern half of its territory to the United States. The Treaty of Guadalupe-Hidalgo as officially agreed upon by Mexico on February 2, 1848, recognized the Rio Grande as its border with Texas, and ceded territory that today is California, New Mexico, Nevada, and parts of Colorado, Arizona and Utah. The treaty gave Mexican nationals one year to choose United States or Mexican citizenship. Approximately 75,000 Mexicans living in what became United States territory were given the choice of becoming Americans or leaving the country. Most chose to stay and became United States residents. The Guadalupe-Hidalgo Treaty also brought large-scale immigration from Mexico into these regions. This treaty guaranteed the land and civil rights of Mexicans in all ceded territory as well as their rights as citizens to retain their language, religion and cultural practices. Individual land titles were ostensibly to be respected.

During the second half of the nineteenth century, the American southwest was physically, culturally, and economically isolated from the rest of the United States. The 1848 gold rush brought a flood of Anglo settlers to California, which became a state in 1850. Settlement in Arizona and New Mexico occurred more slowly, with statehood coming only in 1912, after railroads had overcome their geographic isolation (Barrera, 1979; Cardoso, 1980; Moore & Pachon, 1985). Because land was cheap and easy to acquire, Americans of European heritage moved to the West in large numbers and violated the land-grant protection accorded to Mexican Americans, causing their subsequent economic and social subordination. As more American settlers moved to the southwest, Mexicans began to disappear from public life and leadership roles. In their first fifty years as United States citizens, the newly incorporated Mexicans were affected by two powerful forces which radically altered their social structure. One was the dispossession of real property holdings. Wholesale transfers of land from Mexican to Anglo ownership took place between 1848 and 1900 and shortly thereafter (Barrera, 1979; Cardoso, 1980; Moore & Pachon, 1985). Force, coercion, intimidation, and outright fraud were common means to achieve this end. Land courts and commissions established by the American state provided the legal sanctions and justifications for the process of dispossession, ultimately transferring better than two-thirds of the Mexican land holdings to Anglo-Americans.

The second social force that operated on the Mexican population was that of class displacement. There was a marked and steady growth in the proportion of Mexicans in manual occupations and a decrease in the numbers who were merchants and in commercial pursuits. New occupational opportunities developed in mining, lumber and the railroads. Mexicans were reduced to landless wage laborers who, in times of economic hardship, filled the ranks of the unemployed as a reserve labor pool. The years after the treaty saw the loss of most Mexican property and the beginning of Mexicans as a segregated working class (Barrera, 1979; Cardoso, 1980; Moore & Pachon, 1985). Their contact with American whites usually resulted in subordination. Mexicans stopped being owners and began being *peones* (workers) on the properties of the white ranchers (Moore & Pachon, 1985). The cotton plantations' black slaves were not available to cultivate the crops. There was a demand for cheap Mexican labor. Mexicans were hired by the ones who lived in the region or were brought from Mexico. This new role gave Mexicans a distinct characteristic of being inferior persons belonging to a race entitled to neither political, educational, nor social equity (Barrera, 1979, Moore & Pachon, 1985). By 1910 Mexicans became a minority in the southwest United States.

Between 1880 and 1910 the southwestern part of the United States experienced rapid economic development encouraged by the arrival of the railroad and the commercialization of agriculture and the mining industry. Conditions in Mexico also encouraged emigration to the United States. By the turn of the century, expansion of very large ranches had led to the dispossession of many small farmers, and poverty and inflation were made worse by the considerable political repression under the dictatorship of President Porfirio Diaz. After the Mexican Revolution began in 1910, hundreds of thousands of people fled north from Mexico into the southwest. Between 1910 and 1930, 10 percent of the population of Mexico emigrated to the United States (Barrera, 1979; Cardoso, 1980; Moore & Pachon, 1985). The southwest economy was developing and expanding. Initial labor demands were in agriculture, along with sheep and cattle ranching. The expanding agricultural economy helped create other industries for processing, canning, packing and crating these products. Railroad construction for transporting goods to market increased greatly at this time. Sheep and cattle ranching continued, thereby creating new industries in meat processing and shipping. Mining also gained momentum. Manufacturing of machines for the extraction of ore and its processing was in demand. Housing needs helped stimulate the lumber industry, and it became a major economic force in Texas, California, Arizona and New Mexico.

The expanding economy was highly labor-intensive. Mexicans filled this need. Reasons for this northward flow are several: (a) the mechanization of agriculture served to displace Mexican peasantry, few of whom could be absorbed into the modest industrial sector; (b) Mexico's very high population growth (it increased by 50 percent between 1875 and 1910); (c) The Revolution of 1910 caused a lack of economic opportunities in Mexico. The demand for labor in the southwest, along with social, political, and economic disruptions in Mexico increased the population of Mexicans in the United States to more than one million by 1930. Mexicans began serving the functions of ranch workers, railroad maintenance crews, citrus harvesters and packers, and brick makers. The immigrants of 1910–1930 were more diverse in their socioeconomic status than later Mexican immigrants; they included many political activists, professionals and business owners as well as individuals with limited education and training. They were welcomed in the United States because of the labor needs of an expanding United States economy.

Special rules were developed in 1917 to permit the arrival of temporary Mexican farm-workers, railroad maintenance workers and miners; but up to two-thirds stayed permanently in the United States. Maldonado (1985) summarizes the conditions of Mexican Americans in the southwest when he says:

> Mexicans and Chicanos overwhelmingly were concentrated in the lower reaches of the urban occupational structure. Wage differentials common to the rural sectors persisted in urban areas. Access to particular occupations and industries, however, was limited. Mobility rates were very low out of the unskilled and semiskilled positions in which Chicanos and Mexicans found themselves (p. 149).

In 1990 Mexican Americans were still doing unskilled jobs. That is perhaps one of the reasons why Mexican American children and youth, when asked about future careers, become ambivalent and afraid of identifying blue collar jobs since their history has taught them the sad reality of poor job advancement possibilities.

Mexican Americans came to be mistreated by their adopted country. In Texas, after the Civil War, no provision whatsoever was made for the education of Mexican American children. When they enrolled in schools, they were segregated from white children because of English language "handicaps." Considered by school authorities to be children of an inferior race, they were often punished for speaking Spanish and saw their cultural background systematically ignored in textbooks. Indeed, with the exception of African Americans and native Americans, no other ethnic group has been subjected to quite the same combination of racial and cultural insult as the Hispanics of the southwest.

During the early 1920's, Mexicans began to settle outside the southwest. Many were recruited by northern manufacturing companies: meat packing plants and steel mills in the Chicago area, automobile assembly lines in Detroit, the steel industry in Ohio and Pennsylvania, and Kansas City's meat packing plants (Maldonado, 1985). By 1930, about 15 percent of the nation's Mexicans and Chicanos were living outside the southwest.

With the coming in 1930 of the Great Depression, Mexican workers were no longer welcome. This led to the deportation of more than 400,000 workers to Mexico between 1929 and 1935. Many of those workers had been born in the United States. This action caused a sense of anger against the United States not only by those who were deported, but also by those relatives who were affected, especially children who had begun to function within the cultures and the languages of the two ethnic groups.

With the start of World War II the United States once more needed workers, since labor shortages had been created in the southwest. The United States and Mexican governments agreed on the importation of Mexican workers through the *Bracero* Program. In 1942, the United States began the bracero guestworker program with Mexico, one that would, over the course of the next 20 years, admit an average of 300,000 "guestworkers" a year to pick crops in the western United States (Barrera, 1979, Maldonado, 1985, Moore & Pachon, 1985). The Bracero Program was intended to last only for the duration of World War II. Its advantages to both nations became a powerful inducement for its continuation. For Mexico, it was a temporary solution to high levels of unemployment; it also made for a significant flow of capital to that nation in the form of wages earned and sent home. For the United States, it provided a steady supply of labor easily controlled, minimally paid, and for whom no long term responsibilities were assumed (Barrera, 1979; Maldonado, 1985; Moore & Pachon, 1985). The Bracero Program was designed to legalize (and therefore reduce) the flow of Mexican agricultural workers into the United States. In fact, illegal immigration did not slow down as expected. The Bracero Program was extended annually after World War II in order to ease the labor shortage resulting from United States involvement in the Korean War. By 1954, the illegal alien problem was perceived as so serious that the Border Patrol launched what was officially called Operation Wetback to deport large numbers of illegal aliens to Mexico.

In 1965, Congress abolished the Bracero Program. This action did not reduce the flow of Mexican immigrants, however. Millions of Mexicans, attracted by the promise of work, still entered the United States illegally to fill jobs no one else would take. Peasants had grown dependent on American farmers for employment, and farmers had grown dependent on cheap labor. Large numbers of temporary agricultural workers continued to come to the United States until 1964. Many of these workers never went back to Mexico and are still undocumented aliens. These are the grandparents or parents of a significant group of Hispanic children and youth: individuals that have a sincere interest in staying in the United States; in working and giving their children a better chance to improve their lives. Many of these people cannot help their children due to their illegal status. They have become victims of discrimination and prejudice (Barrera, 1979; Cardoso, 1980; Maldonado, 1985; Moore & Pachon, 1985).

In addition to legal immigrants, an increasing number of undocumented persons have entered the United States from Mexico in recent years seeking work in the low-wage sector of the economy. Estimates of the number of illegal immigrants are unreliable, because they depend upon incomplete census data and reports of apprehensions by immigration officials. The 12.1 million persons of Mexican origin counted by the United States Bureau of the Census in 1988 is a conservative figure that includes some but not all undocumented aliens.

Mexicans are concentrated regionally, especially in California, Texas, Oregon, New Mexico, Arizona, and Illinois. The 1980 Census indicated other states with more than 50,000 persons of Mexican origin: Florida, Michigan, Washington, Indiana and Ohio.

Matute-Bianchi (1986) indicates that there are five major categories by which to identify Mexican-descent children and youth, especially in school. These are:

1. Recent Mexican immigrants. Children and youth who are Spanish-speaking, Mexican-born and, frequently, identified as limited-English-proficient (LEP). They show strong cultural, ethnic and linguistic Mexican ties. These children and youth consider Mexico their permanent home.
2. Mexican-oriented. Children and youth are most often bilingual, with varying degrees of proficiency in English-literacy skills and are usually adept in communication and academic work in classes conducted exclusively in English. Students in this group have strong ties with Mexico and the United States, but they claim an identity of *mexicano*.
3. Mexican American. Children and youth born in the United States of Mexican parentage who identify themselves as either Mexican American or as American of Mexican descent. As a group, they are much more American-oriented than the two groups previously cited and are frequently described by school personnel as totally assimilated.
4. Chicano. Children and youth who identify themselves as Mexican, mexicano, or Chicano. The word Chicano stems from the Mexican Indian Nahuatl word *mechicano*. The first syllable was dropped and Chicano was left. It is an old term for the American of Mexican descent. The term Chicano is not offensive or derogatory but is used to describe people who are politically tied to Mexico and the United States.
5. *Cholo*. Children or youth frequently identified by others as gang oriented or gang sympathizers. Not all children and youth who manifest the symbols of the cholo are members of gangs, but because they reflect the cholo style they are usually considered to be sympathetic to the cholo as a sub-cultural group. These children and youth show stylistic culture symbols. They are held in low esteem by other Mexican-descended children as well as by mainstream children and youth.

All Mexican children and youth groups are discriminated against because of ethnic, color, socioeconomic or language differences. Indeed, in certain communities Mexican American children are the victims of more discrimination and segregation than African Americans.

Mexican American children reflect a variety of cultural patterns, including those created by their parental heritage and the length of time their families have been in the United States. In a way, Mexican American children have inherited the anger of their parents towards the United States because of the way their ancestors were treated. Also, because many of those children are children of illegal parents, they reflect the tendency to think that they or their parents have committed a crime and tend to be shy or not talkative. They share a heritage of *vigilante* justice and border conflict.

Mexicans have contributed to the formation and development of the United States. Mexicans pioneered the west, mapped and named many mountains, rivers and fords, and named California, Colorado, Nevada and New Mexico. Mexicans tend to settle together in Mexican neighborhoods, or *barrios*, in which there is a central area or plaza. The lack of knowledge about cultures other than European is clearly illustrated in the fact that only a few American children learn that the first books printed in America were printed in Mexico, and that much cowboy terminology is Spanish or Indo-Hispanic: *adobe, chaps, mesquite, rodeo.* In most schools the curriculum does not include material with which Mexican American children and youth can positively identify themselves. In history classes, they represent the villains who massacred the courageous Americans at the Alamo. Also, most elementary and secondary schools inflict the final blow on the cultural identity of Mexican American children by forcing them to leave their ancestral language outside the classroom.

Puerto Rican Children and Youth

In 1988, the Bureau of the Census indicated that about 2.5 million, or 13 percent, of United States mainland Hispanics were Puerto Ricans (Bureau of the Census, 1988d). Puerto Ricans are United States citizens by birth. Puerto Rico became part of the United States after the American War with Spain in 1898. Puerto Rico was particularly attractive to the United States, not only because it was a coffee producing island in the Caribbean, but because its location made it of strategic military importance (Moore & Pachon, 1985). The United

States declared Puerto Rico an American territory and imposed a military government. Between 1898 and 1917 Puerto Ricans did not have any status; they were neither United States citizens nor citizens of any other nation. Almost 20 years passed, until in 1917 when the Jones Act was passed in Congress giving Puerto Ricans United States citizenship and making them eligible for the military draft (Wagenheim, 1970; Moore & Pachon, 1985).

Puerto Rico, a Spanish speaking nation, was conquered by an English speaking nation. And immediately, the United States imposed the English language as the language to be learned and taught in the schools of Puerto Rico. However, although English was imposed, Spanish continued to be the language used in the home and in daily communications for the majority of Puerto Ricans. The migration of Puerto Ricans to the United States began on a small scale due to the high cost of transportation to the mainland. An interesting factor in the history of Puerto Rican migration is that by 1900 a large group of sugar cane workers settled in Hawaii, where there is a Puerto Rican group living today.

For Puerto Ricans, paths to economic improvement did not exist. In the 1940's Puerto Rico had a large population per square mile, a high rate of unemployment and poverty. Puerto Ricans thought of moving to the United States as a panacea for their financial problems (Carrasquillo & Carrasquillo, 1979). After World War II, Puerto Ricans began to immigrate in large numbers to the United States encouraged by:

1. Affordable air travel, especially from San Juan to New York City. After World War Two there was a sudden surplus of airplanes. The Puerto Rican government encouraged migration to the United States by arranging low air transportation rates between Puerto Rico and New York City.
2. The need for seasonal farm workers. United States farmers arranged for Puerto Rican male workers to work in the United States during the agricultural months.
3. The need in United States industry for workers (railroads, mines, foundries and mills and agriculture). Newspapers and agencies in Puerto Rico disseminated information about industrial jobs in the United States, especially in the Northeast. Unemployed or underpaid Puerto Ricans moved to the United States to work in these jobs.
4. The demand for unskilled or semi-skilled labor in jobs in garment factories, hotels and restaurants. A significant percentage of Puerto

Ricans from the barrios and the rural areas moved primarily to New York City in search of these jobs.

By 1920, about 12,000 persons in the mainland were migrants from Puerto Rico. By 1930 the number increased to 53,000, most of them seasonal farmers (Maldonado, 1979; Wagenheim, 1970). Between 1940 and 1950, Puerto Rican migration increased even more. The 1950 census counted more than 300,000 Puerto Ricans in the mainland. Puerto Ricans began to settle near workplaces and small *colonias*, or barrios, began to be formed. In New York City, the initial places of arrival for many Puerto Ricans were Manhattan's Lower East Side, Harlem, the southeastern part of Brooklyn and the South Bronx. East Harlem became Spanish Harlem and closely identified with Puerto Ricans. Settlements in New York, New Jersey, Connecticut and Illinois appeared and grew. By 1960, it was estimated that there were about 900,000 people of Puerto Rican origin living on the mainland. The 1970 census counted 1.4 million persons of Puerto Rico origin in the mainland United States.

In the 1970's, due to the recession in the United States economy, there was a decrease of Puerto Rican migration to the United States and an increasing return to the island. This reverse migration included second and third generation Puerto Ricans who had been born on the mainland. The reasons for reverse migration included: a) an economy where there was a declining demand for unskilled labor; b) the deterioration of living conditions in the United States, where crime and drugs were part of daily life (Carrasquillo & Carrasquillo, 1979). However, this reverse migration stopped at the beginning of the 1980's and people have returned to the mainland. This circular migration has created educational, linguistic and social instability and insecurity among them.

In 1952, Puerto Rico became a commonwealth, *Estado Libre Asociado*, which allowed the island a measure of self-government. Puerto Rico's commonwealth government stipulates that Puerto Ricans are subject to military draft, do not pay federal income taxes (which permits the island to offer major tax advantages to qualifying firms), and do not fully participate in federal government political, social and service programs. Puerto Ricans have no voting representation in Congress and cannot vote in United States presidential elections. All of these factors have created a sense of political dissatisfaction and insecurity among Puerto Ricans in Puerto Rico and in the United States.

Politically speaking, Puerto Ricans are divided: some would like to continue with commonwealth status, others would prefer statehood, and still others would like to become independent.

The population is characterized by a pattern of circular migration. To some extent, this phenomenon has had a negative impact on Puerto Ricans' socioeconomic status since it does not provide opportunities to establish a firm foothold in either the mainland or the island's economy and contributes to other problems of adjustment (Carrasquillo & Carrasquillo, 1979, Moore & Pachon, 1985). The flow of Puerto Rican migrants into the continental United States continues due to periods of high unemployment. Puerto Ricans are always going back and forth. During the decade of 1980 a new phenomenon occurred—the migration of Puerto Rican professionals caused by the unavailability of professional jobs in Puerto Rico.

Puerto Ricans on the mainland are highly concentrated regionally, until recently primarily in New York City and surrounding areas and in Chicago. They have concentrated in central cities where their employment has depended on the strength of the local manufacturing and service industries. By 1980, large concentrations of Puerto Ricans also lived in Los Angeles, Miami, Philadelphia and New Jersey.

During recent years, Puerto Ricans have begun to become more ethnically self-aware. In the 1960's, Puerto Ricans began to obtain elective office and with the civil rights movement, young Puerto Ricans began to become activists. Organizations such as the Puerto Rican Forum (formed in 1957), Aspira, (formed in 1961), Institute for Puerto Rican Policy (established in 1982) and the Puerto Rican Round Table (established in the early 1980's) have begun to address the problems confronting Puerto Ricans on the mainland.

The March 1988 Supplement to the Census Bureau Current Population Survey of the status of the 2.5 million Puerto Ricans in the United States indicated that a significant percent of the parents of Puerto Rican children and youth share the following socioeconomic characteristics:

1. More than a quarter of a million Puerto Rican families lived in poverty in 1987, a poverty rate of 37.9 percent. This is close to four times the poverty rate of non-Hispanics and the highest rate among Hispanic groups.

2. The median family income for Puerto Ricans in 1987 was $15,185, less than half that of non-Hispanics and the lowest among the Hispanic groups.
3. The labor force participation rate of Puerto Ricans was only 53.2 percent compared to 64.6 percent for non-Hispanics. For native-origin Puerto Rican women, it was only 40.9 percent compared to 56.2 percent for non-Hispanic women.
4. Forty four percent of Puerto Rican families are headed by single women, 65.3 percent of whom live in poverty.

Puerto Rican children are the poorest of all the United States Hispanic groups. And the degree of Puerto Rican poverty is remarkable. The decline in community economic status is a disturbing fact. As citizens of the United States, often with military experience, with established communities in the United States that predate the Second World War, and coming from a democratic and stable country where English is taught as a second language in all schools and where educational attainment has surpassed all countries in Latin America, it was expected that Puerto Ricans would have an easier route than previous immigrant groups (Melendez & Rodriguez, 1988). Puerto Rican poverty in the United States might be explained by the economic conditions in Puerto Rico and on the unique conditions under which Puerto Ricans have evolved in America. Puerto Ricans are both citizens and foreigners at the same time: citizens since 1917, foreigners because they come from a different land. The situation of Puerto Ricans might have direct repercussions in the United States due to the pattern of high circular migration. In 1988, unemployment in Puerto Rico was 15.2 percent, three times the level of the United States. More than half the island's population lives below the poverty level. About sixty percent of the people receive public assistance because there are not enough jobs to accommodate all who want to work.

Puerto Ricans were the only group to experience a drop in a real family income between 1970 and 1980, along with a steadily increasing concentration in the lowest income quartile (Melendez & Rodriguez, 1988). Their low wages in the secondary labor market, the decline of manufacturing jobs in the northeast, and the high cost of urban living have contributed much to making the parents of Puerto Rican children and youth the poorest of United States Hispanic groups. Presently, the presence of large numbers of new immigrant workers in the Northeast region, many of whom are undocumented and thus highly vulnerable to manipulation, represents yet another arena of conflict and competition in which Puerto Ricans workers must function. An interesting fact is that Puerto Rican women are slightly more likely than other Hispanic women to be in managerial, professional and sales jobs; they also have a strong lead in clerical and administrative jobs.

Puerto Rican children and youth are frequently plagued by problems revolving around acculturation, language difficulties and economic barriers. Puerto Rican children become socially mature at an early age in order to survive in an aggressive urban neighborhood. Sex, violence and crime are familiar to them. Puerto Rican children tend to assimilate in the early years by negating their Puerto Rican background and by speaking only English. However, to the extent that they begin to grow and understand their roots, they become more Puerto Rican and begin to practice and perfect their Spanish. But the flow of Puerto Ricans to the mainland will continue helping to keep cultural, linguistic and ethnic patterns alive. And circular migration also contributes to keeping hopes high and maintaining a sense of closeness and togetherness.

Cuban Children and Youth

By 1988 the Bureau of the Census indicated that there were 1.0 million Cubans or 5.3 percent of the total population in the United States, making them the third largest national origin group of Hispanic Americans. Like Puerto Rico, Cuba was acquired by the United States as a consequence of the Spanish-American War in 1898. But, unlike Puerto Rico, it was ruled by an American government for only three years. Cuba acquired its independence in 1902. Cubans began moving to the United States during the second part of the nineteenth century. The first Cuban migration to the United Sates occurred in 1868 in response to the demand for labor of the new tobacco industry in Key West and Tampa, Florida. This first wave was predominantly white (94 %), averaged 34 years of age, and was well-educated (14 years of school) (Ford Foundation, 1984; Gallagher, 1980; Jaffe, Cullen & Boswell, 1980; Moore and Pachon, 1985). By 1930 there were about 19,000 Cubans living in the United States. By 1950, there were about 34,000. But most Cuban immigration occurred in the last thirty years. Cubans emigrated in large numbers when Fidel Castro took power in

1959. Castro's revolutionary objectives directly affected professionals and business individuals. This brought to the United States many wealthy and middle class Cubans: businessmen, government officials, professionals and managers. This was a more racially mixed group (80 percent white) and younger than previous generations. The census of 1960 counted 125,000 Cubans. In 1966, there were 273,000 Cubans in the United States. By 1970 almost a third of all businesses in Miami were Cuban-owned and operated (Moore & Pachon, 1985). This group was politically conservative since it fled a socialistic revolution. (The Cuban population has grown from 803,000 in the United States in 1980 to 1.0 million in 1988). Cubans have had success in establishing themselves, using their background knowledge and business skills and have done well in the business world, especially in construction, real estate, clothing, tobacco, restaurants, and television and newspapers.

Although Cubans were concentrated mostly in Miami, the Cuban Refugee Program relocated the refugees in communities across the United States in order to relieve the strain that the Cuban influx placed on the economy of Miami. But, by the early 1970's Cubans returned to Miami. About 60 percent of all Cubans lived in the Miami area. The city of Miami offered Cubans a closeness to home, a familiar climate and a well-established community. There is a significant number of Cubans living in New Jersey and in New York City. Other large communities of Cubans may be found in California, Texas and Illinois.

In April 1980 more than 10,000 Cubans took refuge in the Peruvian embassy in Havana, hoping to leave Cuba. This group and other groups were allowed to leave by the Castro government. At least 118,000 Cubans came by boat from the Cuban port of Mariel. This group of Cubans was young, racially mixed (only 60 % white), and poor. The *marielitos* arrived in the United States in an unpleasant atmosphere of resentment in part due to the economic troubles of 1980 and to the press and media accounts that sensationalized the Cuban felons, homosexuals and the mentally ill who were allowed to leave with the immigrants (Gallagher, 1980). The more established Cubans were upset by the exprisoners, street people and homosexuals who tended to destroy the Cuban image as members of a golden exile (Gallagher, 1980; Portes & Bach, 1985). Most of the new arrivals went to Miami and imposed a heavy burden on the resources of the city and the Cuban community.

Cuban children in the United States belong to two socioeconomic groups: the middle class who came in 1959 and the poor group who came in 1980. In many ways, these two groups did not mix and resented each other due to their parents' attitudes towards each other. When the literature mentions Cuban children, it often refers to the economically and socially advantaged group. However, there are many Cuban children and youth, especially from the later immigrant group, who are poor and with the same socioeconomic characteristics of the Puerto Rican and Mexican American children. The middle class children and youth do well in school and in general do not share the social, economic and educational characteristics identified in Chapter 1.

Dominican Children and Youth

Together with Colombians, Dominicans constitute the largest segment of the group labelled "other Hispanic origin" by the United States Census Bureau. Dominicans constitute the fourth largest Hispanic immigrant group in the United States and represent the largest group of immigrants in the northeast since the 1970's. Small Dominican migrations can be traced across several decades. Before 1961, relatively few immigrants came to the United States from the Dominican Republic. In the decade from 1950 to 1960, only about 10,000 Dominicans came to the United States (Leavitt & Kritz, 1989; Ugalde, Bean & Cardenas, 1979). But, Dominicans as a significant group in the United States are considered part of recent migrations that originated in the 1960's following political regime changes in the Dominican Republic, including an intervention by the United States Marines in 1964 (Hendricks, 1977).

In the Dominican Republic, President Rafael Trujillo restricted emigration during his 30-year dictatorship. Trujillo's emigration policies were designed to limit the mobility of the Dominican labor force to insure abundant and cheap labor for new industries and agriculture and to limit contact between the Dominican Republic and other countries. But following his assassination in 1961 a steady flow of migration to the United States, primarily to New York City, began and continues to this day. The United States government considered the migration as an economically motivated one to which regular United States restrictions would apply. The immigration change also coincided with the establishment of the Balaguer government which welcomed the United States migration policy.

From 1967 to 1976 about 12,000 Dominicans annually immigrated to the United States; the total number officially admitted from 1966 to 1977 was over 150,000 (Leavitt & Kritz, 1989). The 1980 Census found that 62 percent of the Dominicans in New York City had arrived after 1965, and about a quarter had arrived between 1975 and 1980 (Leavitt & Kritz, 1989). According to the 1980 Census, 169,100 persons of Dominican birth were living in the United States. They are concentrated in New York City, especially in the area of Washington Heights and the Lower East Side.

While Dominicans have utilized legal immigration to the fullest, they also utilized illegal means, primarily: entry on tourist and student visas and entry without documents through Puerto Rico. Puerto Rico is about a 15 minute flight from the Dominican Republic and trips to Puerto Rico are frequent among Dominicans. Also, undocumented individuals reach Puerto Rico by sea. Puerto Rico is the area of second highest Dominican concentration.

During the 1980's, a period of economic difficulty in the Dominican Republic, many Dominicans migrated to New York City looking for a better way of life. Presently, Dominicans are also settling in other parts of the United States, especially in Florida and Massachusetts. Economic motivation is the main reason for Dominican immigration.

Dominicans who migrate to the United States see jobs and savings as a way to obtain or maintain middle-class status or to attain higher social status when they return to the Dominican Republic by investing their savings in businesses in the Dominican Republic (Leavitt & Kritz, 1989; Pessar, 1987).

Dominican immigrants are neither predominantly rural nor from the ranks of the chronically unemployed. The migration stream is predominantly urban and middle class. Available data indicate that about a quarter of the migrants were from rural areas, and nearly three quarters of the urban migrants were middle class according to Dominican Republic standards (Gurak & Kritz, 1982; Pessar, 1987; Ugalde, Bean & Cardenas, 1979). Dominican migrants were born in urban areas and a large number had lived in urban areas before migrating (Gurak & Kritz, 1982). Dominicans, in general, are literate, relatively well-educated, largely from middle class backgrounds, urbanites and young (under the age of 40) (Ugalde, Bean & Cardenas,

1979). As with other Hispanic immigrant groups, women predominate (Pessar, 1987) and head households. Many Dominican children do not have a father, or the father is still in the Dominican Republic.

Although Dominicans come to the United States in search of jobs, their hopes do not always materialize due to English language barriers or lack of job skills. Kritz & Gurak (1985) found that the Dominican labor force was 75 percent male and 47 percent female. Dominicans typically work as operatives in sewing, textiles, packing, service jobs (especially in restaurants and hotels). The majority of women are employed in manufacturing, especially textiles. About a third of all Dominican workers are employed in firms that provide goods and services to predominantly Hispanic consumers. Leavitt & Kritz (1989) stated that downward occupational mobility appears to be greater for women than for men, and women earn on average significantly less than Dominican men.

Dominican children and youth differ from other Spanish speaking groups in the Eastern United States in that a higher number of them are of illegal status; and in many instances the parents, although they want to, cannot represent them, because they are afraid of being found out and sent back to the Dominican Republic where socioeconomic conditions are extremely poor.

Parents of Dominican children share immediate social, educational and economic needs: housing, jobs, English language development, cultural adjustment, formal education or vocational training and financial and legal assistance (Leavitt & Kritz, 1989). Newly arrived Dominicans, as well as other newly arrived Hispanics, tend to identify schools as the first provider of social services for their children. For the immigrant family lacking solid familiar resources, school is seen as the most available source of emergency services or referrals for food and housing or social security assistance. Leavitt & Kritz (1989) quoting the words of a school principal in New York City whose school had a significant percentage of Dominican students indicated that dropouts are higher among Dominicans than among Colombians or Ecuadoreans whose children are equally represented in the school. A guidance counselor from the same school indicated that the perceptions were that Dominicans were more deficient in educational routines and that they needed more in the way of orientation to what was expected from school.

Central and South American Children and Youth

Central and South Americans are among the most recent of the major immigrant streams. In 1988, the Census Bureau indicated that there were about 2.2 million (or 12 percent) Central and South Americans residing in the United States. Like other immigrants to the United States, many of these persons arrived during periods of political or economic upheaval in their countries. More than half of these immigrants have come to the United States since 1970; less than one third are native born. Often, they have entered the United States through Mexico; some have entered under immigration quotas; others originally came to the United States on tourist or student visas and then stayed in this country without legal status.

Many Central and South Americans have come to the United States in search of a better life for their families; but, since 1979, political disturbances and the existence of armed resistance movements have contributed to large scale migration to other Central American countries and the United States from El Salvador, Guatemala, and Nicaragua. The largest number comes from El Salvador, the second largest are refugees from Guatemala (Melville, 1988). Their exact numbers are difficult to estimate because of their undocumented status. Many Guatemalans, Nicaraguans, and Salvadoreans who have entered the United States in the past seven years consider themselves to be political refugees but have not been granted that legal status.

Recent Central American immigration can be traced largely to economic and political conditions in the native countries, especially during the last two decades. The establishment of the Central American Common Market (CACM) and the growth of the manufacturing sector during the 1960's improved economic conditions in the region. But, in 1969 a border dispute between Honduras and El Salvador created instability, and in the early 1970's the CACM broke down and economic growth slowed. Rapid population rates aggravated these problems even more. Between 1950 and 1985, Central America's population nearly tripled, growing from 9.1 to 26.4 million (Diaz-Briquets, 1986). Unemployment is extremely high and is related to the region's population growth. The increase in the size of the economically active population since the 1960's has been dramatic, and it is likely to continue unabated well into the 21st century.

The Latin American population has increased greatly and has become dispersed in recent years. Latin Americans live in large cities such as New York City, Los Angeles and Houston, but they also relocate to semi-rural areas, from Florida to California. Experts calculate that there are from 500,000 to 2 million such immigrants in the United States today (Melville, 1988). The number of immigrants from Central and South America, legal and illegal, can be expected to increase during periods of political and economical setbacks. The United States democratic government and economic strength offer these immigrants hope for a better life.

Children from Central and South American origins have not received attention in the literature. Very little is known about these children beyond demographic and census data. The largest group of Central American children are from El Salvador, Guatemala and Nicaragua.

Guatemalans are concentrated mostly in Los Angeles and New York City. Guatemala is a territory of 42,000 square miles, about the size of the state of Tennessee. It has a high rate of population growth of 3.1 percent. Its economy depends heavily on agriculture. The unemployment rate in Guatemala is about 33 percent (Suarez-Orozco, 1989). An internal civil war between the poor landless and wealthy government supported groups has affected Guatemala's economic and political stability since the 1970's. Political terror has firmly established itself as the principal means of governance (Suarez-Orozco, 1989). Guatemalans have fled the country in search of political stability as well as for economic reasons. There are not accurate estimates of how many Guatemalans reside in United States since many Guatemalans are undocumented. Suarez-Orozco (1989) indicated that the numbers of legal immigrants have also been on the rise in the past decades: from 1951–60, 4,663 Guatemalans immigrated to the United States; 15,883 from 1961–70; 25,882 from 1971–80, and 15,666 from 1981–84.

Nicaraguans live primarily in Miami, Southern California and San Francisco. Nicaraguans have arrived in the United States in large numbers due to the political situation in Nicaragua. In 1985, Nicaragua had a population of about 3 million people, making it the least densely populated nation in Central America and the largest in area (57,000 square miles). Nicaragua's economy depends primarily on agriculture. From 1934 until 1979 the United States backed the Somoza government which has been described as the longest, most corrupt dictatorship in Latin America. In July 1979, after two decades of guerrilla warfare against Somoza's army, the *Frente Sandinista* ousted the Somozans and eventually installed a nine member directorate of the Sandinista National Front (Suarez-Orozco, 1989). The Reagan administration, arguing that the leftist Sandinistas were a threat to the security of the region, began a campaign to remove the Sandinistas from power.

During the Somoza dictatorship, thousands of Nicaraguans fled the country in search of refuge. Since the Sandinista takeover in 1979, Nicaraguans have continued to leave, although not in the same large numbers as the Salvadoreans and Guatemalans. Until 1990 (when the Sandinistas lost political control of the government) large numbers of discontented youth left Nicaragua to avoid the military draft which they saw as a senseless slaughter. According to 1989 INS statistics, 38 percent of the aliens applying for asylum in the United States were Nicaraguans and 29 percent were from El Salvador. Miami was the most frequent destination given. Miami officials have expressed concern about the financial strain on the public and private organizations providing services to these individuals, especially for education and health needs.

Estimates of the number of Salvadoreans in the United States range as high as 500,000. El Salvador is a country of 8,236 square miles, about the size of Massachusetts. El Salvador is the most densely populated nation in Central America. Its population growth rate of about 3.5 percent per year is one of the highest in the world. El Salvador is not only a country with a civil and internal war, but it is very poor; and many Salvadoreans emigrate for political as well as economic reasons (Diaz-Briquets, 1986).

Legal immigration from El Salvador to the United States has been on the rise in the last three decades: 5,895 from 1951–60, 14,992 from 1961–70, 34,436 from 1971–80 and 32,666 from 1980–84 (Suarez-Orozco, 1989). These are very conservative figures, since the exact number of Salvadoreans uprooted in the context of escalating terror is not well-documented. Estimates indicate that about 1 million people have fled the country. Large numbers of new arrivals are in the United States without the required documentation, since not all apply for political asylum (Suarez-Orozco, 1989). About 30,000 Salvadoreans applied for political asylum in the United States from 1980–85. Salvadoreans are mostly concentrated in Los Angeles, New York and Washington, D.C. Not all Salvadoreans live in the United States. They have settled in cities from Canada to Panama, and there are thousands of refugee camps in Honduras.

The largest concentrations of South American children are from Colombia, Ecuador and Peru. Colombians have come to the United States for economic and social reasons. In 1960, Colombia had an agrarian reform, and the introduction of modern agricultural methods and machinery tended to exclude from the market all those who could not afford the new technology, while the agrarian reform program affected relatively few of Colombia's peasants. Land reform was attempted but not much was achieved. Economic growth did not spread its benefits. Poverty remains acute. A quarter of the Colombians do not have enough to eat. Thousands of children sleep in the streets of Bogota. There was an ever-accelerating movement of people to the cities and, beginning in the early 1960's, to the United States. But a more urgent factor pushing Colombians to leave their country and flee to the United States is the violence created by the *guerrillas* and the drug trafficking. The guerrillas are responsible for killing hundreds of public figures, including politicians, judges and newspaper editors. Others have been kidnapped or forced to flee the country. The rapid growth of trade in cocaine and other drugs has increased violence to new levels even for a country long used to settling political and personal grievances outside the law. Drug dealers almost control Medellin, the country's second largest city.

The Colombian community is more selective than others in terms of where it will settle and is more likely to be dispersed throughout the United States. There are groups concentrated in New York City, Los Angeles, Miami, Washington, D.C., and Chicago. The limited data available indicate that socioeconomic characteristics of Colombians are similar to, though somewhat lower than, those of Cubans. They have higher than average employment rates, a fact which distinguishes them considerably from Puerto Ricans and Mexicans (Gurak & Kritz, 1982). Parents of Colombian children and youth are better represented in both white and blue collar occupational categories than Mexican Americans, Puerto Ricans or Dominicans.

Very little is known about Ecuadorean children. Most Ecuadoreans leave Ecuador for economic reasons. The majority of them come from Guayaquil, a port city with a large population, high unemployment and poverty. Ecuadoreans, like Columbians, are concentrated in New York City, Los Angeles and the Miami area.

Peruvians are leaving their country for economic and political reasons. In 1990, Peru was identified as the South American country with the worst economy among all Latin American countries. President

Alan Garcia, who assumed the Peruvian presidency in 1985, was not able to move Peru toward its desperately needed social and economic progress. Hyperinflation is taking the country to national bankruptcy. Economic performance is central to maintaining the very precarious social peace in Peru. At issue is not only the possible confrontation between left and right. Far more dangerous is the resistance of the Maoist Shining Path Patrulla—*Sendero Luminoso*. This situation exists because of the divisions between rich and poor, the city and the *sierras*, whites and *indios*. Further deterioration of economic performance with declining per-capita incomes, explosive inflation, and real wage cutting make Peru ungovernable. Due to this political and economic instability thousands of middle-class Peruvians are fleeing to the United States, especially to the New York City and Miami areas. Most of those coming from Peru are educated people, professionals and businessmen. It is common to hear Key Biscayne in Miami called "Ancon", the name of an exclusive resort on the coast of Peru.

Refugee Hispanic Children and Youth

The Refugee Act of 1980 established the authority for any alien present in the United States, or at a land border or port of entry, to apply for asylum irrespective of the alien's immigration status. United States law entitles aliens, legally or illegally in this country, to asylum. To be granted asylum, an alien is required to demonstrate a well-founded fear of persecution in the country of habitual residence because of race, religion, nationality, political opinion or membership in a social group. Since 1975, 1,208,767 documented refugees, many of them children, have entered the United States from different parts of the world (National Clearing House for Bilingual Education, 1989a). A number of refugee children come from Central and South America, especially from Nicaragua and El Salvador. In many cases, refugees had to abruptly leave their home culture, language, family and friends, and may never be able to return to their countries (National Clearing House for Bilingual Education, 1989a; Suarez-Orozco, 1989). Refugee students may have suffered traumatic experiences during their escape from their homeland; they may have witnessed parents, relatives or friends die. These events may cause students to have difficulties in coping with the transition into a new culture and society.

Refugee children face other obstacles to success in United States society: employment outside of school hours, legal residency and bureaucracy as well as educational tasks, language barriers and no school documents. Some students were not attending school in their original country, and some may be illiterate. Experts have recognized four phases of adjustment that refugee students may go through that affect their behavior, attitude toward school, and general interactions. They are:

1. Denial—The students may actively disassociate themselves from the past or deny that certain events actually happened.
2. Anger—The students may act out their feelings in inappropriate contexts.
3. Despair—The students may be sullen or non-communicative.
4. Understanding—The students may accept what has happened and begin to integrate themselves more actively into the new environment (National Clearing House for Bilingual Education, 1989a).

In order to meet the educational needs of refugees, the Office of Bilingual Education and Minority Language Affairs (OBEMLA) of the Department of Education provides grant programs under the Emergency Immigrant Education Program and the Transition Program for Refugee Children. The Emergency Immigrant Education Program provides funds for state education agencies to be distributed to local school districts to teach English and other subjects and to provide instructional materials. In 1987, the program served 428,688 students. The Transitional Program for Refugee Children provides assistance on a formal basis depending on the number of refugee students in a given state. In 1987, 80,221 students were served (National Clearing House for Bilingual Education, 1989a). The National Clearing House for Bilingual Education suggested a series of strategies to help refugee students to adjust to United States culture and schooling. Of particular importance are: (a) Enhance students' self-esteem by focusing on their positive abilities and the progress they have already made, (b) Help students develop realistic expectations for adjustment to the United States, and (c) Help students develop coping skills such as not overreacting to stressful situations and making the best of difficult situations.

Conclusion

The diversity of the Hispanic community is exhibited in the distinct communities of Mexican, Puerto Rican, Cuban, Dominican, South and Central American and other Hispanic groups. The Hispanic sub-groups have a unique sense of identity, racial mixture and history. These ethnic and cultural differences may be difficult to understand in a society that tends to identify and categorize people simply as white, African American, Asian or Hispanic. It has been assumed that Hispanics are largely immigrants and that their problems are the problems of all new immigrants, which will disappear when the group learns English and becomes assimilated. Even Puerto Ricans, citizens since 1917, are sometimes perceived as foreigners. Hispanics have come to the United States and been confronted by racial prejudice, a language barrier, and isolation into segregated neighborhoods and schools, locking many of them into low-level, marginal job opportunities.

Hispanics do not share national cultures, nor do they share experiences in the United States. There is a great deal of regional diversity among Hispanic children and youth. Mexican children are mostly concentrated in the Southwest. Puerto Rican children are mostly concentrated in the metropolitan areas of Chicago, Jersey City, Newark, New York City, Orlando, and Philadelphia. Cubans live in Miami, New York and New Jersey. Dominican children are concentrated in the metropolitan areas of New York City and Boston. Central and South American children are more spread out with large concentrations in California, Florida and New York. The Cuban American economic community in Miami is strong in contrast to the subordinate position of Hispanics in other parts of the nation. These "home" areas are different (economically, socially and politically) and these differences are important in understanding the characteristics of each group of Hispanic children. When other children appear in those "home" areas they have to adapt to local circumstances and to the dominant Hispanic group.

Hispanic groups have contributed to make the United States a pluralistic society. All United States citizens need to contribute to help these groups to succeed, by demonstrating a commitment to and appreciation of the value of cultural pluralism. This begins with acknowledging that all people, whatever their ethnic and cultural background, are worthwhile and accepted individuals in American society.

CHAPTER 3

The Culture and Language of Hispanic Children and Youth

Hispanic children and youth, although not a homogeneous group, have much in common because of their shared Spanish language, culture, customs and their ethnic origins. These unique linguistic and cultural characteristics need to be understood in the context of the cultural and linguistic diversity of the United States to accommodate the understanding and respect of both Hispanic and American cultures. The fact that there are general linguistic and cultural characteristics shared by Hispanics does not mean that these individuals are linguistically and culturally alike, but that they share ethnic roots, observed through their specific language characteristics and their cultural traits.

This chapter presents an overview of the unique cultural and linguistic traits of Hispanic children and youth with the purpose of identifying those characteristics shared by all Hispanic groups.

The Hispanic Culture

Culture is the environment that humans themselves have made. It includes the distinctive ways of carrying on life processes: the artifacts, ideas, values, language, attitudes and customs of a particular time and place. Culture includes the most superficial aspects (dress, diet, music, food) and the deepest assumptions that people make about their relationships with other people and their personal values and priorities. Manifestations of non-material culture are much harder to observe but equally important for understanding people's way of life: customs, beliefs, values, means for regulating interactions with other humans and with the supernatural. Culture exists only in relation to a specific social grouping and is created and acquired by human beings only as members of society. The culture of a group of people includes all of the systems, techniques, and tools which make up their way of life. Culture is shared, and defines boundaries, but the exact same culture is not shared by all members of a social group, and the boundaries are highly permeable. The culture is influenced to some extent by geography, resources, climate, and history of the particular society and groups within the society (Hall, 1976; Ovando & Collier, 1985; Spolsky, 1978).

The important cultural dimensions of the Hispanic culture are related to language familiarity and use, interaction with fellow Hispanics, ethnic loyalty and identity, cultural awareness and generational proximity (Fitzpatrick, 1982; Spolsky, 1978). Young people, therefore, do not simply repeat the life processes of their parents; they learn to live according to the demands of the latest developmental stages of the culture. Respect for individual differences and the desire to provide opportunities for every individual to learn and to find a place in society according to their ability and efforts have long been recognized as the essence for societal development. This understanding is not always practiced in the United States, creating much conflict among different cultural groups. Also, many Hispanics themselves do not understand their role in a diverse society like the United States and cannot teach their children what to expect from others or themselves in terms of understanding and respect for individual differences. In many instances, Hispanic children expect every United States citizen or resident to understand that they are linguistically and culturally different, but that those differences are not obstacles to membership in United States society. In other instances, these children believe that such differences do not exist and that, because they were born or raised in the United States, they need to follow only American linguistic and cultural traits. These misunderstandings can cause conflict which in extreme instances result in racial tension or aggression (Fitzpatrick, 1982; Ovando & Collier, 1985; Spolsky, 1978).

Although Hispanics living in the United States trace their roots back to several different countries, there is still a common denominator of Hispanic culture in the United States, especially for Hispanics in the same socioeconomic class. Many elements are shared and enhanced: language, religious beliefs and practices, family structures and roles of family members, forms of artistic expression, food and dietary customs. For example, most Hispanics in the United States are Christians, predominantly Catholics, and celebrate the Epiphany or the Three Kings Day, celebrate Hispanic or Spanish heritage holidays, share similar entertaining habits and communicate in Spanish with each other with no difficulty. Hispanics believe that there is a Hispanic culture in the United States and agree about many specific ways in which professionals can take this cultural factor into consideration when they work with Hispanic children and their parents (Grossman, 1984). The literature (Fitzpatrick, 1982; Ovando & Collier, 1985; Pifer, 1979; Seda Bonilla, 1975; Spolsky, 1987) has identified several life patterns and basic beliefs shared by a significant group of Hispanics. These are among others: (a) Interpersonal relationships based on interdependence and cooperation, (b) The importance of emotional relationships—worth and affection are openly expressed, (c) The concept of self-pride and individual worth, (d) Importance of the immediate and extended family, and (e) Acceptance of life as it exists—spiritual and social aspects of life are valued. Hispanics tend to retain their unique ethnic characteristics longer than immigrants from Europe and Asia. There are several theories that justify that retention: (a) Hispanics are in constant circulation from and to their not-distant home land; (b) There is a continuous high rate of new immigrants and visitors from home; and (c) Hispanics tend to live together and this closeness helps to preserve the culture (Moore & Pachon, 1985; National Council of La Raza, 1986a; Ovando & Collier, 1985; Seda Bonilla, 1975; Valdivieso & Davis, 1988).

At the same time that there are universal cultural characteristics of Hispanics, there are stereotypes of Hispanic children and youth. Stereotyping is used to establish social distance and social boundaries to maintain and rationalize the Hispanic subordination to the dominant culture or to identify those dominant culture characteristics Hispanics lack. Stereotypes—Hispanic *machismo*, Hispanic time, Hispanics only think and plan for the present—can usually be recognized by the negative statements made by people who do not understand the cultural traits of Hispanics. For example, machismo is not demonstrated by all Hispanic males. There are some who say that although Hispanic women in general are not very outspoken, they are the ones who make the final decisions in the home. Furthermore, the idea that Hispanics emphasize the present rather than the future, intangible gratifications rather than material rewards, and enjoyment rather than the "run-run" of whites is not always true. The Hispanic stereotype of being serene, not anxious, perhaps just a bit improvident in planning for the future and living, may be true to some Hispanics and false to other Hispanics (Hall, 1976; Moore & Pachon, 1985).

There are indeed real differences between groups of people, and those differences need to be recognized, understood, and respected. For those dealing directly with Hispanic children and youth, it becomes a process of balancing an awareness of general cultural or subcultural traits with an affirmation of the absolute uniqueness of every individual.

Hispanics form a cultural, social and historical mosaic. Hispanic immigrants bring variants of national cultures. Mexican Americans represent a Hispanic culture distinct from Puerto Ricans, Cubans or Dominicans. Their eating habits are different. They have different religious beliefs, different Spanish language characteristics and show different migration patterns. For example, taking the simplistic trait of foods, a rich variation of dishes is found. Puerto Ricans' main food is rice and beans, yellow rice with pigeons, *pernil*, and *pasteles*. One of Dominicans' main plates is *mangú* (mashed plantains) and *moro* (yellow rice with beans). Cubans' black beans and *congri* (yellow rice with beans) are unique dishes. Ecuadoreans are famous for their *cebiche*. But, the Ecuadorean cebiche is different from the Peruvian cebiche.

Puerto Ricans are United States citizens, but with different historical, linguistic and cultural traits than other Americans. The Mexican Americans' history in the United States includes their being conquered, their land being taken and attempts to deprive them of their culture. Cubans in general feel grateful to the United States for accepting them when they were forced to leave their country. The attitude of Cubans, Puerto Ricans and Mexican Americans toward the culture of the United States is different in many ways due to their different forms and patterns of immigration. The Spanish spoken in the United States, although relatively homogeneous, presents linguistic varieties. These linguistic characteristics are mostly seen in the vocabulary and in daily expressions. For example, the word for bus in Puerto Rico is *la guagua* and *el bus* or *autobús* in Colombia, Ecuador and Mexico.

Not only are there differences between national origins and regions of Hispanic cultures, there are differences within regions (Barrera, 1979; Moore & Pachon, 1985; Seda Bonilla, 1975) and generations. New immigrant Mexicans live according to Mexican values in some ways more than do second and third generation Mexicans. Puerto Ricans coming from Puerto Rico's rural areas will live according to Puerto Rico's rural values in many ways. Third generation Dominicans will tend to live according to the values of a local *barrio*, such as Washington Heights in New York City, retaining the cultural values that they have absorbed from first and second generation Dominicans. There are variations of these cultural elements from one sub-group to another. Some of these variations may be traced to contrasting conditions and customs in different regions of the homeland of the family's forebears, the difference in rural and urban life. The members of the particular ethnic group do not all follow the same religion in the same manner, even in cases where one religion dominated in the original homeland, as Catholicism with most Hispanics. Hispanics bring to the United States their specific cultural traits which are learned and practiced by their children in several ways and degrees. Second- and third-generation Hispanics, caught between the Hispanic and the dominant cultures, particularly experience conflict which may result in deviance (Grossman, 1984).

It is important to emphasize that although the Hispanic culture shares certain common elements of life patterns and basic beliefs, there are also significant differences in the attitudes, interests, and goals that children internalize by interacting with their families and by interacting with the American culture. Also, it is necessary to state that due to factors affecting rate of assimilation, differing composition by region, status or background, uniformity in Hispanic cultural life patterns and basic beliefs cannot be defined easily. Values, for example, involve individuals' beliefs concerning the world and their position in it. Values have a universal referent and a judgmental character. For example, Hispanic children and youth have been taught certain values that are part of Hispanic culture, but they also acquired other values inherent in American culture by their interaction with both cultures. And, at times, the cultural values of both cultures are unconscious assumptions children and youth take about the appropriateness or inappropriateness of ideas or actions. These assumptions in no way make them guilty of adapting more cultural traits of one culture or abandoning the other culture's traits. In some instances they adopt interpersonal communication patterns of both cultures focusing frequently on body language as a mode of communication and upon values of dignity, respect, honesty, aggression and subservience which are communicated differently by different cultures. The fact that Hispanic children and youth retain some values from both cultures can create conflicts between them and their parents or other individuals.

Hispanic children's and youths' culture should be presented in a positive way to help them understand that they can live in the so-called *American culture* without necessarily rejecting their *Hispanic culture* (Grossman, 1984; Ovando & Collier, 1985). This harmonious concept of accommodating the understanding and respect of both the Hispanic and the dominant culture is called biculturalism or cultural pluralism. Biculturalism exists when a person has the volition and capacity to negotiate two conformable sets of cultural assumptions, patterns, values, beliefs and behaviors. Biculturalism, in essence, says that a person has to come to terms with two world views, usually one which is learned from one's parents and another one which is adapted. Being bicultural suggests the individual's ability to respect each culture's values, openness and adaptability in their interaction with one another, enhancing the ability to function effectively as both members of an ethnic group and participants in American society (Grossman, 1984; National Council of La Raza, 1986a; Ovando & Collier, 1985; Spolsky, 1978).

Cultural pluralism is more related to a society in which members of diverse, social, racial or religious groups are free to maintain their own identity and yet simultaneously share a larger common political organization, economic system and social structure. Collier & Ovando (1985) cited Havighurst's (1978) definition of cultural pluralism as meeting the following conditions:

1. Mutual appreciation and understanding of every sub-culture by the other ones.
2. Freedom for each sub-culture to practice its culture and socialize its children.
3. Sharing by each group in the economic and civic life of the society.
4. Peaceful co-existence of diverse lifestyles, folkways, manners, language patterns, religious beliefs and practices, and family structures (p. 111).

In the United States, Hispanic cultural norms are partially in conflict with those of the larger host society. For example, the American educational system itself is a cultural intervention, which serves primarily to prepare middle class children to participate in their own culture; and, as a result, most teachers are trained to meet the needs of only this group of students. Children and youth from other cultures, such as the Hispanic culture, are usually perceived as disadvantaged or deficient to the degree their cultural experiences differ from the mainstream, middle class norms. Because of this conflict, behavior which is normally acceptable in Hispanic culture is viewed as deviant in the larger society. Hispanic children and youth living and learning in the United States suddenly find that their normal behavior is automatically defined as deviant by the dominant society and the school. This tendency has been known to occur in relation to recreational activities such as gambling, religious practices such as spiritism ceremonies, attitudes toward property, and patterns of interpersonal communication, frequently misinterpreted by those unfamiliar with Hispanic culture. Hispanic children and youth may demonstrate cultural values and beliefs that may not accommodate the values of the United States middle class society. Some of the differences in values may create conflict for Hispanic children in their interaction with non-Hispanic individuals. In school, for example, there is importance given to cooperation versus competition, to compliance versus aggression, to anonymity versus self-assertion. Conflict of values is a real problem for Hispanics. Test taking requires competition; and cooperative behavior may be interpreted as cheating in such contexts.

Hispanic children's and youths' demonstrated behaviors need to be understood by those who have the direct responsibility for their well-being and development. Also, parents of Hispanic children need to be aware of these cultural or behavioral differences among groups in order to be able to prepare their children to live and learn in two cultures and two languages.

Hispanic Cultural Change and Acculturation

Acculturation refers to a complex process whereby the behaviors and attitudes of the immigrant group change toward the dominant group as a result of contact and exposure to a cultural system that is significantly different. In other words, one cultural group takes on and incorporates one or more cultural traits of another group, resulting in new blended cultural patterns. Acculturation has been used to describe such diverse behaviors as the generation of migration, recency of migration, familiarity with the host language, factual knowledge of the host society, interaction with persons belonging to the host society and value orientation such as ethnic pride and identification with a cultural heritage (Grossman, 1984; National Council of La Raza, 1986a). Concerns about acculturation frequently are seen in public worries about whether new immigrants will learn English. Too often, this translates into a fear of bilinguals. In fact, having Americans who can speak two or more languages is not a threat. For immigrants to learn English at the expense of their native language is a serious waste of national resources. Hispanics follow the same acculturation process as other immigrants. By the third generation, the vast majority of Hispanic Americans are English dominant. Another public fear is that Hispanic immigrants will pursue the goal of separatism. But, Hispanic groups are unanimous in their advocacy of opportunities to become bilingual citizens.

Sometimes fear of bilingualism can lead to policies which make acculturation more difficult. Because of the fear that bilingual education programs will somehow keep children from learning English, attempts have been made to eliminate these programs and replace them with English-only programs. Disparities largely occur between first generation parents and second or third generation children, because the children are more likely to be exposed to influences of United States culture and society in school and through the mass media. The meaning of children's cultural background is the depth of their identification with their particular ethnic group. How long the family has been in the United States may have considerable bearing on the degree and nature of a child's ethnic awareness.

Hispanic culture changes and it persists. Change primarily affects the minority ethnic group because culture is expected to become more and more like the white majority's culture. This process has been called *Americanization*, Anglo conformity and assimilation. It is assumed that traits of the Hispanic culture disappear and are replaced by traits of a white culture. It has been suggested that with each passing decade Hispanics are being brought closer to the mainstream of social change and economic development of the larger society until eventually there will be a merging with the general United States population (Jaffe, Cullen & Boswell, 1980; National Council of La Raza, 1986a). This is generally a difficult process even for parents whose organization of their behavior patterns was developed in the culture in which they grew up. For their children, who are still trying to internalize one culture when they are expected to take on the ways of a brand-new culture, the transition is even more difficult. Cultural conflict is the term frequently used to denote the frustrations individuals experience in such circumstances. Whether they are assimilating more or less quickly with other groups, they do seem to retain a sense of their original cultural identity more tenaciously than do other ethnic groups (Ford Foundation Report, 1984; National Council of La Raza, 1986a). It often happens that first-generation immigrants are encouraged by their children to dispense with all the old things they have brought with them from the old country home. The third generation, interested in their ethnic heritage, may bring back the cultural traits and heritage that their parents and grandparents had valued and maintained.

For many Hispanics in the United States confusion and stress can result when traditional values come into conflict with the majority culture. The Quest International (1987) position paper gives an example when it says: "In a culture in which youth is virtually worshiped, respect for elders declines" (p. 7). Other conflicts may arise when Hispanics identify with the American or white culture. For example, the Latino emphasis on interdependence and cooperation can be antithetical to the mainstream culture's preference for competition and individual achievement. A suggestion for ameliorating cultural conflict may be an understanding by Hispanic children and youth that the traits of the primary culture that are not needed may be dropped, with the result that there can be two modes of functioning. Thus, it is possible to gain white cultural traits without totally losing Hispanic ones. Acculturation may be a means by which biculturalism can develop in certain circumstances, but it can also result in total assimilation, because it is a process in which an individual or group completely takes on those traits of another culture, leaving behind the original cultural identity. Hispanic children and youth may show different degrees of acculturation or changes in the adoption of American styles, loss of Hispanic styles, and biculturalism. For example, in some instances, Hispanic children adopt interpersonal communication patterns of both cultures focusing frequently on body language as a mode of communication and upon values of dignity, respect, honesty, aggression and subservience which are communicated differently by different cultures (Barrera, 1979; Hall 1976; Grossman, 1984; Ovando & Collier, 1985; Ramirez, 1985).

Language is a key component of culture. It is the primary medium for transmitting much of culture, making the process of language learning in children a linguistic dimension of culture. Children learning their native language are learning their own culture. Learning a second language also involves a second culture to varying degrees that may have profound cognitive and psychological consequences for children and youth.

Language Characteristics of Hispanic Children and Youth

Hispanic children of parents whose native language is not English, particularly immigrant children, have a broad range of language characteristics and needs that impact on their development. Language is recognized as the means for representing thought and as the vehicle for complex thinking. But children use the language they understand best to explore, interpret, construct meaning and to manipulate complex concepts (Brown, 1980; Chomsky, 1965; Diaz, 1983; Sapir, 1921). Language is a very important component of Hispanic children's and youths' cognitive development and growth since it is a reflection of their underlying thought; it expresses and defines their ideas, concepts and logic. Proficiency in two languages is desirable because it enables students to think in two systems, shifting language codes as necessary to solve problems. Capable bilinguals have a problem solving advantage over monolinguals (Cummins, 1984; Diaz, 1983; Peal & Lambert, 1962). Language serves to facilitate or amplify intellectual growth because the individual's intellect interacts with things and people in the environment. An extensive vocabulary, broad concepts, and command of grammatical construction facilitates learning, memory and manipulation of complex concepts (Brown, 1980).

Sapir (1921), a famous linguist, defined language as a purely human activity used to communicate ideas, emotions, and desires through a system of voluntary-produced symbols. This definition emphasizes a number of important aspects of language that need to be discussed and understood when describing the language of Hispanic children and youth in the United States as a complex and unique characteristic of their culture. In essence what this definition states is that:

1. Language is a purely human activity. Every physiologically and mentally normal person acquires in childhood the ability to make use of a system of verbal and nonverbal communication, as both speaker and hearer. Speakers possess abstract abilities that enable them to produce grammatically correct sentences in a language, and they actively engage in a gradual subconscious and creative process of discovery through which they acquire the rule system of their language.
2. Language is used to interact or communicate with other members of the same speech community. In other words, Puerto Rican Spanish speakers interact or communicate without difficulty with Spanish speakers from the Dominican Republic, Peru or El Salvador.
3. Language is a means of individual expression. Individuals use language to impart information, express feelings and emotions and to influence the activities of others. The language produced by children has a particular purpose; i.e., to convey a need, to get an object, to express joy or sadness. Language is also used to share friendliness or hostility towards persons who make use of a similar set of voices.
4. Language is transmitted culturally, that is, it is learned. Authorities such as Brown (1980) and Chomsky (1965) suspect that language is universally acquired in the same manner. Children learn the language by relating their understanding of the new to what they already know and by changing or elaborating the knowledge they acquire.
5. Language normally does not operate without meaning or function. Language learners are learning all the time, using social or cognitive strategies. The acquisition of meanings and concepts is a process that continues well beyond the primary years.
6. Language production is usually less than language comprehension. Language learners show more receptive language than the language they are able to produce. Perceptually, children need to have some comprehension of the language system they are trying to internalize. Physiologically, children must feel conformable about using the language productively. Once they feel ready to orally express their thoughts, they will communicate in the desired language.

Cummins (1984), Krasher and Biber (1988) identify two kinds of language that need mastery: conversational language, the language used for informal, interpersonal communication; and academic language, the language used in school for learning. Limited-English-proficient (LEP) students can acquire conversational English fairly rapidly, in two years or less. However, it takes much longer than that to reach grade level proficiency in academic language (Krashen & Biber, 1988). According to Cummins (1984) academic language includes written and oral components. The second language learner requires between six and 12 years to achieve the cognitive academic language proficiency (CALP) necessary for classroom success by LEP students. CALP is strongly related to the ability to use language in a decontextualized situation in order to provide a coherent, comprehensible, informationally adequate account without signals from an interlocutor (Cummins, 1984).

Hispanic children and youth reflect a large variation of spoken language. The greatest educational harm to Hispanic children is the false assumption that they are fully English proficient, when, in fact, the children have only developed a superficial command of the English language. In many states, the language needs of Hispanic children are grossly underestimated, resulting in the placement of children in all-English classrooms where they do not fully comprehend the language of instruction (Arias, 1986; Cummins, 1984; Ovando & Collier, 1985; Ramirez, 1985).

The principal characteristic that is widely shared by Hispanics is the Spanish language; it is the single most unifying element of Hispanics in the United States. The retention of Spanish is the most obvious and visible sign of retained Hispanic cultural characteristics. Over half of the people who speak a language other than English in United States speak Spanish; and it is spoken in four-fifths of all Hispanic households (Brown, Rosen, Hill & Olivas, 1985). By 1980, approximately 10.5 million United States Hispanics spoke Spanish at home. Oxford-Carpenter, Pol, Lopez, Stupp, Hendell & Peng (1984), describing the demographic projections of non-English language background (NELB) and limited English persons in the United States to the year 2000 by state, age and language group, conclude the following about Hispanics:

1. The Spanish non-English language background population increases from 10.6 million (38 percent in total) in 1976 to 18.2 million (46 percent) in 2000.

2. Growth of the Spanish group (by 7.6 million) accounts for two-thirds of the total growth of the NELB population (by 11.5 million).
3. There is heavy concentration of NELB's in California, New York and Texas.
4. Spanish NELB's are much younger than other NELB groups (ages 5–14).

Spanish persists in the Hispanic population longer than other languages have remained with immigrant groups. It is continually invigorated by linguistically high contact situations. The use of Spanish in the United States has increased considerably. For example, the number of Spanish radio stations grew from 60 to 200 between 1970 and 1980, Spanish language newspapers from 40 to 65 and Spanish television stations from 12 to 167 (Moore & Pachon, 1985; Valdivieso & Davis, 1988). The use of Spanish in school is seen as an instructional means to advance Hispanic students' academic advancement. Before the 1970's, Hispanic children were put directly into mainstream (English-only) classes and forced to learn the language or fail in school (swim or sink). That process caused much stress and hardship and resulted in high drop out rates. Hispanic children suffered humiliation and physical punishment if they used Spanish. Today, school districts are to some extent penalized with threats of the loss of funds if they deny the children of Spanish-language background access to any school programs, including programs that make use of Spanish for instructional purposes.

But, not all Hispanic children have Spanish language proficiency. Language proficiency is not a unidimensional construct, but it is a multifaceted modality, consisting of various levels of abilities and domains. Hispanic groups have different degrees of Spanish language exposure and usage. Hispanics who were born outside the mainland of the United States are more likely to come from homes in which Spanish is spoken and are more likely to speak Spanish rather than English as their usual language. Spanish is not the language of the home of all Hispanics residing in the United States. Perhaps, the earlier categorization of Hispanics as "Spanish surname" can account for the popular assumption that all Hispanic children speak Spanish (Arias, 1986). The following section includes a brief description of the language groups of Hispanic children and youth.

Bilingual Children and Youth

Students' English language needs are expressed in the research at various levels of complexity. Estimates of the number of limited-English-proficient students vary widely. The Department of Education estimates that there are 1.2 to 1.7 million LEP school-aged children ages 5–17 (United States General Accounting Office, 1987b). The Report mentioned all LEP's to include Hispanic children and youth. This estimate is based on the number of children who: (a) Score at or below the 20th percentile on a national English language proficiency examination, and, (b) Demonstrate a dependence on their native language. Other estimates are higher estimating up to 2.6 million LEP students. The number of Spanish LEP's aged 5–9 will increase at a rate 20 times faster than Spanish LEP's aged 10–14 between 1976 and the year 2000 (900,000 to 1.4 million) (Oxford-Carpenter et al., 1984). States with the largest concentration of LEP students are California, Texas, and New York (United States General Accounting Office, 1987b).

There are variations in the definition of what makes an individual bilingual. There is a range of definitions forming a continuum from a strong to weak bilingualism. Ovando & Collier (1985) listed some of these definitions. These definitions are:

1. Can use two languages alternately (Weinreich, 1953).
2. Can produce meaningful sentences in L2 (Haugen, 1969).
3. Can use two languages alternately; but the point at which a person actually becomes bilingual is arbitrary or impossible to determine (Mackey, 1962).
4. Can engage in conversation in more than one language (Fishman, 1966).
5. Possesses at least one language skill (listening, speaking, reading or writing) in L2 to a minimal degree (MacNamara, 1967).
6. (An "incipient bilingual") can use a passive knowledge of L2 to transact businesses in L2 (Diebold, 1961).
7. Speaks only one language but uses different varieties, registers, and styles of that language (Halliday & Stevens, 1964; Collier & Ovando, 1985, p. 66).

The variety of definitions arises because the purposes for using two languages vary depending on the groups or individual goals and preparation to use that language. Since bilingual students are not a linguistically homogeneous population, a continuum of proficiency or degree of bilingualism can be determined according to the students' language skills. Along this continuum there are Hispanic bilingual individuals with varying degrees of proficiency in English and Spanish. There are several levels of bilinguals among bilingual speakers: (a) Proficient bilinguals, (b) Partial bilinguals, and, (c) limited bilinguals. These levels are listed and described below.

Proficient Bilinguals

Bilingual Hispanic students may be defined as individuals who are exposed, formally or informally, to two languages and who engage in conversation in more than one language. To be bilingual means that a person has at least some level of competency in the native language (L1) and the second language (L2), in this case English. These individuals are not expected to have equal mastery of both languages, but it is assumed that they are able to understand the communication of others and to communicate and achieve goals in English and Spanish. Valdivieso & Davis (1988) and Veltman (1988) indicated that as immigration continues bilingualism may persist longer among Hispanics than it did among other immigrant groups. Valdivieso & Davis (1988) also say that immigration does not delay the acquisition of English by the native born or by the immigrants themselves. Theorists suggest that most Hispanics appear to regard knowledge of English as a prerequisite to success in American society and yet retain their Spanish. Ramirez (1985) indicated that the degree of bilingualism can be depicted according to the individual's knowledge of the two languages in three broad areas: (a) the knowledge of different aspects of language, such as grammar, vocabulary and pronunciation, (b) The receptive and productive control of language skills, such as listening, speaking, reading and writing, and (c) The use of language in different varieties, styles, domains and functions, depending on the audience of the language.

The majority of Hispanics in the United States are bilingual. In a survey conducted among Mexican Americans, 75 percent indicated that one of the most important characteristics of Mexican culture is being bilingual (Brown et al., 1980). Hispanics do shift to English, but it is a three-generational process rather than one- or two-generational as experienced by other immigrant groups (Arias, 1986). The preference for Spanish or English also depends on one's job, neighborhood and lifestyle (Valdivieso & Davis, 1988). Valdivieso & Davis indicated that 75 percent of all Hispanic immigrants speak English on a daily basis by the time they have been in the country for 15 years. More than half of the immigrants who arrived in the United States before they were 14 have made English their everyday language. The United States-born children of Hispanic parents usually become fluent English speakers. Most retain knowledge of Spanish as well, because Spanish is spoken at home or in the neighborhood (Valdivieso & Davis, 1988). Most of these Spanish speakers are also fluent in English (Valdivieso & Davis, 1988; Veltman, 1988). Veltman (1988) projected that the number of Spanish speaking Americans, including those bilingual in Spanish and English will reach 16 to 18 million by the year 2000. Half of the growth will occur in Los Angeles and New York. Veltman projected that Spanish-speaking population in these two cities could reach 2.5 to 3.0 million by 2001, and about 1 million in the cities of San Antonio, Chicago and Miami. Most language theorists agree that children have great facility in becoming bilingual, or even multilingual. Most Hispanic children acquire English skills through their every day involvement with English out of necessity or through school. In order to develop bilingualism in Hispanic children the maintenance of the weaker language is essential.

A significant number of Hispanic children and youth are proficient bilinguals. Proficient or fully bilingual (or equally Spanish and English superiors) describes a level of bilingualism at which individuals attain native-like proficiency in the full range of understanding, speaking, reading and writing skills in both languages. The degree of bilingualism is measured by students' performance on language proficiency exams.

Partial Bilinguals

These individuals exhibit a level of bilingualism at which individuals attain native-like proficiency in the full range of understanding, speaking, reading, and writing in one language, but achieve less than native-like skills in some or all of these skills areas in the other language. A partial bilingual or limited-English-proficient (LEP) student is defined by the Bilingual Education Act as an individual who comes from a home environment where a language other than English is most relied upon for communication and who has sufficient difficulty understanding, speaking, reading and writing English to deny the individual the opportunity to learn successfully in all-English classrooms. There are two partial bilingual groups: the more English dominant and the more Spanish dominant.

Projections concerning students with Spanish, non-English backgrounds for the year 2000 note that 29 percent of California, 27.5 percent of Texas, and 11 percent of New York State school enrollment will have students whose language at home is Spanish (Arias, 1986). Veltman (1988) found that approximately 43 percent of Spanish speakers relied on Spanish predominantly; the remainder preferred English. There is a significant group of immigrant Hispanic children, as well as the United States born children of immigrant parents who enter school speaking Spanish. Their dominant language is Spanish. Dominance results from measuring language proficiency in two languages in which the language receiving the highest score is said to be the dominant one. In the case of monolingual Spanish speakers, their English proficiency does not exist or is very limited. They lack a working command of the English language in situations where the medium of instruction, textbooks, wordbooks, libraries and the spoken word, is English.

There is also a group of Hispanic children and youth for whom English is their only medium of communication. These individuals represent a small group since most of those Hispanics who are English proficient also speak Spanish. Use of English by Hispanics depends in part upon whether they are foreign- or native-born, and for the native-born how far removed they are from the immigrant experience. With increasing age, Hispanic children use less Spanish as English becomes the language of instruction and as they continue to live in an English-speaking nation.

Limited Bilinguals

These individuals have attained a level of bilingualism less than native-like proficiency in both languages. The National Assessment of Educational Progress (1986) has stated that socioeconomic variables and language are related to achievement. They indicated that Puerto Rican students are negatively affected as compared to Cubans in regard to frequency of use of Spanish in the home. They indicated that the effects of bilingualism on achievement appear to differ both within ethnic groups (being positive for Hispanic children from middle and high socioeconomic groups, but negative for low socioeconomic Hispanic children) and between ethnic groups, depending on the achievement being measured. One explanation for this finding is the fact that low socioeconomic children do not receive the language foundation in any language to be successful in school. There are two limited bilingual groups among Hispanic students: the more English dominant and the more Spanish dominant. There is a theory, not fully explained, that suggests that first-generation immigrants speak their native language and learn some English; their offspring learn English and will not use Spanish often. On this issue, Ramirez (1985) listed Fishman's four stages of language shift patterns that may help to explain Hispanics' change to English. These are:

- Stage 1:   Immigrants learn English through their mother tongue. English is utilized in only those domains (e.g. work), where the mother tongue cannot be used. (This may be the case in the first generation).
- Stage 2:   Immigrants learn more English and can use this language on their own in various domains (e. g. neighborhood or recreation). There is still a dependency on the mother tongue.
- Stage 3:   Speakers become bilingual, being able to use both languages with almost equal ease. Language separation does not occur by domain. (This is usually the case of the second generation).
- Stage 4:   English displaces the mother tongue, except in the most intimate domains (e.g. family affairs or religious services). (This may occur in the third generation) (P. 9).

Conclusion

Hispanics constitute a very important minority group with a large and constant presence in the United States. Their cultural and language characteristics represent different varieties and levels due to Hispanics' historical, socioeconomic and immigration experiences in the United States. Within Hispanic subgroups, cultural and linguistic variations are factors that make them a diverse and unique population. In planning educational programs for Hispanic children and youth, decisions need educational programs for Hispanic children and youth, decisions need to be made in terms of the varied cultural and linguistic characteristics of these populations. Some of these characteristics are related to size, demographic concentration, age and the diversified language abilities within the group.

Hispanic ethnic groups represent different degrees and levels of language proficiency in English or Spanish or in both languages. With an increasing number of Hispanics speaking both English and Spanish, the United States is being enriched with the addition of the Spanish language, a valuable personal and national resource that should be nurtured and shared. Ways must be found to encourage Hispanic children and youth to become bilingual. These bilingual individuals will represent the United States in monolingual Spanish countries as business and political entrepreneurs, where translators will no longer be needed.

Spanish-language LEP's will become an increasingly important factor in educational planning to the year 2000 because Hispanics have a higher birth rate than most other language minority groups and Hispanics are younger than other language minority groups. Recognition must be given to the need to provide enriching bilingual curriculums and experiences that will enable these Hispanic students to participate fully in the United States educational system; and an emphasis must be placed also on devising strategies for enriching the language of monolingual English speaking students who can acquire Spanish-language skills that they can benefit from in the society of the twenty-first century.

CHAPTER 4

The Family of Hispanic
Children and Youth

The Hispanic family, more than other social institution, has been affected by the Hispanic presence in the United States. A variety of family experiences has emerged due to the diversity of times and ways in which Hispanic families have entered the United States. The role of the Hispanic family is very important in insuring the success of their children. Therefore, Hispanic children and youth face challenges related to family structure and organization, family education, income and occupation, housing, family arrangements, and family social and economic dependence.

This chapter presents an overview of Hispanic children's and youths' families. It discusses the Hispanic family structure and organization, its socio-educational status, housing, and family arrangements. It also presents a discussion of how the status of the family has pushed the Hispanic family into social and economic dependency, and into other problems such as child abuse and neglect, foster care and teenage pregnancy. Although these elements do not have a cause and effect relationship, they are interrelated, especially the socioeconomic status of the family.

Family Structure and Organization

The family is in some respects a microcosm of society, reflecting within it many facets of the whole social, economic and legal environment of the society at large. The family is still the primary agent in passing on social skills, especially as they relate to its children. Child-bearing and child care also remain primary functions of the family. The child is totally in the care of the parents or grandparents during the first few years of life when the basic characteristics of personality are being formed. The family is responsible not only for socializing the children but also for ensuring that children conform to or share certain basic values of the family's culture and society. An important function of the family is to provide emotional security. Companionship and parenthood seem to be the most important sources of psychological security. Family members protect each other, care for the sick or injured, provide one another with shelter, warmth, food and clothes. The literature also indicates that neighborhood is important to the pattern of the family's social activities. Families are eager to find the right kind of neighborhood with a school that suits their children, a church responsive to their religious and mental needs, and the provision of social activities to meet the family's social needs. This ability to choose is not the case for the majority of Hispanic families. Hispanic families' choice of neighborhood is not by preference, but mostly by convenience or because it is the only neighborhood alternative for them. Therefore, in many instances, Hispanics do not participate in the neighborhood social activities, due to language and cultural barriers.

Just as there is no uniform white/Anglo or African American family, there is no one Hispanic family in the United States. Rather, there are a number of family types that vary according to region, recentness of migration, education, social class, age, urban-rural locale and cultural assimilation. The Hispanic family in the United States presents a variety of family structures and organizations mostly closely related to socioeconomic and educational status (Andrade, 1983). In other words, Hispanic middle class family characteristics tend to be more alike than those of Hispanic low socioeconomic families. Also middle socioeconomic level Hispanic families tend to share more characteristics of middle class white and African American families. Because the majority of Hispanic families are poor most of the characteristics mentioned in this chapter describe Hispanic low socioeconomic families.

The Hispanic family is a relatively young one. In 1988, the median age of the Hispanic family was only 26 years of age, while the median age for the total population was 32 years of age (Bureau of the Census, 1988d). The youngest of all of the Hispanic groups are the Mexican Americans, with a median age of 24 years. Puerto Ricans are close at

25 years of age. Both Mexican Americans and Puerto Ricans have comparatively fewer older people and more children. The younger Hispanic population is in part a result of high fertility levels and migration rates.

Hispanic families tend to be larger than those of the general population; for example, Hispanics are more than twice as likely to have three or more children in the average household. As a result, the median household size for Hispanics is nearly one third larger than for the general population. Hispanic families are more likely than non-Hispanic families to have children. In 1980, two-thirds of Hispanic families had children compared to one-half of non-Hispanic families. But, both groups show declines from 1970 to 1980. The averages have decreased since 1970, but the decline was less for Hispanics than for any other group. The consequence of high fertility is large families. In 1988, the average number of persons per family was larger among Hispanics than non-Hispanics: 3.7 compared to 3.1 of non-Hispanics (Bureau of the Census, 1988a). Mexican American families had the largest families with 4.1 persons.

It has long been recognized by anthropologists and sociologists that alternative types of family structure may fulfill similar kinds of functions such as discipline and socialization. Typically, there is a tendency in the literature to view a two-parent nuclear family household as a model type and to give little attention to the variety of family arrangements which exists in non-two-parent households. In the United States, there is a significant group of Hispanic children who do not enjoy a two-parent, nuclear family household. Thus, there is no model type of family structure and organization. In Hispanic families, for example, the mother's brother may substitute in various ways for an absent father.

A significant number of Hispanic households are headed by women. The proportion of Hispanic families maintained by married couples decreased between 1982 and 1988 from 74 percent to 70 percent. During the decade of the 1980's, almost one out of five school-age children lived with a single parent. Nine of ten single parent families were headed by women, and about one third of female-headed families were at the poverty level (Andrade, 1983, Moore & Pachon, 1985, Valdivieso & Davis, 1988). Thus, in 1988, 23.4 percent of all Hispanic families were headed by women, compared with 16.3 percent of all American households. Family type varies among the Hispanic subgroups (Bureau of the Census, 1988d). Cuban and Mexican origin families had the highest proportion maintained by married couples. Puerto Rican families had the highest proportion maintained by a woman without the husband present.

Decisions in the family depend on the family structure and are determined by who is the leader, or head of the family. There is an increase in the proportion of households headed by women due to the rising divorce rate, the number of illegitimate births, and the number of women who emigrated without their husbands. This is similar to the trend for the rest of the nation. By 1983, 23 percent of Hispanic families were maintained by women, higher than the 15 percent for non-Hispanic families. Among Hispanic families, the proportion maintained by women was noticeably higher for Puerto Ricans (about 44 percent) than for other Hispanic groups (Valdivieso & Davis, 1988). Compared with other family types, the female-headed, single-parent family is generally the most limited with respect to financial and personal resources to cope with family tasks.

Grandparents are likely to remain with the family. Contrary to common practices of non-Hispanic groups in the United States, grandparents are welcome to live with the family. They are not seen as a burden, but as a blessing due to their knowledge, as role models for the children, or as people who can take care of the children during the parents' absence. Grandparents play a significant and highly respected role in the lives of Hispanic children, many times being the only adult who interacts with the children for most of the day and part of the night.

The structure within the Hispanic family has been one of the most criticized and yet least understood aspect of family life. The male has been viewed as the ultimate and unquestionable authority. However, male superiority is maintained formally and publicly, legally and socially, but within the home, the woman quietly exerts her will and remains the focus of her children's life.

While the impact of the Hispanic family may have been eroded somewhat by urbanization and acculturation, it is still a central institution for the Hispanic individual. Hispanics put great emphasis on family relationships. For example, in Hispanic terms the word *family* means not only the nuclear parent-child family, but an extended family of several generations including cousins and *compadres*. *Comadres* and compadres play an important role in the social and affectional development of the Hispanic family. Compadre is a term used to describe the relationship between two adult couples who are bound through a ritual kinship related to the baptism of a child. Compadres also help to formalize ties of friendship and are very important individuals in case of the absence of the natural parents. In the United States, the word family is used only in reference to that nuclear model of father, mother and children living in one house. In Hispanic countries, such as Colombia, the Dominican Republic, El Salvador and Puerto Rico, the word *family* includes all the relatives, including those who do not live in the same house and those who live in their homelands. This cultural trait was brought to the United States, where it is very common to see a Hispanic family composed of a mother, grandmother, children, aunts, uncles, grandparents and cousins, all of them living in the same house or apartment. On many occasions these individuals stay with a given family for a long period of time until these individuals improve their economic situation or find an apartment of their own. Relatives play an important role in affecting the economic adaptation of the family. Relatives are welcomed to live with Hispanic families because they may represent the second salary of the household: as another financial resource desperately needed to cover the expenses of the family. Among Colombian and Dominican women with children, the presence of other adult women helps distribute the burdens of child care and household maintenance and results in a higher probability that a woman can add to the economic resources of the family through employment (Gurak & Kritz, 1982). Social policy has not always adapted to the survival needs of the Hispanic extended family. Housing policies and sizes make it difficult for three generational families to live together.

There are, too, social and cultural tensions between Hispanic parents and their children. For example, a significant group of Hispanic parents are still living in the culture of their homeland, and would like their children to follow their lifestyles. The children are brought up in the American society and attend American schools where American values and lifestyles are being presented, worshiped, and encouraged. Because American values are strongly emphasized by the school, by society at large, and by children's peers, and because these life-styles appear as the most appropriate ones, children tend to deviate from traditional Hispanic life-styles creating tensions and conflicts with their parents. At times, it looks as if the parents do not understand their children and their children do not understand their parents (Fitzpatrick, 1982). Fitzpatrick, describing transitional family patterns of the Puerto Rican family in the United States, stated that the group most affected by these changes is the children. He stated:

> Puerto Ricans families have frequently lamented the patterns of behavior of even good boys in the United States. Puerto Rican parents consider them disrespectful. American children are taught to be self-reliant, aggressive and competitive, to ask why, and to stand on their own two feet. A Puerto Rican child is much more submissive. When the children begin to behave according to the American pattern, the parent cannot understand it (p 53).

This section ends with the observation that when speaking about the structure of the family of Hispanic children and youth it is difficult to identify only one or two structures. At the beginning of this section it was made clear that the Hispanic family indicators or generalizations to be presented were more related to low socioeconomic Hispanic families since they represent the higher percent of Hispanic families. Most Cuban families do not match all the characteristics discussed in this section since a high percent of Cuban families belong to the middle socioeconomic level. Also, many South American, Central American, Dominican, Puerto Rican or Mexican American families do not reflect the above characteristics, either.

Parents of refugee children and youth do not fall into the characteristics previously discussed. Many parents of refugee children stayed in their countries and sent their children to the United States for safety purposes. Parents, in many instances, suffer great hardships and, often, invest precious and limited resources to finance the journey north (Suarez-Orozco, 1989). These children living in the United States perceived their parents as having made sacrifices. Suarez-Orozco (1989), referring to this family commitment, stated: " The strong desire in many immigrants to work and study, to remain in an educational system, unlike their own, to learn English, to enter college or professional training or to secure a good paying job was firmly rooted in a familial matrix of reciprocity and mutual nurturing" (p. 75).

Generalizations about the Hispanic family are relative to indicators of the historical, demographic and socioeconomic status of Hispanics in the United States. There is no such thing as only one structural characteristic of the Hispanic family in the United States. There are, however, a variety of organizational and structural traits in many Hispanic families, especially those that live in low socioeconomic neighborhoods.

Education, Occupation and Income

Family factors such as education, income, English language proficiency, technical and specialized training are socioeconomic conditions affecting the welfare of Hispanic children and youth. The family is the most common economic unit, involving a relatively efficient division of labor between the members of the family. Although, traditionally, the husband has been the breadwinner and the wife has taken care of the home, the household and the children, this is not the case in many Hispanic families, where that husband often does not exist, and a significant number of households are headed by women.

Hispanic children's and youths' economic and social status is below the level of non-Hispanics, since living standards for Hispanics did not improve during the 1980's, especially in terms of income, education and employment. Data indicate that the Hispanic family lags behind that of whites in critical areas such as education, employment and earnings (Bureau of the Census, 1988b; Valdivieso & Davis, 1988).

The Hispanic family is less educated than white families. For those persons 25 years of age and over, whites had completed a median of 12.7 years of school and Hispanics 12.0 years. There are a great many inter-group differences. Mexican Americans are the least educated achieving only 10.8 median years, Puerto Ricans 12.0 and other Hispanics 12.4 years. The Hispanic adults most likely to have school age children are in the 25–34 year age bracket. In 1988, this group was over three times as likely not to have completed high school as other non-Hispanic groups (Bureau of the Census, 1988b, Valdivieso & Davis, 1988). Some United States Hispanics are more likely than others to have high school diplomas. In 1988, nearly 83 percent of Cubans age 25 to 34 had completed high school compared to only 67 percent of Puerto Ricans and 54 percent of Mexican Americans (Bureau of the Census, 1988b; Valdivieso & Davis, 1988). Although the educational attainment of Hispanics has improved, it remains below the level of their non-Hispanic counterparts.

There are major differences in educational attainment between native- and foreign-born Hispanic families. A survey conducted in the middle of the 1970's indicated that 45 percent of Puerto Ricans and 55 percent of Mexican Americans between the ages of 14 and 30 who were born outside the mainland United States were not enrolled in school and were not high school graduates. This number contrasted with 16 percent of the Puerto Ricans and 18 percent of the Mexican Americans who were born in the United States (Moore & Pachon, 1985). Most of the recent literature indicates that Hispanics with an English background and proficiency complete high school at higher rates than English limited children and youth, a significant number of whom are foreign born.

The Hispanic family is poorer than the white family. Since the end of the last economic recession in 1982, the real median family income of Hispanic families has risen by 6.9 percent compared with 12.3 percent for non-Hispanic families. The poverty rate of Hispanic families in 1987 was 25.8 percent. About 26 percent, or 1.2 million Hispanic families were living below the poverty level compared with 10 percent of non-Hispanic families (Bureau of the Census, 1988c; 1988d). Among Hispanic subgroups, Puerto Ricans families had the highest poverty rate at 38 percent. Cubans, Central and South American families had the lowest poverty level at 13.8 and 18.9 percent.

Hispanic children in two-parent families are twice as likely as white children in two-parent families to live below the poverty level. Hispanic children have the highest poverty rate among children in the states of New York, New Jersey, Texas and New Mexico. The median income of Hispanic families reported in the 1988 census was only $20,310, below the national median of $31,610 for non-Hispanic families. Hispanics on the average earned slightly more than African Americans, but only about three-fourths as much as other non-Hispanic groups. The lowest of the Hispanic family groups were the Puerto Ricans, earning $15,190. Hispanics did not improve their relative standing between 1970 and 1980. The Mexican Americans lost slightly, the Puerto Ricans dropped, Cubans and other Hispanic groups gained (Bureau of the Census, 1988d). Hispanic unemployment rates are always higher than those of whites. The Hispanic unemployment rate is 40 to 60 percent higher than the total for the rest of the United States population. The increasing rate of unemployment is a major factor in the rise of poverty among Hispanic children and youth. A factor which affects the economic situation of Hispanic families, in addition to unemployment, is the potential earning power provided by two parents.

Housing and Family Arrangements

Poor housing is a direct consequence of poverty, but low income alone cannot fully explain the poor housing conditions in which many Hispanics live. Factors other than income contribute to poor Hispanic housing conditions. One of these factors is housing discrimination (Dolbeare & Canales, 1988). Discrimination against minority groups, Hispanics as well as African Americans and others, is a common occurrence in the United States housing market. Since 1968, federal law has prohibited housing discrimination. But enforcement procedures are very weak. The law does not provide protection to families with children or handicapped persons. Hispanics are severely affected by restrictions prohibiting families with children from housing units. Very few Hispanics own their own homes, and they pay a high proportion of their income in rent. Most Hispanics in the United States are renters, live in housing that is more than 25 years old, in single family structures, or in low-rise apartments located in urban areas. A monograph of the National Council of La Raza (1988) indicates the following housing characteristics among Hispanics. According to the authors Dolbeare & Canales (1988) in 1983:

- One Hispanic family in 20 (five percent) occupied housing classified by the United States Department of Housing and Urban Development as having severe physical problems, and another one in eight (12.5 percent) lived in housing with moderate physical problems.
- Among Hispanic sub-groups, Puerto Ricans appeared to have the greatest incidence of housing problems in 1980.
- One in ten (10 percent) paid more than 70 percent of its income for housing; nearly two in five (37 percent) paid more than 30 percent.
- Hispanics are less likely than other Americans to be homeowners. Only 43 percent of Hispanic households were homeowners in 1983, compared to 65 percent of the general population.

In 1980, less than half of the Hispanic families lived in homes they owned compared to two-thirds for the non-Hispanic households (Bureau of the Census, 1980). Dolbeare and Canales (1988) analyzed data from the 1980 Census that clearly indicated a significant difference in housing status among the major Hispanic subgroups. Puerto Ricans appear to have the greatest incidence of problems. Five percent of Puerto Rican households did not have complete plumbing facilities. Puerto Rican homeowners with or without mortgages had the highest housing costs (Dolbeare & Canales, 1988). Home ownership is much higher for Mexican Americans and Cubans (49 and 44 percent respectively) than for those of Puerto Rican origin (21 percent) (Bureau of the Census, 1980). By 1980, home ownership rates for Hispanic households showed no improvement over 1970 despite gains by Cubans and Puerto Ricans because home ownership for Mexicans declined.

Housing quality is a major problem for Hispanics. Hispanic families are twice as likely to live in housing that is physically inadequate. It is most likely to suffer from poor maintenance, poor heating, uncollected garbage, rats and dilapidation. Inadequate heating is a major problem affecting more than 60 percent of all such units, while almost one third of the units have upkeep or maintenance problems (Dolbeare & Canales, 1988). More than one in six (18 percent) Hispanic housing units showed signs of rodent infestation, almost one in eight (12 percent) had open cracks or holes in interior walls or ceilings, one in ten (10 percent) had broken plaster or peeling paint or rooms without electricity, and almost one in ten (9 percent) showed evidence of roof leaks (Dolbeare & Canales, 1988).

The poor living standards of many Hispanic children have required a higher degree of home sharing and cooperation among Hispanic families. As of 1983, one fourth (25 percent) of all Hispanic households had five persons or more; only 15 percent consisted of single persons (Dolbeare & Canales, 1988). More than one half of all Hispanic households contain children under the age of 18, but there was almost no difference between owners and renters in this regard. In 1983, almost half of all Hispanic homeowners and nearly 75 percent of renters were under the age of 45. Mexican Americans had the largest household size at 3.74 persons per unit, Puerto Ricans ranked second with 3.27, while Cubans had 2.94 (Dolbeare & Canales, 1988).

Hispanic housing is likely to be overcrowded. Extended families are common, in which a grandmother, for example, absorbs her daughter's family into the household as a way of arranging to pay the high cost of housing or as a care taker of the child while the mother works. Related data suggest that Hispanics are much more likely than whites or African Americans to live with their children where the children—not the elderly persons—are the householders. In 1980, among non-Hispanics 37.4 percent (including 14.4 percent of men and

54.0 percent of women) lived in families; about 39.1 percent of Hispanic elderly were widowed in 1985, and of this group, more than one third (34.4 percent) were not in households, but lived in family groups, with relatives (National Council of La Raza, 1987). Hispanic culture places a high priority on keeping the elderly with the younger generation, a factor that results in many multigenerational families.

Paternal Support

Historically, Hispanic children and youth have had to depend upon multiple sources of economic and social support, different from the white ideal home of nuclear family self-sufficiency. An important source of economic and social support for Hispanic children and youth should be their fathers. The literature is not clear in identifying how much financial support Hispanic children and youth receive from their fathers. It is assumed that perhaps they do not receive sufficient paternal financial support. Most of the children who are in economic dependency lack paternal economic support. There are several reasons for this lack of financial support:

1. Hispanic children in families headed by a male are more likely to be poor than non-Hispanic children in male-headed households. Although the father may live with the children, he may not have the economic means to appropriately support the children. If the father has re-married, the burden of supporting the children from a previous marriage will put the father's current family in jeopardy since he will have to share whatever economic means he has with two families. In most instances, the father chooses not to contribute to the support of the children of the previous marriage.

2. Many Hispanic males are unemployed, and they cannot support their children and their families. While the unemployment rate for the total population of non-Hispanics was 5.8 percent, for Hispanics it was 8.5 percent; it was 9.8 percent for Mexicans and 9.2 percent for Puerto Ricans (Bureau of the Census, 1988d).

3. Because divorce and separation rates are very high among Hispanic migrants, many of the fathers remain in the homeland, and only the mother and her children immigrate, making it difficult for United

States officials to enforce child support. Most of these children end up in social dependency programs.

Social and Economic Dependence

For much of America's history, social welfare needs were addressed exclusively through the family, voluntary organizations and local governments. Federal dependency in the United States began in 1930 and most recipients were white, African Americans and widowed mothers. The Great Depression of 1930 with its widespread loss of jobs and property led to the creation of President Roosevelt's new programs such as Social Security, Unemployment Insurance, and Aid to Families with Dependent Children (AFDC) (Ford Foundation, 1989, O'Hare, 1987, Wilson, 1987). The second movement was in the 1960's, when a re-thinking of welfare issues brought about President Johnson's War on Poverty and the Great Society Programs, such as Medicare, Medicaid, Food Stamps and Headstart (Wilson, 1987). In time, minority mothers were included, many of whom were bearing children out of wedlock. This aid to minorities has produced a mixture of racism and resentment that contributes to the current stigmatization of the welfare population (Moore & Pachon, 1985).

The public image of social dependency programs and the people who use them is riddled with misconceptions. Welfare programs are usually thought of as government handouts for poor people. Only 60 percent of the population below the poverty level receives welfare. In 1960 most welfare recipients were families with dependent children. AFDC is a federal/state program established by the Social Security Act of 1935 for the care of dependent children in their own homes by providing cash to needy families with payment levels determined by each state. In all states, eligible families are those with children under 18 where one parent is absent due to death, desertion, divorce, incapacitation or incarceration.

The term welfare is used to refer to government programs which provide money or services to people with low incomes. Supplemental Security Income (SSI) was established by 1972 amendments to the Social Security Act. This program provides monthly cash payments to needy aged, blind and disabled persons to help to bring their incomes up to a federally established minimum level. Medicaid was established in 1965 as a program by which the federal government provides open-ended payments to states to help to cover the costs of medical services for members of AFDC families and most individuals eligible for Supplemental Security Income payments. The Food Stamp program began in the 1960's and currently operates under the Food Stamp Act of 1977. This program distributes coupons redeemable for food to individuals and families with incomes below the poverty line. The bulk of government spending on social programs is not for welfare programs, but for programs like Social Security, Unemployment Insurance and Medicare. Welfare programs require applicants to demonstrate need through a means test based on income, family size, and age. Welfare typically serves low-income families with children, the disabled, or the needy elderly, and accounts for 11 percent of the annual federal budget. Most Welfare benefits are not cash, but services like food stamps, medical care or subsidized housing.

The two ethnic groups that have received welfare for the longest period of time are African American families headed by women, and Hispanic families headed by women. Women, especially with dependent children, are more likely than men to receive welfare; African Americans and Hispanics more likely than whites, and children and young adults more likely than the elderly (Ford Foundation, 1989, Wilson, 1987). Divorce, out of wedlock births, and loss of income are major reasons people seek welfare (Ford Foundation, 1989; O'Hare, 1987, Wilson, 1987). Three fourths of the families headed by an African American or Hispanic woman received welfare in 1986 (Ford Foundation, 1989; Mercado, 1986; O'Hare, 1987). Hispanic families on welfare fall into the category of long-term poor, live in single parent households, especially those formed when unmarried women have children and are out of the labor force. Women account for 56 percent of the welfare population, most being single mothers with dependent children and elderly widows below the poverty level (O'Hare, 1987). African Americans and Hispanics have a much greater likelihood than whites of going on welfare. Over one half of all African Americans and 43 percent of Hispanics received welfare in 1986 compared to 16 percent of whites (O'Hare, 1987). Families headed by an African American or Hispanic woman often fall into the two highest risk groups: the young minorities and female-headed households.

Welfare and poverty are closely linked in the minds of many, including policy makers. Poverty is characterized by conditions of not having enough money, food, clothing, adequate housing, prestige or hope. Hispanic families' economic sources are inadequate; therefore, it is the state and federal governments' responsibility to supplement family support. In 1985, 33.1 million people (14 percent of the population) lived in poverty (Ford Foundation, 1989). About one in five children live in poverty.

The American public has the stereotyped idea that most Hispanic families are welfare dependent, especially in Los Angeles and New York City. Poor Hispanics are less likely to benefit from federal welfare programs than are poor African Americans, but more likely to benefit than whites (Mercado, 1986; Valdivieso & Davis, 1988). Not all Hispanic children and youth benefit from social dependency programs. Cubans are the least dependent. Puerto Ricans are the most dependent since they are the poorest and their parents have a large number of children. In many instances, there are many Hispanic families who are not receiving these benefits, especially those who are too proud to ask for assistance. Also, undocumented Hispanic families by law are not allowed to participate in these programs. These families have to survive by other financial means. The percentage of poor Hispanics served by federal welfare programs fell slightly between 1980 and 1988, partly as a result of federal budget cuts. In 1988, the only major program that reached a majority of poor Hispanics was the subsidized school lunch program, serving 92 percent of poor Hispanic children (Valdivieso & Davis, 1988). In the same year, only 30 percent of poor Hispanics received cash assistance , 13 percent lived in public housing, 49 percent received food stamps, and 42 percent received Medicaid (Bureau of the Census, 1988d). Because there are many single-parent Hispanic households, child care responsibilities make it difficult for many single parents to work. Also, under the current rules for AFDC, a single parent who works often experiences a drop in disposable income. The parent loses health care coverage under Medicaid for the whole family. Given the prevailing wages for entry-level work for single parents, most of whom are women, and the difficulty of working full time, many persons will be better off, at least in the short run, by not working.

Negative public opinion about the program results partly from concerns that recipients are long-time citizens who are unwilling to work and who require numerous other people to work for them. This negative opinion has also brought on political pressures. Presently, there are several social dependency reform bills in the Congress.

Child Abuse and Neglect

It is universally the rule that natural or adoptive parents have a primary duty to raise, protect and care for their children. In general, parents take this responsibility very seriously. However, there is a significant percentage of parents who abuse and neglect their children. Child neglect and abuse are growing. More than two million cases are reported each year, of which about 900,000 are verified (Ford Foundation, 1989). Hispanic children are overrepresented among children reported as abused and neglected. Environmental circumstances such as social isolation and stress seem to be the most likely causes of maltreatment.

Poverty, racism and insensitivity to cultural differences serve to prevent Hispanic children and families from receiving the protection they need. A successful approach to the prevention of child maltreatment in Hispanic communities must address community conditions caused by deep-seated cultural and social practices rather than focusing solely on individual problems.

Foster Care

Foster care is a term that refers to the boarding of a child with a non-biological family. Children in foster care are separated from their biological families by state agencies to protect them from crises of familial difficulties that threaten their well-being. The state has the legal obligation to intervene when the parent cannot or will not provide for the safety and welfare of the child, or when the child is orphaned or abandoned. In general, the decisions concerning removal of a child from his/her home are made by an agent of the state who is usually called a social worker, and who works as the paid functionary of an agency. Foster care is meant to be a temporary arrangement that seeks familial stabilization and a smooth and early return of these children to their homes.

Children may arrive in foster care by being brought by their parents, by a relative or neighbor, by the police, by workers in institutions such as hospitals, welfare agencies or schools. The children may have been abandoned, malnourished, abused or neglected. Care is often requested by parents, either because of a devastating family problem or because the child's own behavior or disability is beyond the parents' abilities to handle (Gurak, Smith & Goldson, 1982). Approximately half of the children entered into foster care because of abuse or neglect in their homes.

Hispanic children and youth are twice as likely as white children to be living in institutions or group quarters. In the United States, an estimated one-half million children live separated from their biological parents in foster homes and institutions as wards of their respective states (Gurak, Smith & Goldson, 1982). Despite the unique characteristics of extended families and care-taker behavior among Hispanic families, Hispanic children are still more likely than white children to live in homes away from their parents. Overall, Hispanic and African American children comprise about one-third of the children in foster care (Washington & La Point, 1989). The over-representation of ethnic minority children in foster care is likely to be related to their over-representation among the poor. Once in foster care Hispanic children tend to remain there longer than do white children. Children in foster care systems tend to suffer from psychological and social maladjustments. Being in a strange house with a strange family creates low self-image, a sense of guilt, feelings of rejection and abandonment by their biological family. Hispanic children are faced with the exchange of family ties and customs for a new home, new ways of living, a new family's effective and instructional styles and child-rearing practices. The family change impacts on the children's emotional development as well as their social relationships and behaviors which, in turn, affect their chances for successful re-entry into the family of origin or for permanent adoption elsewhere.

One of the problems of welfare agencies is the lack of permanent homes for Hispanic foster children. A significant number of Hispanic foster care children reside in non-Hispanic homes. Many of these children are relocated in foster care outside their cultural environment, creating in them a serious disadvantage that affects their ego identity and strength. The first preference for placing Hispanic children in the foster care system would be to exhaust every possible available alternative to foster care in the immediate or extended family as the most appropriate placement. Relatives such as grandparents, godparents, uncles and aunts should be contacted first before sending these children to other ethnic and cultural homes.

The potential trauma of foster care placement for Hispanic children and their families has not been determined. It is a serious problem in the

Hispanic community because of the social and psychological effects it has on children and their parents. Therapists say that children grow up thinking that they are not liked. Parents see their children being separated from them and feel guilty. However, very few studies exist on the subject of Hispanic foster care and its effects on the Hispanic family.

Pregnancy among Hispanic Teenagers

Teenage pregnancy is a big concern in the United States today. Early child-bearing disrupts a young person's life by interfering with the normal preparation for adult living. Early child-bearing is associated with many problems for young parents as well as their parents including, for some, a lifetime of poverty or welfare dependency and the likelihood that the next generation also will become adolescent parents. A disproportionate number of women receiving public support and other public services are teen mothers or women who had their first child as a teenager. Some 3.3 million children are living with their teenage mothers. The proportion of out-of-wedlock births has soared during the past twenty years (Ford Foundation, 1989; McGee, 1982). Typically, an adolescent pregnancy is pre-marital and unintended. Almost half of all births to teenage mothers occurred outside marriage; and another 20 percent of all babies of teenage mothers were conceived before marriage but delivered within marriage. Teenage mothers are likely to be the school-aged girls from poor, immigrant families, isolated from a viable or supportive family, living on their own or in an unstable housing situation or in a tenuous relationship with the child's father, low achievers in school or high school dropouts (Ford Foundation, 1989). Young mothers tend to experience poorer medical outcomes during pregnancy and delivery, have large families and little family stability, inadequate education, unemployment or intermittent employment in occupations with low wages and little mobility, and dependency on government services and support.

For the young woman who engages in sexual intercourse of her own volition, the school hardly offers a more understanding environment than the home, should she become pregnant. Young women who are less able intellectually, or who are having problems with school, are more likely to choose parenthood than are young women not similarly situated. A teenage parent may find it difficult to finish school, acquire employment skills, or hold down a job. Teenage childbirth increases the probability that parents will become poor or remain poor. It appears that early childbirth directly affects the total number of children born to a woman, her marital status, her educational attainment, and the type of man she may marry. Since many young parents have trouble acquiring the education, training and experiences they need to perform adult roles, they become frustrated and overwhelmed by the experience of parenthood. The stress of early parenthood can exacerbate the normal intergenerational conflicts of adolescence. And if these challenges are not enough, many teen mothers soon experience a second pregnancy: 17.5 percent of teen mothers experience a second pregnancy within twelve months of their first birth (Ford Foundation, 1982). The majority of teen births occurred to women 17 or younger. Since birth rates are declining for every age group except young teens, a greater proportion of American children are now from young-parent families. In addition, half of all births outside marriage occur to teens. Most teenage mothers become pregnant outside of marriage, and today over 90 percent keep their babies.

From a Hispanic cultural dimension, the problem of adolescent pregnancy is exacerbated by the fact that most young Hispanic women come from Catholic families, where pregnancy or abortion invoke familiar negative attitudes and religious beliefs. Hispanic families tend to be close-knit and religious; and expectations of moral performance are usually more rigorous than for the society at large. Pregnant Hispanic teenagers not only face problems with their families, but they may view their pregnancies as proof of their own immoral character, resulting in guilt, depression and low self-image. This low self-image may act as a propellent of young Hispanic females into delinquency.

There is a need to develop programs to educate Hispanic teenagers to avoid early pregnancies. Programs to address adolescent pregnancy and parenthood must come under the mantles of family planning and anti-poverty programs. If pregnant, these teenagers are urged to enroll in tutoring programs or go to a home for unwed mothers. However, these two approaches have not resolved the problem of teenage pregnancies. There is a need to develop programs that, once these girls are pregnant, help them to cope with the situation. Unfortunately, many teenagers become immersed in the street culture of the urban ghetto and are likely to develop serious problems—by remaining undereducated, unskilled, or having frequent run-ins with the police that may translate into involvement with the juvenile justice system. One service that might help the children of teenagers is child care, although many young mothers have difficulty using child-care services consistently and appropriately.

Conclusion

Hispanic families face many challenges to their survival and development. Children and youth of Hispanic families are not well-served by American institutions. Hispanic children are at risk simply by living in the United States. The system has not found solutions to the many problems facing these children and, in many instances, it seems to reflect an attitude of giving up on them, assuming that their parents are less likely to profit from services designed to enhance their ability to maintain responsibility for their children. Hispanic families are interested in the well-being of their children, but socioeconomic conditions in many instances do not allow them to fulfill their obligations to their children.

The Hispanic family structure is similar to that of other families in the desire of parents to provide the best spiritual values and material means for their children. However, the socioeconomic conditions of the Hispanic family—especially for Mexican Americans and for Puerto Ricans—do not always allow them to provide the best housing, the best schools and the best neighborhoods for their children. For that reason a significant number of families, especially female-headed households, depend on social programs. The number of Hispanic welfare recipients in future years depends on the health of Hispanics as a group in the United States. All Hispanic children need permanent and stable living conditions. Whenever possible, they should live with their parents; but their families are not always in the best socio-educational position; and this poverty may affect these children's educational and social development. If they cannot stay with their parent, attempts should be made to place children with Hispanic foster parents.

The United States needs to provide the means to help the Hispanic community. Most Americans still live in the traditional nuclear family, with two parents to share in producing income, caring for the children, and maintaining the home. But, more and more Hispanic families are headed by single parents who find it much harder to cope. In an economy that demands more and more highly skilled workers, those who are well-educated can count on commensurate rewards; and those who are not prepared will continue to fall behind. The Hispanic family is a precious human resource that needs to be nurtured and helped to share the same advantages as a large percentage of other American families. Welfare does not contribute to the breakups of families or promote out-of-wedlock births, but it does not pull many families above the poverty line either. The poverty gap or the hurdles necessary to bring the income of the poor families up to the poverty line persist despite high annual government welfare expenditures.

CHAPTER 5

The Education of Hispanic Children and Youth

Education is generally regarded as the principal means of promoting social mobility. Educators and policy makers have expressed concern about the poor achievement of students as a whole in the United States in comparison to those in other industrialized countries. Throughout the United States, schools are now preoccupied with educational excellence and retention rates. But the United States is undergoing a remarkable demographic change which has direct implications for the education of Hispanic children and youth. Hispanic children and youth represent a significant percentage of the Hispanic population. However, Hispanics have had to face serious barriers to acquiring educational excellence in order to improve their community and individual lives. Low educational achievement has been a major barrier to their advancement in the United States society. The education system in the United States does not treat students as diverse individuals; on the contrary, schools tend to be homogeneous places in which many educators push students to think in only one way.

The past decade has shown an increase in the number of Hispanic children and youth in the United States. School enrollment has changed. In the 1970's, the ethnic representation in the public schools of the United States was about 85 percent white, about 10 percent African American, and about 4 percent all other minorities. The total of all minorities was only about 15 percent. By 1980, the proportion of whites had dropped to 72.5 percent, while the total for minorities had risen very rapidly to 27.5 percent of individuals under age 14 years (Banks, 1982, Bureau of the Census, 1982, Davis, Haub & Willette, 1983, Oxford et al., 1984). This number though is too conservative, and the number of Hispanics will be at least as great as that of African Americans by the year 2000, each group making up about 17 percent of the school population. Minorities will make up 43 percent of the total group of public school children aged 6 to 14 years (Duran, 1983, Olivas, Crown, Rosen & Hill, 1980, Oxford et al., 1984, Valdivieso & Davis, 1988). Hispanic students may become the majority of the school-aged population in several big cities throughout the country. Whether these predictions are presently confirmed or not, there is no doubt that minority children, especially Hispanics, are flooding into the nation's schools in increasing numbers. These children and youth challenge educators to place their attention on maximizing the cognitive, academic and social skills of children in ways compatible with social, linguistic and cultural diversity. The success of the United States public schools will depend, in large measure, on how well they are able to serve minority children, in particular Hispanics, thus making new demands for school spaces and educational services. Schools will need to search for the best ways to motivate Hispanic students to stay in school and to engage them in the educational process. This chapter presents an overview of the educational status of Hispanic children and youth and the responsibility of the schools to utilize the cultural differences Hispanic children bring to the educational process. Parental involvement is discussed as an important factor in achieving changes in the educational system to guarantee equal access and opportunities to Hispanic children and youth.

The Educational Status of Hispanic Children and Youth

Language minority students vary markedly in the degree to which they achieve access to economic, educational, occupational and social mobility in the United States (National Advisory and Coordinating Council on Bilingual Education, 1988; Bureau of the Census, 1984). The significant numbers of Hispanics in the United States have profound implications for educational policies and practices. Although there are Hispanic students in every state, the largest concentrations are found in Arizona, California, Florida, Illinois, Massachusetts, New Jersey, New Mexico, New York, and Texas. In these states, Hispanic students represent a significant group within the school population. For example, in New York City, Hispanic students represent 34 percent of the total school population. Due to communities' and school districts' educational policies, services provided to Hispanic students vary from district to district and from school to school. A high percentage of Hispanic students are failing academically, indicating that these children and youth are not receiving an appropriate education and are at risk. Hispanic children and youth as a whole have not done well in the public school system. A large group of the Hispanic population living in the United States suffers most from social, educational and economic disadvantages, and education is one of the areas where the gap between Hispanics and other groups is the widest. There are four factors that need to be mentioned in discussing the educational status of Hispanic children and youth: educational attainment, academic achievement, access to quality programs and school retention.

Educational Attainment

Educational attainment is measured by the degree to which students are able to complete their elementary and secondary schooling and are accepted in an accredited college. Low educational achievement has been a major barrier to the advancement of Hispanics in the United States. Many Hispanic children and youth face four major obstacles in attaining a quality education, they: (a) are at a low socioeconomic level, (b) belong to a minority group (c) may not understand English well enough to keep up with their English-speaking counterparts, and (d) come from a home environment that has not prepared them for school.

Hispanics have made small gains in educational attainment since 1970. By March 1988, three out of five (62 percent) Hispanics aged 25 to 34 had completed four years of high school, while 89 percent of non-Hispanics had completed high school (Bureau of the Census, 1988b, 1988d). Only 12 percent of Hispanics in the 25 to 34 age bracket had completed four or more years of college, less than half the percentage of non-Hispanics. The range within Hispanic groups is even more striking, from a low of 8 percent of Mexican Americans to a high of 24 percent of Cuban Americans with four or more years of college (Bureau of the Census, 1988b; 1988d). Fewer Hispanics complete high school than either whites or African Americans. While 77 percent of the white population and 63 percent of the African American population complete high school by age 19, only 50 percent of the Hispanic population graduates by age 19 (National Advisory and Coordinating Council on Bilingual Education, 1988). Hispanics were nearly two years behind African Americans, with a median completion of 10.3 years. Hispanics aged 14–19 were twice as likely as whites not to have completed high school (Bureau of the Census, 1988c; 1988d).

Recent research suggests that Hispanics are in lower educational tracks, where students are taught with different objectives and with different methods from students in higher tracks. Teacher expectations for students are lower in these tracks; higher order thinking skills are not developed; and students are taught mainly by drill and repetition (Orum, 1988). Students in lower tracks spend most of their time practicing language mechanics and computation. Almost half of the Puerto Rican and Mexican American students do not stay in school long enough to earn diplomas from any track, and some of these youths probably re-enroll in programs for General Educational Development (GED) certificates.

There are noticeable differences in educational attainment between young adults of selected Hispanic-origin groups. Non-completion rates were considerably higher for Mexican Americans and Puerto Ricans than for the other Hispanic sub-groups. Mexicans were the least educated (9.9 median years) and Puerto Ricans were close behind them (10.2) (Bureau of the Census, 1988d, Orum, 1988). In 1983, 71 percent of the Cubans were high school graduates, as compared with 53 percent of Mexicans and 55 percent of Puerto Ricans (Bureau of the Census, 1988d, Orum, 1988). New York City, for example, enrolls more than 77 percent of the African American and Hispanic students, and as many as three out of four African Americans and four out of five Hispanics fail to complete high school within the traditional four-year period (New York State Education Department, 1988d). In general, the functional illiteracy rate among Hispanics (a person with less than five years of elementary school or no school at all) is high. The national illiteracy for whites is 2.7 percent, for African Americans is 9.6 percent, and for Hispanics it is 17.6 percent. A study on the education of youth conducted by Cardenas, Robledo and Waggoner (1988), based on data of the 1980 census in the context of trend data through 1985, indicated that more males (54 percent) than females are undereducated. The term undereducated refers to youth aged 16 to 24 who were not enrolled in school between February 1 and April 1, 1980 and had not completed twelve years of schooling with some who had passed the GED test.

Males are 1.2 times more likely than females not to be enrolled in school. Specifically, the data indicate that:

1. Hispanics (32.2 percent) are more likely to be undereducated than other minority groups: Native Americans (29.2 percent) and African Americans (20.4 percent).
2. Hispanic young people are more than twice as likely to be undereducated as all the other ethnic groups combined. In 26 states, Hispanics have a higher undereducation rate than the 15.4 percent average rate for all other ethnic groups.
3. Young people from non-English language backgrounds are 1.5 times more likely than their English language counterparts to have discontinued school before completing twelve years of education. Hispanics are the most likely group to have a non-English language backgrounds (49 percent).

Although a significant number of Hispanic children are limited-English-proficient, this fact alone does not explain poor academic performance. Among Hispanics, Cuban students are the most likely to speak Spanish at home, yet have the highest educational levels; clearly, for these students the benefits of the middle class professional background of the majority of United States Cuban parents outweigh their limitation in English proficiency (Valdivieso & Davis, 1988). There is a slight improvement for younger Hispanics who are graduating from high school. In the 10–24 year old group, the rates of graduation are: (a) California, 55 percent, (b) Florida, 75 percent, (c) New York, 58 percent, and (d) Illinois, 48 percent (Moore and Pachon, 1985). In 1983, 58 percent of young Hispanic adults, 25 to 34 years old, (compared to 88 percent of non-Hispanic adults) were high school graduates, compared to only 45 percent in 1970. This improvement also appears in the proportion of college graduates, which was 10 percent in 1983 compared to 25 percent for non-Hispanics, but only 5 percent in 1970. Despite these gains, Hispanics have not reached the level of non-Hispanics, especially when data are analyzed by sub-groups. In 1985, Hispanics made significant gains in the Scholastic Aptitude Test, one of the traditional yardsticks of academic success (Cardenas, Robledo & Waggoner, 1988, National Clearinghouse for Bilingual Education, 1989b, Plisko and Stern, 1985). However, Hispanics are still behind in all levels of educational attainment.

Academic Achievement

Academic achievement indicates the degree to which students are able to demonstrate mastery of basic skills and achieve grade level competency in achievement tests. School achievement, though slowly improving, is a serious problem for all Hispanics, but most troublesome for Mexican Americans and Puerto Ricans. Mexican Americans were the least educated (Bureau of the Census, 1988b; 1988d). Orum (1988) indicated that:

> Hispanic students graduating from high school in 1980 had completed fewer Carnegie Units than white students in almost every type of academic subject. Hispanic high school graduates were also less likely than white high school graduates to have received "A's" in school and were almost twice as likely to have received grades of "D" or "F". Hispanics were also most likely to report failing or below-average grades in core academic subjects: mathematics (33.3 percent), natural sciences (34.6 percent), social sciences (34.2 percent), and English (31.4 percent) (p. 7).

The reading proficiency of African American and Hispanic students in grades 4, 8 and 11 is far below the national average; however, African Americans achieve at a higher level than Hispanics. The National Assessment of Educational Progress (NAEP) (1986) data on literacy skills of young adults age 21 to 25 found that a significant number of Hispanics' educational level of performance is below that of white young adults, although it is midway between African American and white peers. The average performance of Hispanics in the nation as a whole slips further behind the performance of non-Hispanics as the children advance through the grades. Young Hispanic adults score consistently lower than whites on tests of writing performance, reading and prose, document and qualitative literacy.

In 1983–84, the National Assessment of Educational Progress (NAEP) measured the writing of American school children. The assessment was administered to nationally representative samples of 4th, 8th and 11th grade private and public school students. The Writing Report Card (New York State Education Department, 1988d) concluded that most students of all racial/ethnic backgrounds were unable to write well except in response to the simplest of tasks. In general, American students can write at some minimal level, but cannot express themselves sufficiently well to ensure that their writing will accomplish the intended purpose.

There are several factors that contribute to the low academic achievement of Hispanics. One of them is the decision to use English as the exclusive language of instruction for all students regardless of their English proficiency, a policy that works to the disadvantage of Hispanic children for whom English is not their native language. The schools exclude those children by presenting them with a hostile school environment of incomprehensible English and unfamiliar culture. The children's intellectual development, oral and written expression and access to content areas are frustrated by their unfamiliarity with the English language. In such circumstances, many language minority students fall so far behind in their education that they cannot recover. And, yet, these students are judged on English-speaking achievement tests standards and are expected to compete on equal terms with English-speaking students.

A very important factor in the low educational attainment of Hispanics is the fact that Hispanic students lack the cognitive and linguistic foundation necessary for schooling. The preschool experiences of prototypic Hispanic and poor students do not equip them to undertake learning activities as well as non-minority and non-poor students do.

Another factor contributing to Hispanic educational failure is the fact that many Hispanic high school students do not have the necessary academic achievement to enroll in specialized programs and most of them participate only in general educational or vocational programs that lack the academic emphasis needed to prepare them for college entry. These factors added to the negative expectations of the school affect the educational attainment of Hispanic students. Educators who expect little from Hispanic students do not provide the motivation and challenge for students to academically advance in school.

Access to Quality Programs

Access to quality programs can be viewed as an extension of the equal education opportunity movement. Equal educational opportunity has a history that dates back to the founding of the United States, the Declaration of Independence and the Fourteenth Amendment of the Constitution, which ensures equal protection under the law. Hispanics are entitled to the same quality of education as any other ethnic group. Under federal and state civil rights laws, Hispanics cannot be excluded from public education programs nor segregated into isolated programs or facilities.

Baca & Cervantes (1989) mentioned cases that have substantially influenced educational policy regarding equal educational opportunity. They are *Brown vs. Board of Education of Topeka* (1954) and the "Coleman Report" (Coleman, Campbell, Hobson, Weinfield & York, 1966). In the Brown vs. Board of Education decision the Court ruled that the segregation of African American and white children in state public schools denied African American children equal protection guaranteed by the Fourteenth Amendment. The Court held that the doctrine of separate but equal education was inherently unequal (Baca & Cervantes, 1989). This court rule can also be applied to Hispanic students. The Coleman Report (1966) stressed that all students be treated the same and placed the responsibility for achieving equality upon the students. Unfortunately, too many low-income Hispanic families are not becoming productive contributing members of society due to disproportionately high academic failure. One of the reasons for this failure is that Hispanic students are not attending the most successful schools. They are often in segregated schools, made up of mostly Hispanic and African American students, in which educational resources and physical facilities are mediocre. At times Hispanic students are placed in programs not suited for their needs. Equality becomes the responsibility of the school rather than the student (Baca & Cervantes, 1989, Crawford, 1989). Quality programs as well as financial programs are not offered in most of the schools that Hispanic children and youth attend.

Hispanic students have the right to an education appropriate to their needs. Providing an appropriate education in a language that is familiar to the students, appropriate instructional methods and materials and competent teachers are part of the concept of appropriately meeting needs. Baca & Cervantes (1989) see this concept as an extension of a more basic concept and fundamental right referred to by the courts as the *right to education*. Hispanic children are more likely than non-Hispanic children to be enrolled in special education or vocational programs (Ortiz, 1988). They are less likely to be enrolled in programs for gifted or talented students. More Hispanics are identified as having learning disabilities and fewer as being gifted and talented than whites (4.5 percent versus 4.2 percent of whites who are identified as learning disabled; 2.1 percent of Hispanics versus 4.7 percent of whites are identified as gifted and talented).

All the above aspects affect negatively the enrollment and retention of Hispanic students in school. Educational organizations and policy makers have criticized the limited educational resources and programs available to schools attended by Hispanics. But, in spite of these claims, Hispanic access to successful schools and programs is still limited.

School Retention

Increasing the percentage of Hispanic students who finish high school is a necessary first step to the overall advancement of Hispanics. Ideally, Hispanic students are supposed to stay in school until they graduate from high school and then attend at least four years of college or begin working in a full-time job. Of concern to educators, policy makers, and the business world is the high dropout rate among all students, especially Hispanics, and the development of programs and strategies to decrease the number of dropouts. The term *dropout* is often defined as a pupil who leaves school, for any reason except death, before graduation or completion of a program of studies without transferring to another school (Office of Educational Research and Improvement, 1987). Steinberg, Blende and Chan (1984) advised that reported dropout rates should be taken as rough estimates because official statistics may not accurately represent dropout rates by not including students who drop out before high school or by including as enrolled students with sporadic attendance, who, in effect, have left school. A student is reported as a dropout in the school year if the individual is absent for a period of consecutive school days (usually 30 or more) without approved excuse or documented transfer from the school or if the student fails to re-enroll during the first 30 consecutive school days in the following semester or school year. The American public school dropout rate is reported to be 25 percent, and as high as 40 percent in urban areas (National Advisory and Coordination Council of Bilingual Education, 1988; Office of Educational Research and Improvement, 1987; Orum, 1988; Strother, 1986). The media have focused on the high dropout rate for Hispanic youngsters, which is as high as 50 percent nationally and over 70 percent in some major cities.

Hispanic dropout rates are nearly double those of African Americans and whites between the ages of 14 and 25 years. Based on

United States Census Bureau (1988d) data of 1987, 29 percent of Hispanics aged 18 to 21 were not enrolled in high school and were not high school graduates, compared to 13 percent for non-Hispanic whites. The situation is more acute in certain states where Hispanic dropout rates range from 45 to 62 percent (Applehome, 1987; Fernandez & Velez, 1989; Finn, 1989). The National Commission on Secondary Schooling for Hispanics (1984) found that 45 percent of Mexican American and Puerto Rican students who enter high school never finish, compared to 17 percent of white students. Forty percent of all Hispanic students who leave school do so before reaching tenth grade. In 1989 the State Board of Education of Texas reported that from 1.36 million elementary and high school students, 88,000 of these students (a number larger than the population of Brownsville) dropped out during the 1987–88 school year (Texas Education Agency, 1989). These figures translated to an annual state-wide dropout rate of 6.4 percent which is small when compared to the state of New York's dropout rate of 40 percent (Institute for Puerto Rican Policy, 1989). According to the Texas Education Agency, Hispanic students have the highest dropout rate in Texas, with an annual figure of 8.6 percent, compared to 7.5 percent for African Americans, and 5.0 percent for whites. The largest concentration of dropouts is at the ninth grade (9.6 percent). The ninth-grade Hispanic dropout rate was 13.6 percent compared to 11.3 percent for African Americans and 6.7 percent for whites. This report suggests that there is a tendency for Hispanic students to drop out earlier, while whites tend to drop out later. The study found a significant correlation between minority percentages of students enrolled and the number of dropouts; the greater the minority percentage, the higher the dropout numbers reported. Typically, most dropouts have enrolled in high school. Steinberg, Blende, and Chan (1984) pointed out that students from homes where a language other than English is spoken drop out at a rate of 40 percent, compared to a rate of 10 percent of students from homes where English is spoken. The statistics indirectly suggest a very high dropout rate for limited-English-proficient students. Competency in English seems to be directly related to academic grades and mathematical achievement (Baratz-Snowden and Duran, 1987).

A number of personal, family and school factors have been identified as indicators of risk for dropping out of school. Personal and family factors that students may face include frequent health problems, above or below average intelligence, difficulty in relating to authorities, coming from a single-parent home, lack of financial resources, and low parental expectations (Finn, 1989; National Clearinghouse for Bilingual Education, 1989b). A large percentage of Hispanic children are born into families that have neither the experience nor the resources to encourage learning from the start. School factors, particularly for Hispanics, have been associated with school environment, language used for instruction, and teachers' characteristics. De la Torre (1988) cited the Hispanic Policy Development Project *Make Something Happen: Hispanic and Urban School Reform* that indicated the following characteristics of the school environment that can affect Hispanic students' attendance and retention in school: (a) Poorly equipped and overcrowded schools; (b) Lower per pupil expenditures; (c) Segregated schools; (d) Schools at times understaffed and with limited basic resources; (e) High rate of grade repetition; (f) Lower expectations by the school system; (g) High enrollment in vocational and general educational programs. Other factors that contribute to dropping out of school are those related to school and school-related risk factors. They may include being older than one's classmates, poor grades, lack of school support, and lack of extracurricular activities.

The characteristics of the schools that dropouts attend are also important factors in why students leave school (New York State Education Department, 1988a; 1988c). Orum (1988) identified some of those school characteristics: attendance, discipline, promotion policies, the language used for instruction, availability of special instruction to meet special needs, and provisions to ensure parent involvement. By the time such children enter kindergarten, they already have fallen behind other children who have been exposed to books and whose intellectual curiosity has been stimulated in different ways. As the learning gap widens throughout elementary school, Hispanic children become more discouraged about school. Upon reaching the age at which they no longer are required by law to attend school (even before, in many instances) they stop attending school and become dropouts.

The dropout rate not only hurts Hispanics, it constitutes a massive waste of human resources society needs in this era of international economic competition. Moreover, because educational attainment is strongly associated with social and economic status, the high dropout rate is certain to contribute to Hispanic poverty in the future (Fernandez & Velez, 1989; Finn, 1989; Johnston & Parker, 1987, Valdivieso & Davis, 1988). Generally, Hispanic students are blamed for dropping out because they fail to see education as an avenue to future opportunities or because their social status creates pressure to drop out. The school's structure presents conditions that exacerbate the minority students' sense of powerlessness; school work becomes meaningless because it does not break the cycle of economic and political disenfranchisement. As a result, many dropouts become further alienated and turn to antisocial behavior as a means of economic survival. Attempts by Hispanics to take advantage of opportunities inherent in the educational process are frustrated by practices that maintain racial segregation. For example, Hispanics are placed in classes for the mentally retarded for reasons other than handicapping conditions; they are typically assigned to low tracks; they are allocated fewer funds for education, are the object of lower expectations, and are not considered as important as their more affluent peers (Calabrese, 1988).

Many of the dropout prevention techniques have not worked. For example, in New York City, despite the million dollars allotted for special Stay in School programs, the Board of Education was unable to lower the high school dropout rate during the 1987–1988 school year. Programs did not improve daily attendance and fewer students were able to graduate from high school. Only 54 percent of New York City students who entered high school in 1982 graduated six years later (New York State Education Department, 1988d). It is estimated that the actual dropout rate in New York City approaches 50 percent.

Designers and implementers of dropout prevention programs have to begin to look at the causes of the lack of Hispanic students' school retention. Prevention programs need to look at the school and the family of Hispanic students and to the potential dropouts: teenagers who may have lost their belief and trust in the school as well as their self-esteem (Calabrese, 1988).

Another emphasis of dropout prevention that is gaining impetus is directing efforts toward the lower grades where children have yet to fall behind in reading and mathematics. Prevention programs cannot target only 14 or 15-year olds who are already two years or more behind their class mates, because for many of them it is probably too late. The early years cannot be ignored, beginning in preschool and developing a strong parental component. What many policy makers are indicating is that a meaningful dropout strategy will take time if effective dropout prevention strategies are to reach the community and family and change the characteristics of the schools (Banks, 1982; Calabrese, 1988; National Clearinghouse for Bilingual Education, 1989b). But the alarming number of dropouts cannot be reduced by the educational system alone. The inability of the labor market in economically depressed areas to provide jobs for students who graduate from high school makes persistence seem futile to students, particularly those who are struggling.

Schools and Hispanic Children and Youth

The central purpose of education is to learn the basic disciplines, become able individuals and citizens who can use skills and strategies to contribute to the country's and the world's well-being. The purpose of education is the development of critical thinking, effective communication and creative skills, and social, civic, and occupational competence. The American people regard education as a means of improving themselves and their society. Schools are charged with fostering the development of individual capacities that will enable students to become useful citizens. Hispanic parents and leaders, despite the past record of the public schools, place great hopes for the future of their communities on the school's ability to educate their children.

A very important aspect of the life of a community is the education it gives its children. It is widely recognized that it will take the combined and coordinated efforts of many agencies to solve Hispanic children's and youths' educational problems and that schools are expected to play a major role. No public institution has a greater or more direct impact on future opportunity than the school. But schools cannot fulfill this role by trying to impose on Hispanic students educational programs designed for white and middle class children. A public school system that discriminates against minority students is in violation of their right to equal protection of the law under the 14th Amendment to the United States Constitution when it fails to educate them in a language and culture they understand. The right of children and youth to be different imposes many obligations on their schools and their teachers.

The literature on effective schools delineates a set of factors believed to positively correlate with student gains in achievement. These factors include strong leadership by the principal, high expectations for student achievement, emphasis on basic skills, an orderly environment, systematic evaluation of students, and increased time on task, among others (Ortiz, 1988). For language-minority students, these characteristics need to be seen in a broad perspective and should not isolate parents, curriculum, and teachers in their quest for more innovative curriculum activities and higher level skills. Effective schools acknowledge the ethnic and racial identity of their students and reinforce this identity by providing role models. School personnel need to involve parents in their children's learning and provide mechanisms for all parties interested in collaboration in governance. Programs need to be academically rich to include tasks that capitalize on the students' personal experiences. Schools that respect this right do not expect all children to learn at the same rate, with the same materials, and in the same language. Studies of Mexican American students in junior and senior high schools conclude that in many instances the negative self-images adopted by Mexican Americans are simply coping devices. Recent studies also illustrate the detrimental effects on students of negative perceptions that teachers and administrators hold. Students become aware of these negative views and, in some instances, play the role of people with negative images in order to minimize conflicts in school (Andrade, 1983; Arias, 1986; Matute-Bianchi, 1986).

Just as poor living conditions, employment problems and family instability contribute to the unproductive environment of Hispanic youth, so the schools often fail to counteract these forces which draw individuals toward crime and violence. The public school has been viewed as a major institution for the transmission of legitimate values and goals of society. Recent studies, however, have pointed out that the school system is failing to reach all youth equally and is, thus, contributing to low achievement and school dropouts (Andrade, 1983, Applehome, 1987, Arias, 1986, Calabrese, 1988, Divoky, 1988). Back in 1966 one of the conclusions of the Coleman Report was that minority group pupil achievement appeared to be more affected by the school environment than was the case for majority groups. The factor most strongly associated with pupil achievement was the educational background and aspirations of the other students in school. The report indicated that:

> . . . if a white pupil from a home that is strongly and effectively supportive of education is put in school and most pupils do not come from such homes, his achievements will be little different than if he were in a school composed of others like himself. But, if a minority

pupil from a home without much educational strength is put with schoolmates with strong educational backgrounds, his achievement is likely to increase (page 22).

American schools have failed to educate Hispanic children and youth. The schools have done too little to understand and utilize the cultural differences Hispanic children bring to the educational process. The lack of Hispanic role models among the teachers and other school staff, the limited attention counselors give to Hispanic students, the provision of work-study and cooperative education programs which underserve Hispanics, the lack of appropriate programs to meet language needs and involve parents, and the fact that many Hispanics attend schools in districts with low per pupil expenditures are some of the factors that negatively affect students' educational attainment (Orum, 1986; 1988).

The lack of knowledge about cultures other than European is clearly illustrated in the fact that only a few American students learn that the first books printed in America were printed in Mexico, and the first one, *Doctrina Cristiana en Lengua Mexicana* published in 1540 was written in Nahualt, the language of the Aztecs. Also, few students know that cowboy terminology is Spanish or Indo-Hispanic. In most schools the curriculum does not include material with which the Hispanic students can positively identify. For example, in history classes Mexican Americans represent the villains who massacred the courageous Americans at the Alamo. Puerto Ricans are represented only as low-skilled workers. In other words, educational material presented to Hispanic children and youth is often both negative and unrelated to their experiences, thereby making learning difficult. The quality of education offered by ghetto schools is diminished by the use of curricula and materials poorly adapted to the life experiences of the students. Designed to serve a middle class culture, much educational material appears irrelevant to Hispanic children and youth. Until recently, few texts featured any Hispanic personalities. Few books used or courses offered reflected the harsh realities of life in Hispanic neighborhoods or the contributions of Hispanics to United States culture and history.

Nationally, Hispanic students have fewer of some of the facilities that seem most related to academic achievement. They have less access to physics, chemistry, and language laboratories; there are fewer books per pupil in their libraries; their textbooks are less often in sufficient supply. Most elementary and secondary schools inflict the final blow on the cultural identity of Hispanic students by forcing them to leave their ancestral language at the school door. Thomas (1974), a Puerto Rican writer and someone who lived through the lack of linguistic and cultural understanding of the school, wrote the following:

> I can remember my mother first taking me to school, leaving me in a classroom, and the only identification I had with that room was other children who looked like me—also dark-skinned and Puerto Rican. The teacher said something to me and I looked very blank-faced as I struggled hard to understand the meaning of her alien language. With a great sense of controlled impatience, she gritted her teeth and pointed a long white finger towards an empty desk. I smiled politely and whispered a courage filled "muchas gracias," she smiled sort of tightly and said what sounded like "we speak on-lee Engleesh here" (p. 13).

Many students react to similar negative school experiences by adopting a defense mechanism called ethnic self-hatred. The factor of discrimination most surely assumes a major share of the responsibility for the academic deficits of Hispanic students. For instance, school discrimination toward Hispanic students may be reflected when schools shunt them into educational tracks designed for low achievers, by classifying them as mentally retarded or learning disabled, by denigrating their Hispanic heritage, by giving them the message that they cannot or are not expected to succeed. Schools as a whole have neither welcomed Hispanic students nor been willing to deal with their learning, linguistic and cultural differences.

Hispanic students have long been discriminated against in the public school systems, have been segregated from non-Hispanic origin children and punished for using Spanish even in casual conversation. They have attended schools that are poorly staffed and equipped. Mexican, Puerto Rican and Dominican students often found their schools to be overcrowded and poorly equipped, and generally unprepared to handle the sudden infusion of culturally distinct children. A 1983 study showed that although school segregation for African Americans decreased in this country, with the exception of the Northeast, the segregation of Hispanic students was on the rise from already high levels (Olfield, 1983). The regulations issued under Title VI of the Civil Rights Act of 1964 stipulate that no person shall, on the basis of race, color, or national origin, be subjected to discrimination in any program receiving federal financial assistance. But this legal mandate is seldom followed when dealing with Hispanic students.

Schools have failed to understand the culture of the Hispanic community and its children. For example, Puerto Rican children are taught very early to respect their elders by bowing their heads. In the schools, however, teachers insist that pupils look at them when giving verbal responses. Teachers fail to understand that in some families illness in the family requires everyone to remain home until the sick person's health is restored. Ignorance of such differing cultural norms, or the inability to understand them, results in unjustly labeling students as belligerent or docile or not interested in school.

President Bush has mentioned on several occasions that expanding parents' rights to choose their child's public schools is a national imperative. Choice enrollment policies have become one of the most controversial and widely discussed education reform initiatives of the 1980's. Choice supporters claim that open enrollment encourages increased parental involvement. In an open educational marketplace, parents will be taken more seriously by school officials and policy makers. Moreover, choice empowers parents, while diminishing state or city control of the child's education. On the other side, opponents of open enrollment view it as a way of disenfranchising parents due to distance and extended travel time. Parents need to be aware of enrollment reforms and how these reforms affect their children. One of the more disturbing trends in existing choice plans is that they exclude bilingual students. Most Hispanic students will have no significant choice until all schools participating in choice plans are required to provide bilingual instructional services. These choice limitations severely limit options for Hispanics and, once again, segregate Hispanics from the rest of the student population.

Overrepresentation of Hispanic Children and Youth in Special Education

Children come to school with a variety of abilities—due to heredity, social class, group experiences—or they are determined by teachers' and administrators' attitudes. Educationally, children who differ negatively from the normal or average characteristics are called *handicapped* or *exceptional* children: that is mentally, physically, emotionally and socially. Within this category they are further broken into several groups: mentally retarded, learning disabled and emotionally handicapped.

Hispanic children and youth have not had a positive experience with special education. Historically, Hispanics have been misplaced and over-represented in self-contained special education classes—particularly those for the mentally retarded and learning disabled (Cummins, 1984, Mercer, 1973, Ortiz & Polizoi, 1988). Mexican American children have been placed in classes for the mentally retarded at a rate that was much higher than expected (Cummins, 1984). The principal reason for the over-representation has been biased assessment practices. The available assessment and evaluation instruments do not fairly measure Hispanic children's handicaps and confuse language deficits with language deficiencies (Cummins, 1984; Ortiz & Polizoi, 1988). Another factor has been the ignorance of teachers, psychologists and other school personnel about factors that influence learning of language minority students. Regular educators seem to have difficulty distinguishing Hispanic students who have learning problems which can be addressed by adapting the regular education program from those who should be referred for comprehensive assessments because of suspected handicapping conditions. Ortiz & Polizoi (1988) found that accurately identifying handicapping conditions among Hispanic students is difficult. Available assessment procedures do not provide adequate information to distinguish characteristics of second language learners from those of handicapped students. This lack of appropriate assessment data, particularly regarding students' native language and English language proficiency, may lead to inaccurate placement of Hispanic students in special education. Ortiz & Polizoi (1988) cites data identifying this over-representation:

> In 1978, 74 percent of Hispanic students in special education were in programs for the learning disabled (44%) or the speech/language impaired (30%) (USGAO, 1981). In Texas, Ortiz and Yates (1983) found that representation of Hispanics in speech and language therapy was below national estimates of prevalence (2.4 percent as opposed to 3.2 percent) but that there was a serious over-representation of Hispanic students in learning disability programs (page 33).

It may be argued that this over-participation of Hispanic children and youth in special education classes has contributed to students' low academic performance, since the teachers' expectations of them are low and challenging activities are not present in many of these classrooms.

Hispanic Parental Involvement

There have been efforts to change the educational system to accommodate the needs of Hispanic children and youth. Community and parental pressure have been an important factor in achieving changes in the educational system. Increased power of citizens in the governance of the schools helps create more effective and responsive schools. The passage of the Elementary and Secondary Education Act of 1965 (ESEA), Title I, Headstart and the Bilingual Education Act, was the mandate for community participation in federal programs. These programs' regulations required the creation of Parent Advisory Councils designed to assist local school officials in the planning, implementation and evaluation of the specific federally funded programs. The term participation was widely used to make provisions for maximum participation by all citizens whenever feasible. Since that time parents have a voice in the education policies which directly affect the lives of their children.

The literature points to the important relationship between early home influences and a young child's school performance: what goes on at home and parents' attitudes toward education are of vital importance in determining whether children succeed or fail in school. What parents do in their interactions with their children at home, rather than parents' status, source of income, type of dwelling or some other demographic variable, is the key determiner of students' success in school. The environmental variables include: (a) The climate created for motivation and achievement—parental aspirations for the child's education, (b) Opportunities provided for verbal development, (c) Assistance provided in overcoming academic difficulties, (d) Level of intellectuality in the environment, (e) Stimulation provided for intellectual growth.

It is essential that parents know what goes on in school. Without parent collaboration it is not possible to coordinate the partnership role of home and school. A higher level of parental education is associated with greater academic knowledge and increased perceptions of school, both of which may have an impact on children's knowledge and motivation for learning. In addition, by providing differential opportunities for parents' participation in society, there may be indirect effects upon the child via parental attitudes and child-rearing behaviors acquired through such experiences. Parents with low educational levels, high rates of English illiteracy, and previously unsuccessful experiences with school often have a difficult time knowing how to help their children succeed in school. Furthermore, with the language of the parent being Spanish and the language of the school being English, communication is not feasible. While studies conclude that Hispanic parents have high aspirations for their children, many lack the skills and confidence to provide their children with the academic benefits that come from active parent involvement (Orum, 1988).

There are indications that Hispanic parents desire closer participation in the education of their children. Parental school-supportive activities include visiting the school, participating in classroom activities, knowledge of the children's functioning in school, higher expectations for their children's educational attainment and, in some cases, parents' involvement in their own continuing education.

Hispanic parents in general are not part of the educational process, and the school and home become conflicting institutions. While some parents are aware of their roles as the child's first teachers, others are not cognizant of their teaching role, remaining unaware of how to interact positively with their children in ways that lead to academic success. In general, Hispanic parents, especially Puerto Ricans, Mexican Americans, and Dominicans, give little support to schools because they are preoccupied with the problems of learning English, finding housing, securing employment and otherwise trying to survive. When they do turn their attention to the schools, they feel powerless to improve them, controlled as they are by white administrators and teachers. Hispanic parents need encouragement to become involved in the schools attended by their children.

Bilingual education has served as a stimulus for Hispanic parents to begin playing an active role in the schools, for the first time taking part in decisions affecting the quality of education their children receive. Parents believe that bilingual education has already helped to improve the way in which the educational system deals with their children. A small group of Hispanic parents have been advocates for their children who have suffered discrimination at school because of their ethnic or language background, challenging school administrators who punish children for speaking Spanish. Parents have objected to placement of their children in slow-learning groups or their retention in grade solely because of language differences.

Conclusion

Changes in demographic patterns and labor market demands have contributed to renewed national attention to the problems that confront Hispanic youth. Resident Hispanics and Hispanic immigrants will continue to represent the greatest percentage of the increase in the population and the work force until at least the year 2000. The largest number of jobs will be found in occupations that require the highest education and skill levels (Johnston & Parker, 1987). The need for adequate and effective schooling of Hispanics is therefore critical. Many Hispanic children and youth face four major obstacles in attaining education: They (a) Are from a low socioeconomic group, (b) Belong to a minority group, (c) May not understand English well enough to keep up with their English-speaking counterparts, (d) Have home environments that have not prepared them for school programs.

Educational outcomes for Hispanics are well below those for other United States students. Hispanic students experience the need for more Hispanic role models in the schools; textbooks to which Hispanic children can relate; the need for access to classrooms in which teachers can speak Spanish; elimination of the stereotyped perception that they are slow learners, working (males) more hours a week while attending school less than any other group.

It is the responsibility of the schools to meet the educational needs of all these students. Schools must operate under the assumption that all of these students can and must learn to become part of the mainstream of the United States. Schools must also provide methods for the development of cognitive and academic skills to permit overall scholastic success.

Schools must search for ways to motivate students and engage them in the educational process. Schools need to better serve the needs of Hispanic students by creating a climate of excellence, not just by demanding a great deal of their students, but by involving parents in positive, constructive ways and responding effectively to the unique needs of their communities. For planners and administrators in school districts in which new immigrant children are enrolled, the data suggest the importance of assembling socioeconomic information, as well as linguistic and cultural information and information on English language proficiency of immigrant children from each specific group before programs are prepared and implemented for educating them. Early intervention tends to reduce the large number of Hispanic students dropping out of school as well as improve the self-image of students. Teachers are seen as the heart of the educational system. Although the Hispanic population is growing and more Hispanic students will be enrolled in schools, the number of minority language teaching candidates is declining.

The role of parents in the educational process is increasingly emphasized in educational reports. Parent involvement has been shown to benefit students' achievement and improve parents' attitudes toward themselves, their children and their children's schools and teachers. The benefits of parental involvement are enormous regardless of the parents' level of education or socioeconomic or marital status. When parents are involved in their children's education, the knowledge they gain about the school and its program enables them to assist their children and to assess the quality of the school and teachers more effectively.

Policy makers, educators, private and public agencies and the community in general should recognize the following:

1. Schools must respond to demographic changes in the student population. Hispanic students are fast becoming a majority of all American students. In terms of growth, Hispanic students represent the most dynamic sector of our student population. Today, nearly one half of the children entering kindergarten in the nation's two largest school districts—Los Angeles Unified and New York City—come from Hispanic homes.

2. Many Hispanic students are educationally at risk. They are at risk because of socioeconomic factors including poverty, lack of parental education, poor health and nutrition, crime, drugs and social discrimination. Schools need to compensate for these out-of-school problems, but schools must be accountable for those children.

3. Schools put many Hispanic students at risk. Schools do so by treating social differences as educational deficiencies; by engaging in self-fulfilling prophecies of low expectations.

4. Schools must adopt a positive approach toward the education of Hispanic students—toward the education of children who are culturally or linguistically different. These children are different, they are not inferior. Nowhere is the need for change more evident than in the way in which schools treat language-minority students. Today, these students are commonly known as Limited-English-Proficient. Most schools fixate on the language deficiencies of these children, rather than on their positive communication skills. Most schools employ a wrecking-ball rather than a building block approach to English-language development for language-minority students. Teachers waste their energy and frustrate students by trying to take away, to eradicate, the communication skills language-minority students bring to school, rather than using those communication skills as building blocks for academic learning and the mastery of English. Hispanic children and adults can make contributions to internationalizing our schools and to developing a multilingual country.

5. Quality of teaching needs improvement. There is a need to both expand and upgrade the nation's teaching force. More minority teachers must be recruited, and more teachers must be trained and retrained so that they have the experience, sensitivity, and outlook required to successfully instruct the children of the future.

6. There is a need to involve Hispanic parents in their children's education, to ensure that the schools will succeed and all students will learn.

CHAPTER 6

Language Issues in Educating Hispanic Children and Youth

Since bilingual education was first given official recognition and support by the federal government in 1968 it has stimulated both excitement and controversy in the discussion of programs for language-minority students. During the past 22 years, educators have been called upon to make some dramatic programmatic and curricular changes in their policies and practices to take into account the cultural diversity inherent in United States society. One of the challenges they faced was to find the best educational programs for Hispanic children and youth. Specifically, educational literature has described effective second language instruction within the context of the public school system, while simultaneously nurturing the native language development and socio-cultural traditions of Hispanics.

This chapter briefly summarizes some of those instructional language policies giving particular emphasis to bilingual education and second language programs. The issue of the availability of bilingual teachers is discussed with the idea of presenting a rationale for the need for more qualified school teaching personnel. The issue of United States English is briefly described to awaken people to the idea that "English only" policies are a menace to Hispanic linguistic and cultural diversity in the United States.

Bilingual Education

Objective discussion about bilingualism and bilingual education becomes difficult due to the politics and emotionalism surrounding the topic (San Miguel, 1984; Santiago, 1985). Bilingual education is a general approach used in a variety of instructional programs in schools in which subjects are taught in two languages, using the native language and culture, and English is taught as a second language. In the United States, bilingual education is an instructional tool to help students, whose first language is not English, to overcome their linguistic and academic difficulties and, it is hoped, to perform as well as their English-speaking peers in school. All bilingual programs include instruction in English as a second language (ESL), but some provide specialized instruction in English with native language support for content area instruction. While non-English speakers learn English, they can also learn social studies and mathematics, among other subject areas, in their respective languages. The goal of bilingual education is to facilitate education of students and youth by fostering a positive self-concept while facilitating students' cognitive, academic and language expression. Instruction in English in cognitive areas begins when the student can function in that language and experiences no academic handicap due to insufficient knowledge of the language. A major aspect of it is the inclusion in the curriculum of the students' historical, literary and cultural traditions for purposes of strengthening identity and sense of belonging and for making the instructional program easier to grasp (Cummins, 1984; De la Torre, 1988; Krashen & Biber, 1988; Wong-Fillmore & Valadez, 1986).

In the United States, bilingual education is intended to permit limited-English-proficient or non-English-speaking students to develop enough proficiency in English to be able to learn in English. The duration of bilingual instruction will vary among different communities, depending on the number of years language minority children need to develop proficiency in English and learn content through English along with the community's desire to continue a program so that students will maintain skills in the minority language.

The term "bilingual education" covers a wide range of programs from school to school and from district to district. The most well-known are transitional bilingual, maintenance bilingual, and two-way bilingual programs. Transitional bilingual programs emphasize the development of English-language skills in order to enable students whose proficiency in English is limited to shift to an all-English program of instruction. Maintenance bilingual programs provide instruction in both content areas and language skills in the students' native language and in English. Instruction is designed to provide improved language skills in English as well as in the native language. In two-way bilingual programs classes include native English speaking students as well as native speakers of another language. The English speakers learn a second language at the same time as the non-English speakers are learning English. A major strength of two-way bilingual programs is that both groups of students act as linguistic models for each other.

Contrary to popular belief, bilingual education is not new in American education. Its implementation began in the nineteenth century in private schools and some public schools in communities settled by German, Scandinavian and French immigrants. Between 1840 and 1917, schools in Cincinnati offered classes in German to German pupils who did not speak English. From time to time, New York City used Yiddish, German, Italian or Chinese to educate new waves of immigrant children. It was around the First World War, when anti-German sentiment swept the country and speaking English became a kind of index of political loyalty, that the use of bilingual instruction was forbidden in the schools.

The modern revival of public bilingual education began in the early 1960's, when schools in the Miami area, faced with a sudden influx of refugee Cuban students, responded by offering instruction in Spanish until the children were able to learn English. Bilingual instruction also began to be employed in New Mexico and Texas.

There is a variety of legislation and court decisions that guarantee the right to access to a comprehensible education, which includes bilingual education. These are: (a) *Lau vs. Nichols* (1974), (b) Title VI of the Civil Rights Act of 1964, (c) The Equal Education Opportunities Act of 1974, and, (d) Various bilingual education laws in force at the state level (De la Torre, 1988). Bilingual education received new interest in the wake of the Civil Rights movement and a new national interest in ethnicity. The concept of cultural pluralism which became very popular allowed minority groups to take a new outspoken pride in their heritage and their contributions to American life.

Federal funding of bilingual education and federal protection of the educational rights of language minority students trace their roots to political pressure brought to bear by Mexican Americans from Texas. The legal basis for federal help under Title VI of the Elementary and Secondary Education Act of 1965 is the result of complaints to the Department of Health, Education and Welfare's Office of Civil Rights in 1964, which resulted in prohibiting the recipients of federal aid from discriminating against racial groups. Complaints indicated that school districts on the Texas border held back Spanish-speaking students because of their lack of English language ability, and this practice increased the dropout rate among Mexican American students. The then Department of Health, Education and Welfare (HEW) asked school districts to comply with the legislation through its Office of Civil Rights (OCR). In May, 1970, the Office of Civil Rights issued a memorandum to all school districts stating that those districts with an enrollment of more than 5 percent national-origin minority children will be required to rectify the educational deficiencies of those unable to speak or understand English (Pottinger, 1970). Political pressure urged senator Ralph Yarborough to introduce and support the Bilingual Education Act of 1968. The act established a competitive categorical grant program in the Department of Health, Education and Welfare for school districts wishing to start a bilingual program to aid the education of low-income and limited-English-proficient students. The original aim of Title VII was modest: to give seed money to local educational agencies for new and innovative elementary and secondary programs designed to meet the special educational needs of children of limited-English-speaking ability in schools having a high concentration of such families with incomes below $3,000 per year. The income requirement was later eliminated. In addition, the Bilingual Education Act, when it was re-authorized in 1974, minimized the compensatory aspects of the program and stated that the aim in the act was to establish equal educational opportunity for all children.

In the 1970's, and after the enactment of title VII, parents of non-English-speaking students accused the San Francisco Unified School District of language discrimination because their children were receiving instruction only in English, a language they could not understand and were not helped to learn. They claimed that the programs designed to meet their special needs violated both Title VI of the 1964 Civil Rights Act (which contains a provision forbidding discrimination on the basis of natural origin) and the equal protection clause of the 14th Amendment of the Constitution. In 1974, the Court agreed to the charge of language discrimination. In its ruling, the Court held that school districts must take affirmative action to remedy the English language deficiencies of minority children or lose federal funds. If school districts fail to fulfill such a responsibility, they violate students' rights to equal educational opportunities under Title VI of the United States Civil Rights Act. The United States Supreme Court upheld the Department's positions affirming that schools must provide compensatory education for those who were not native speakers of English to be in compliance with the Civil Rights Act. The impact of *Lau vs. Nichols* was enormous. For the first time, language rights were recognized as a civil right. And federally funded schools were legally obligated to provide special assistance to students with limited-English-speaking ability in overcoming their language difficulties. Furthermore, schools were told that students must not be denied full participation in the educational process while they were learning English. The Court, however, did not specify the type of remedy. In 1976, the Office of Civil Rights (OCR) commissioned a task force of experts who formulated a set of guidelines that became known as the *Lau Remedies* for school districts to follow. The Lau Remedies were widely distributed to school officials and the general public, but not published in the Federal Register. Lyons (1989) indicates that the Lau Remedies ". . . quickly evolved into the de facto standards that OCR staff applied for determining an education agency's compliance with Title VI under Lau. Between 1975 and 1980, OCR carried out nearly six hundred. Title VI compliance reviews that led to the negotiation of 359 school district Lau plans by July 1980, with virtually all of them based on the Lau Remedies" (p. 11). President Reagan's secretary of Education, Terrell H. Bell, withdrew the proposed Lau Regulations, giving school districts the flexibility to use any instructional approach to educate children deficient in English. Lyons (1989), citing the court decision, indicated that the court's unanimous decision in Lau established two significant points:

1. Equality of educational opportunity is not achieved by merely providing all students with the same facilities, textbooks, teachers and curricula, for students who do not understand English are effectively foreclosed from any meaningful education.
2. The Office of Civil Rights has the authority to establish regulations for Title VI enforcement, which among other things prohibits discrimination . . . which has that effect even though no purposeful design is present (p. 3).

The Court's decision and the Lau Remedies provided the legal foundation for law suits brought by organizations speaking for the rights of children from linguistic minorities, resulting in a number of court mandated bilingual programs.

Several years after the federal government enacted the Bilingual Education Act of 1968, a number of states enacted similar legislation or established state policies that provided special instruction for limited-English-proficient students. Massachusetts was the first state to establish such policies, followed by Oregon, Alaska, and the Virgin Islands (Bennett, 1988).

Bilingual education received further impetus in the Northeast under legal actions filed by community organizations. In 1972, Aspira, a New York community based Hispanic educational advocacy group, sued the Board of Education of the City of New York charging unequal treatment of Hispanic children. Aspira charged that as a result of language barriers, many Puerto Rican children of limited English proficiency were prevented from fully participating in the instructional program of the public schools (*Aspira of New York vs. Board of Education of the City of New York*, 1972). Aspira won the suit in 1974, resulting in a consent decree that required the implementation of a transitional bilingual educational program that included: (a) intensive English language instruction, (b) instruction in subject matter in Spanish, and (c) Spanish language instruction. Although the decree has been in existence since 1975, the New York City Board of Education has failed to: (a) provide the program to large numbers of children, (b) systematically monitor the implementation of the program, and (c) evaluate the educational outcomes of the decree for limited English proficient students (Santiago-Santiago, 1986).

In 1988, a federal court approved a plan as part of a settlement of a suit against Lowell, a city of 95,000 residents, 35 miles northwest of Boston. The suit was brought by the parents of Southeast Asian and Hispanic students in 1987, charging that school officials had deliberately segregated the children and provided them with an inferior education. In 1989, with federal court approval, the public schools of Lowell, Massachusetts started instructional programs for students and parents whose first language was not English. A school for bilingual instruction was established, bringing together students of all degrees of competency in English with an emphasis on American, Asian and Hispanic cultures.

Many Hispanic parents and organizations want bilingual education for children, not only to help them master English-language skills but to help them maintain their first language. Bilingual education is a major objective of Hispanic political and social organizations. It has been supported by Hispanic legislators and national Hispanic organizations such as the National Association for Bilingual Education, National Council of La Raza, Aspira of New York, and the Institute for Puerto Rican Policy. They have built a national constituency for it, with a leadership that has played a significant part in the formation of bilingual education policy. Bilingual education has served as a vehicle to enable Hispanic people to press for their language rights while, at the same time, giving them a major point of entry into all other issues having to do with opportunities and rights for Hispanics, and providing an avenue for their participation in the political process through election to school boards and other offices. Since the concept of language rights gained legal status in the 1970's, Hispanics received, through the bilingual education movement, visibility in terms of their pride in their heritage as seen in the rise of Spanish language instruction in the schools. Spanish is no longer regarded as an inferior language. Although in 1985, Secretary of Education, William Bennett placed part of the blame for high Hispanic dropout rates on bilingual education programs, an independent Government Accounting Office (GAO) study in 1987 found evidence that these programs are effective.

The amount of funding and the number of school districts receiving federal funds have decreased in the last decade. Districts rely upon a varied number of funding sources. Some local districts' programs are funded by federal sources such as Chapter 1, the Bilingual Education Act (Title VII), the Emergency Immigrant Education Assistance Act, The Transition Program for Refugee Children, and the Vocational Education Act. Programs are also funded by state and local sources. Districts use combinations of funding sources—federal, state, and local—to sustain their programs. Few new bilingual programs have been established. Bilingual education has been redefined to mean ". . . any special efforts used to teach language minority children even if the children's primary language is not used in their instruction. Under this definition such single language programs as English as a second language or immersion programs are considered to be options within the category of bilingual education" (San Miguel, 1987, p. 108).

Despite all the attention it receives, bilingual education serves a small fraction of Hispanic students. Baratz-Snowden and Duran (1987) indicated that in 1984 only about 25 percent of Hispanic fourth graders who needed language assistance were enrolled in special programs to learn English and basic skills. Very few students participate in bilingual programs. There are several reasons for the lack of participation of Hispanic children and youth in these programs. One reason is the lack of bilingual programs available to students in their school communities. A second reason is the requirement of bilingual programs to be of a transitional nature, and students who demonstrate a certain level of English proficiency are moved into mainstream classes. A third reason is the ignorance of many parents about the linguistic and cognitive benefits of bilingual education, causing them to refuse to allow their children to participate in bilingual education programs.

English as a Second Language

English as a Second Language is the recommended instructional approach when there are many language groups represented in one classroom or when bilingual education is not feasible. There is little disagreement that learning English is essential to economic and social mobility. In the 1960's there was a growing recognition that Hispanic children needed some kind of special assistance if they were to have an opportunity to succeed in school. In the last thirty years several methodologies have been developed and proven to be useful in teaching English to Hispanic children and youth. The two most popular methodologies are the English as a Second Language (ESL) and the immersion approaches.

English as a Second Language (ESL) is a teaching approach designed to meet the immediate communication and academic needs of the students whose proficiency in English is limited or non-existent by providing them with the language skills they need to communicate with teachers and peers and to receive content matter in English. Their instruction is based on a special curriculum that typically involves very little or no use of the native language and is usually taught only in specific school periods. For the rest of the school day, students may be placed in regular (or submersion) instruction, in an immersion program, or in a bilingual program. ESL is designed to complement the practice and exposure to English that students receive outside the class. ESL classes provide students with instruction at their level of English proficiency. Differences in the development of oral English skills among language minority children exist due to the influence of such factors as sex, age of the learner, verbal flexibility, sociability, attitude toward the target language group, anxiety level, and instructional approaches.

The application of the theories of linguistic science to the teaching of English as a Second Language has been increasing steadily since the 1940's. This approach to language learning as a tool of verbal communication gained impetus during World War II when the United States government needed personnel with a practical knowledge of foreign languages. It became necessary for the government to set up its own language training programs for military and civilian personnel who would be working in various parts of the world with people who spoke foreign languages. The widespread use of tape recorders and other audio devices made it possible to provide authentic spoken language examples. By the early 1950's, teachers responsible for teaching English to non-English speakers were using some of the methodologies used in the military such as pattern practice techniques, use of meaning in aural/oral practice, and the learning of language structures.

In its early development, ESL teaching involved small numbers of foreign students in the United States who were taught only by specialized language teachers. But, in 1964, the federal government, through Title IX of the National Defense Education Act (NDEA), officially recognized that, in addition to foreign students abroad and in this country, there were thousands of students in the United States whose native tongue is other than English and who need specialized instruction in English if they were fully to understand or participate in the American cultural, social and economic way of life. ESL programs grew through the NDEA. The ESL program included instruction in English at all levels and courses in the students' culture. The aim of the instructional program was to assist native-speaking students designated as disadvantaged because they spoke a non-standard variety of English. Most of the ESL programs were offered at the adult/college level. Training in ESL methodology was provided for the preparation of ESL adult or college teachers. English as a second language spread very rapidly, requiring teachers and professors to meet to discuss issues pertaining to the profession. The first of three ad-hoc conferences in TESOL was held in March of 1964. The professional organization TESOL (Teachers of English to Speakers of Other Languages) was established in 1966; the development of ESL textbooks increased; and several ESL methodologies were created. The organization was created out of professional concern over the lack of a single, all-inclusive professional organization that might bring together teachers and administrators at all educational levels with an interest in English for speakers of other languages. During these two decades the ESL profession expanded in response to increasing numbers of immigrants and refugee children and youth entering the United States, as well as the growing number of international students coming from countries around the world to attend universities in the United States (Alatis, 1987).

Appropriate ESL instruction put into practice the following principles: (a) Emphasize communication of meaning. (b) Integrate the four areas for functional contexts of learning and communication development: understanding, speaking, reading and writing. (c) Recognize students' prior linguistic, conceptual and cultural experiences to build proficiency in English. (d) Respect the values and traditions of students' cultural heritage. (e) Provide for the continuation of conceptual development for functional contexts of learning and communication. In the past, ESL programs were criticized for not following the above guidelines for recognizing students' strengths and building on these strengths. They have recently made tremendous efforts to do so.

There are different ESL instructional approaches. One recent popular approach is sheltered English, which emphasizes simplified vocabulary and sentence structure used in teaching school subjects in which students lack enough English-language skills to understand the regular curriculum. In this model, every lesson in every subject becomes, in part, a language lesson. Vocabulary and language skills are taught in tandem with relevant concepts.

Hispanic students represent a large percentage of ESL students in the United States. Their presence is seen at all levels, but most noticeably at the college level. In many colleges, ESL courses are non-credit bearing, and students who enroll in ESL programs take a longer time to complete their academic degrees. However, the programs, in general, are effective in preparing students to be able to do academic work in English.

The Immersion Program

Immersion is a general term for teaching approaches for language minority students not involving children's native language. A general description of immersion is that students are taught in a second language from the first year of school, with first language instruction introduced possibly as late as the second or third year. First-language instruction may be increased in the upper grades, or it may be limited to one to two hours per day. The second language is added with no negative effect on first language development. Since a student is a member of the dominant social class, he or she encounters positive attitudes about and continues the development of their first language from both parents and the community.

The Immersion Model has been used successfully and tested extensively in Canada, in areas in which speakers of the dominant language (English) receive their schooling largely in French (Krashen & Biber, 1988; Cummins, 1984). These French immersion language programs in Canada began as an experiment to counter parental dissatisfaction with conventional second language teaching approaches. Students have achieved high levels of proficiency in French at no cost to English or other academic skills. Immersion bilingual education works very well for speakers of the dominant language, especially for middle class students who receive parental support and resources.

Immersion programs in the United States are not numerous, and the few being implemented have not been as successful as those in Canada. Cummins (1984) states that "what many policy-makers and media commentators appear to understand by the term immersion is some form of high-intensity monolingual English programs which would simultaneously Americanize minority students while teaching them English: in other words a programme not very far removed from submersion but with the possible addition of an ESL component" (p. 155). In other words, immersion programs in the United States do not provide support or structured ESL instruction and may unconsciously place language minority students in a position subordinate to monolingual English-speaking students and teachers; it may lead to low achievement and high dropout rates, especially among Hispanics who sometimes perceive their status as low relative to the majority. Cummins (1984) indicated that the immersion programs in the United States may not work, since the program does not respond to the needs of language minority students. He stated that "there is considerable evidence that academic progress is facilitated by means of programs that slightly reinforce students' cultural identity and promote language and literacy development" (p. 157). Cummins concluded that: "For the many minority students whose academic future is much more deeply rooted, monolingual immersion programs appear to have only limited potential" (p. 157). Immersion programs teach subject matter and language simultaneously. Non-English speaking Hispanic students would be taught in English and the necessary vocabulary in English would be introduced as the subject matter required its use.

There are several programs related in some way to the immersion program. These are submersion and structural immersion. A submersion program is one in which students whose proficiency in English is limited are placed in ordinary classrooms in which English is the language of instruction. They are given no special program to help them overcome their language problems, and their native language is not used in the classroom. Also called "sink or swim", submersion was found to be unconstitutional by the Supreme Court decision in *Lau vs. Nichols*. Structured immersion teaches English in an instructional environment where teachers understand the native language and students may speak it to the teacher, although the teacher generally answers only in English. Knowledge of English is not assumed, and the curriculum is modified in vocabulary and pacing so that the context is understood by the students. This model is more effective for language majority students attempting to learn a second language than for language minority students (Cummins, 1984).

A Case for Bilingual Hispanic Teachers

Teachers are a very important component in the development of a country's future since they are, after the parents, the most influential force in children's and youths' academic and social development. Teachers help students grow in self-awareness and in the ability to relate to others, clarify values, and promote moral development in addition to teaching the basic skills. Two assumptions are discussed in the following paragraphs: (a) there is a need for more Hispanic teachers in United States schools to be proportional to the number of Hispanic students; and (b) since there is a large number of limited-English-proficient students attending schools in the United States, it is necessary to hire more bilingual (English/Spanish) teachers. Presently, there is an imbalance in the ethnic make up of personnel of schools in the United States. Since there is a high percentage of Hispanic students attending schools in the United States, there is a need to offer these students more human resources to motivate them to improve their cognitive, linguistic, and academic skills learned at home.

The schools need to provide an atmosphere, curriculum, and staff that enrich Hispanic students' language, culture, and academic development. Students need to understand instruction—in a language that they can understand—and which includes the learning of English and learning through English. If students understand the school curriculum they will learn more and will be motivated to stay in school. Well-trained, Hispanic bilingual teachers can offer all these learning incentives to students.

The effectiveness of the instruction will depend on the training, preparation and continued development of the instructional staff. If students understand the school curriculum they will learn more and may be motivated to stay in school. Hispanic bilingual teachers are better equipped to help Hispanic children and youth in the following areas: (a) personal growth of the students, (b) social development, (c) national and world citizenship development, and (d) mastery of academic subjects, including the basic skills of reading, writing, and computation, skills essential to contemporary life. To carry out these multiple responsibilities, Hispanic bilingual teachers are better equipped to engage in several professional roles, often simultaneously: counselors, facilitators, instructional managers, curriculum designers, academic instructors, evaluators of instruction, and reluctantly, disciplinarians. The need for Hispanic/bilingual teachers in the United States comes about not only because there are many Hispanic students for whom English is not the dominant or native language and who need to learn content through their native language. Hispanic/bilingual teachers are also needed to teach those Hispanic students for whom English is their dominant language but need a sensitive, Hispanic bilingual individual, one who can teach in both languages and who can enrich the school curriculum with content from the Hispanic culture and Spanish languages. There are few Hispanic teachers. For example, in 1986–87 in New York State 14.2 percent of the students enrolled in schools were Hispanic, but only 3.4 percent of public school teachers were Hispanic. In 1988, in New York City, 34 percent of the school population was

Hispanic, however, only 8.7 percent of the classroom teachers are Hispanics (New York State Education Department, 1988b). There are few Hispanic teachers in the nation's teaching force: only 2.6 percent of elementary school teachers; 1.7 percent of secondary school teachers, and a similar small proportion among administrators; 2.5 percent of central office staff, 2.0 percent of principals, and 2.7 percent of guidance counselors (Orum, 1988). Thus, there are few role models among school personnel, and few educators who are familiar with the Spanish language and the cultures of Hispanic children.

There are non-Hispanic teachers who speak Spanish and are familiar with the cultures of these children; this is a small group, most of whom work in bilingual education programs. Most Hispanic students are taught by teachers who know little about Hispanics and were never trained to provide instruction to Hispanic students. Orum (1988), citing data from the 1983 Survey of Teacher Demand and Shortage conducted by the National Center for Education Statistics, indicated that at that time there were 3,590 uncertified teachers teaching in bilingual education programs, accounting for 12 percent of all uncertified teachers in the schools. The same survey found that bilingual education had the greatest proportional shortages of any field of education, and that the fewest special recruitment and training incentives were offered by public schools to attract teachers to that field. Traditional training programs for teachers have not prepared educators to be effective in educating Hispanic students who may have different language and cultural characteristics and needs from the mainstream students; and many school employees feel frustrated and unequipped to teach these students. Unfortunately, some have translated this frustration, along with their inability to understand or effectively teach Hispanic students, into low expectations of these students.

Competencies required of an effective Hispanic bilingual (English/Spanish) teacher include knowledge of language methodology, knowledge of the Spanish language, knowledge of the American and Hispanic cultures, sensitivity to Hispanic students' learning and cognitive styles, mastery of the subject area to be taught, and mastery of language teaching skills in the classroom. Macias & the Tomas Rivera Center (1989) has listed the most significant skills for bilingual teachers as follows:

1. Use of both languages for instruction, assuring not only understandable instruction, but a clear and positive environment

and status for each language. Bilingual teachers need to be proficient in both languages, be knowledgeable of bilingual and second language instructional methodologies.

2. The integration of English language development with academic skills development. Bilingual teachers need to be able to use appropriate language methodology in the content areas to facilitate the acquisition of the content to be learned.

3. Understanding and appropriate use of the cultural background and diversity of the students to mediate learning and classroom management. Teachers need to be able to address individual and social group diversity through the teaching of cultural and multicultural understanding to the benefit of the students, the community, and the whole United States.

The quest for more bilingual teachers continues. However, the federal and local educational agencies, although aware of the shortage, have not done enough to recruit and keep bilingual and Hispanic teachers.

Official English: A Growing Menace to Hispanics

Hispanics have been attacked by several movements that are forcing a constitutional amendment to make English the only official language of the United States. Among them, the two most aggressive forces are the English-Only and the U.S. English organizations. The English-Only organization was established in 1983 as an offshoot of the Federation for American Immigration Reform (FAIR), a Washington, D.C.-based lobby that advocates greater restrictions on immigration. The first sponsors and founders of English-Only were former Senator S. I. Hayakawa and Dr. John Tenton, a Michigan ophthalmologist, environmentalist and population-control activist. The United States English advocates convince people by stating that the United States' common language is threatened by a movement toward a bilingual society. They state that the English language is the unifying factor that has held United States citizens together and allows them to resolve their differences. They claim that bilingual education and bilingual voting rights are beginning to weaken these ties. In November of 1986,

California passed a referendum declaring English the state's official language. The ballot instructed public officials to ensure that the role of English as the common language of the state of California is preserved and enhanced. Between 1987 and 1988 similar referendums or proposals were presented in 39 states, and 16 states have passed them (Crawford, 1989).

At the federal level, a Constitutional English Language Amendment has been presented and has been in committee since 1981. President Reagan's policies toward bilingual education have, in a way, helped to support United States English objectives, and provided funding for English only programs under the Bilingual Education Act. The Bush Administration, through the former Secretary of Education, Lauro Cavazos, is opposed to the English-only movement. Hispanic leaders see the United States English movement as anti-Hispanic because it is a threat to civil liberties. An example is Arizona's Proposition 106, passed in 1988, which requires that "This state and all political subdivisions of this state shall act in English and no other languages" (cited by Crawford, 1989). The Amendment may curtail government activities such as driver's license tests, public information, and other social services (Crawford, 1989). However, in 1990 a Federal district judge in Phoenix declared that the state's constitutional amendment making English the language "of all government functions and actions" in Arizona was a violation of federally protected rights of free speech. The decision was the first legal set-back for the official English movement. Judge Paul G. Rosenblatt ruled that the Arizona amendment "is a prohibition on the use of any language other than English by all officers and employees of all political subdivisions in Arizona while performing their official duties." As such, Judge Rosenblatt said, it could inhibit legislators from talking to their constituents or judges from performing marriages in a language other than English.

According to bilingual education advocates, the U.S English movement is a divisive movement whose purpose is to foster division among rather than to integrate the United States people. Senator Hayakawa indicated that unless English is legally protected the United States will find itself increasingly polarized. He indicated that immigrants need to understand that English-speaking ability is an obligation of American citizenship.

Opponents of the Official English Movement state that there are legal and political implications of official English measures. The official language-measures will make it even harder for immigrants who have not yet mastered English to enter the social, economic and political mainstream of the United States. Hispanics will be greatly affected since there is a significant percentage of Hispanics in the United States for whom English is not a spoken language.

For Hispanics in the United States this is a very dangerous movement: federal, state and local governments will be forced to curtail a range of services they now provide in Spanish. Crawford stated this very clearly: "At various times, leaders of United States English have advocated elimination of bilingual 911 operators and health services, endorsed English-only rules in the work-place, petitioned the Federal Communications Commission to limit foreign language broadcasting, protested Spanish-language menus at McDonald's, and opposed Pacific Bell's *Páginas Amarillas en Español* and customer assistance in Chinese" (p. 55).

Lately, the United States English movement has begun to distance itself from the English Only label, denying any interest in interfering with non-public uses of other languages or in curtailing emergency services for non-English speakers. Official English opposes bilingualism and bilingual education. The English Only officials frequently stated that bilingual education breeds and fathers a separatism mentality which has both economic and political implications. The U.S. English movement is against bilingual programs for limited English proficient students. In 1988–89, when the New York State Board of Regents was considering its "Position Paper on Bilingual Education," and passing regulations to implement bilingual education, the U.S. English movement developed an intense campaign in New York State that lasted eleven months. But the Board of Regents did not let U.S. English consultants intimidate them and approved the regulations in November 1989.

Conclusion

When describing educational programs for Hispanic children and youth, discussion of language issues is appropriate. The concern of the 1960's to provide all children with equal educational opportunity led to the 1968 Bilingual Education Act that provided the children from low income families with programs to meet the "special needs" of large numbers of children of limited-English-speaking ability. But even though bilingual education has been widely accepted, some of its original proposals have been passed over, particularly the value of bilingual education for all children and the importance of literacy in the non-English language. Today, at the public school level, bilingual education is provided only to students who are limited-English proficient. Once students are able to survive educationally in English, they are mainstreamed into regular English-only classrooms. And, in many instances, the bilinguality achieved by the students stops there. When students are mainstreamed, most of the time, they are sent to classrooms for the low achievers, in which students' cognitive and academic skills are not challenged. The ideal goal would be to allow students to grow cognitively and academically in a bilingual classroom environment. But, the transitional goal of bilingual education does not permit students to remain in bilingual classrooms. And in many instances, when the effectiveness of bilingual education is questioned, researchers do not address this issue.

Second language programs play a key role in the education of Hispanic students. Every bilingual program in the United States must include an English as a second language component, and ESL programs must recognize the importance of the mother tongue. Effective second language programs need qualified teachers who make the classroom environment attractive to students and one in which they will feel motivated to learn content areas and the second language.

A great menace to the development of Hispanic children and youth are official English Only policies. In the last decade, Hispanic advocacy groups have been fighting the United States English and English Only movements. Hispanics need to be alert to every movement of these groups since they will not rest until they see the eradication of Spanish from the schools, the media, and the public service domains.

CHAPTER 7

*The Health of Hispanic Children and Youth**

Health refers to a condition of optimal physical, social and mental well-being, not just the absence of disease. This century has witnessed an unprecedented explosion in the phenomenal capacity of physicians to diagnose, treat, and cure disease. Concomitantly, advances in social and behavioral science research have elucidated relationships among biological, behavioral and social factors that affect health and illness. As a result, the health status of all American citizens has improved tremendously since the turn of the century. Although such tremendous strides have been made in improving the health and longevity of the United States population, certain subgroups of the American population have not benefited fully or equitably from the fruits of science or from those systems responsible for translating and using health science technology. Included in these minority subgroups are Hispanics, African Americans, Native Americans and those of Asian/Pacific Island heritage. This chapter discusses the health of Hispanic children and youth in the United States by summarizing some of the most recent data available about their health status. Areas addressed in this chapter are: infant mortality, maternal/childbearing factors, Acquired Immune Deficiency Syndrome, chemical dependency, and mental health.

---

*
I wish to thank my son, Olveen Carrasquillo, a student at NYU Medical School, for his help in the research and writing of this chapter.

Limited Data Sources

One of the most disturbing facts that emerges when one tries to discuss the health of the Hispanic population in the United States is that there is actually a very limited amount of data on Hispanics as an ethnic group. It has only been in the last two decades that the government has begun making attempts to get a better picture of the health of the second largest minority group in the United States. In 1974, a congressional mandate, PL 94-311, called for the active production of data on the health of America's Hispanics. One of the main reasons why data were not readily available before the 1970's was that before then health data were collected in terms of white or black; and Hispanics had to decide to which of those two groups they felt they belonged. Even to this day, despite intensive efforts to develop a significant body of knowledge regarding Hispanic health issues, there still exist significant gaps, partly because the white or black mentality still exists in many of the data sources on health.

Major data sources used to obtain information about the health of Hispanics are the National Health Interview Survey (NHIS), the Hispanic Health and Nutrition Examination Survey (HHANES), vital statistics, and independent scientific studies. The National Health Interview Survey (NHIS) is the principal source of information on the health of the civilian non-institutionalized population of the United States. Its three main assessments are short-term disability measures, long term disability measures, and measures of health service utilization. Unfortunately this source of data does not sample enough Hispanics to allow precise estimates for Hispanic national groups. Realizing the need for Hispanic data, in 1984, the United States Department of Health and Human Services released a report in which three years of data (from 1978–80) were combined to produce reliable estimates for Hispanics. One of the most important findings of the report was the need to collect and present Hispanic data by national origin, since, in many measures, Hispanics of different national origins differ more from each other than they do from non-Hispanics, African Americans and whites (Trevino, 1986; Trevino & Moss, 1984).

Another important source of data on the health of Hispanics is the Hispanic Health and Nutrition Examination Survey (HHANES). As a result of the National Health Survey Act of 1956, a National Health and Nutrition Examination Survey (NHANES) has been periodically administered to a national sample in the United States. The NHANES relies on five principal data collection methodologies: physical examination, diagnostic testing, anthropometry, laboratory analysis and personal interviews. It is one of the prime sources of prevalent data for specifically defined diseases or conditions of ill health. Like the NHIS, though, the NHANES does not sample enough Hispanics to make any precise calculations. Realizing this lack and the need for Hispanic health data, in the late 1970's it was recommended that a special NHANES be carried out for Hispanics. The HHANES was the first special population survey ever undertaken by the National Center for Health Statistics and probably the last based on the cost of its development and implementation. The HHANES did not use a national sample but, instead, focused on the three major Hispanic subgroups in the geographic regions where they are found in largest concentration. Thus, three separate surveys were conducted of Mexican Americans in the Southwest, Puerto Ricans in New York City, and Cubans in Dade County (Miami), Florida. HHANES was a one-time study carried out from 1982–84, and unless future NHANES oversample Hispanics, there will not be further HANES data from Hispanics. Finally, since a comparison survey was not done at the time, in order to compare HHANES data one would have to use data from NHANES carried out several years before or after the HHANES took place (Munoz, Lecca & Goldstein, 1988). At present, the data from the HHANES are still being analyzed. Reports for certain measures comparing different Hispanic subgroups have been made as well as some comparisons to non-Hispanic, African Americans and whites. An overview of preliminary results for Puerto Ricans and Mexican Americans has also been published.

Another popular measure used to determine the health of the general population is vital statistics, that is, data from birth and death certificates. These data are collected at the state level, and, although states vary in their vital statistics compilation records, agreements between the National Center for Health Statistics (NCHS) and the states on uniform registration practices have led to the use of these records on a national level to compute national statistics. In the past, Hispanics have been considered an ethnic rather than a racial minority and are often included in vital statistics information as white. It was not until 1978 that the NCHS recommended that a Hispanic identifier be used on these records. At present, about 23 states use such an identifier, covering 90 percent of the Hispanic population. The only problem that arises is that due to privacy laws, the state of California makes such information optional, a fact that hospital staff interpret as meaning that they do not have to inquire about such details. For this reason, only half of these records in California have the Hispanic identifier item completed. Other states with large Hispanic populations such as Florida and New Jersey also do not require such information.

To solve these discrepancies among states in reporting ethnic data on a national level, the NCHS decided not to include Hispanic identifier information from any state in its data use tapes. As a result, national Hispanic mortality rates, which are the simplest and most essential estimates in public health, cannot be determined in this country. For example, one can easily look on a chart and find the infant mortality rate for whites and minorities such as African Americans, Native Americans, and Asian/Pacific Islanders. However, the present national infant mortality rate for Hispanics is not known. Despite this lack of national vital statistics data, one can still examine the records of individual states which often tabulate their data with the Hispanic identifier to get a picture of Hispanic health in that state.

The last important source of data on Hispanics used in preparing the information presented in this chapter comes from independent studies done by individual researchers. These studies usually focus on one or a few particular health aspects and they are usually limited to one Hispanic subgroup or geographic area and often do not distinguish among Hispanics; but, together, they can provide a valuable source of data on Hispanic health issues. Thus, anyone seeking data about certain aspects of health in the Hispanic population should make an especially careful review of the recent medical literature.

The Health of Hispanic Infants

Throughout the world, the families most vulnerable to health problems are those with the lowest household incomes. Such a situation applies to many of the Hispanic youth in this country. The economic, social and educational levels of Hispanic children and youth have a tremendous impact on their physical, social and mental health. The health status of Hispanics can be related to many socioeconomic factors such as education, income, occupational status, lifestyles and attitudes toward health care and treatment. It is also related to the role that health care, schools and welfare institutions play in the lives of these children and youth.

Young children comprise one of the vulnerable health groups most susceptible to nutritional, physical and cognitive deprivations. These hazards are especially intense during the earliest stages of life: from conception through the first year. Health and nutritional deficits, inadequate childhood stimulation, and parental neglect have been linked to underachievement and antisocial behavior as the child grows up. Studies have shown that these deficits are linked to impaired intellectual and emotional development, and, in some children, to delinquent juvenile and adult behavior.

Infant Mortality

One the most important measures in public health is the role of infant mortality, which measures deaths in the first year of life. A high rate has been taken to indicate unmet health needs and unfavorable environmental factors such as economic conditions, nutrition, education, sanitation and medical care. The infant mortality rate can be further broken down into two rates—the neonatal mortality rate (deaths in the first 28 days of life) and the postnatal infant mortality rate (deaths from 28 days to one year). The postnatal mortality rate is generally perceived as a reflection of living conditions, quality of care for children and medical care for treatable conditions such as infections. The neonatal mortality rate, on the other hand, is felt to be a more accurate measure of pre-existing health conditions of the mother and the medical care she and her baby received during pregnancy.

Another indicator is low birth weight (less than 5 1/2 pounds), which is a specific predictor of child mortality and morbidity. Low birth weight has been implicated as the cause of two thirds of the neonatal deaths and sixty percent of all infant deaths (McCormick,1985). Among the low-birth-weight births there are two subgroups—preterm deliveries and those which are small for gestational age, not always, possible to distinguish in the data. Low-birth-weight babies also run a great risk of retarded intellectual and emotional development. Since they are generally less active, they tend to interact less with their parents than do higher birth weight babies, and thus tend to be deprived of the early intellectual and emotional stimulation necessary for health and mental development. For Hispanics, birth data are available for 22 states, which include about 90 percent of all Hispanics in the United States; thus, low birth weight figures are available and have been separated into different Hispanic ethnic subgroups. As mentioned , national data on infant mortality, neonatal mortality and postnatal mortality are lacking, and one must look at state data and independent studies.

One can get an idea of the infant mortality rate from the fact that in 1983 the infant mortality rate for whites was 9.7 deaths per 1000 live births while the infant mortality rate for African Americans was more than double at 19.2 deaths per 1000 live births (United States Department of Health and Human Services, 1986b). Although these numbers represent tremendous drops in death rates for both groups since the turn of the century, where the national infant mortality rate was about 65, the black infant mortality rate is similar to that found today in some developing countries and not indicative of one of the most advanced countries in the world. Similarly, the neonatal mortality rate was 6.4 for whites and 12.4 for African American, while the postnatal mortality rate was 3.3 for whites and 6.8 for African Americans (United States Department of Health and Human Services, 1986b).

For Hispanics, although the data are fragmented, one of the most apparent findings is how much they differ among themselves. For example, most studies focused on the southwest where most Hispanics are Mexican Americans. These studies have found that Mexican American infants do relatively well, which is surprising given their social and economic conditions. For example, cohort data reported the infant mortality rate to be 8.5 deaths per 1000 live births for white infants and, similarly, 8.8 for Hispanic infants. It should be mentioned that for African Americans in that study, the rate was only 10.2 (Villarreal, 1986). Likewise, the neonatal mortality rate for Mexican Americans generally appears favorable. One study using linked birth-death records in California from 1981–83 found that the neonatal mortality rate among whites was 4.24; deaths per 1000 live births among African Americans was 7.28; for United States born Hispanics it was 4.39; and for Mexican-born Hispanics it was 4.65 (Binkin, Rust and Williams, 1988). This slightly higher neonatal mortality rate for Mexican-born Hispanics, as opposed to United States-born Hispanics (most of whom are of Mexican descent), persisted even when separated by birth weights. These data suggest that births to Mexican-born, Hispanic mothers are not as favorable as those for United States-born, Mexican Americans. The authors of the study noted that even though

Hispanics had lower rates of death from factors such as congenital abnormalities, Mexican-born Hispanics had more deaths due to conditions in which more aggressive monitoring and intervention might have helped prevent some of these deaths. As an example of lack of aggressive measures, they cite that the caesarean section rate for Mexican-born Hispanics was only 13.3 percent as opposed to 18.3 percent for United States-born Hispanics, 17.9 percent in whites, and 16.8 percent in African Americans (Binkin, Rust and Williams, 1988). It should be kept in mind though that the above neonatal mortality rates are still much better among Mexican born Hispanics than for African Americans.

In terms of birth weight, Mexican Americans also appear to do well. In 1981, using data from 22 states, the estimated national low birth weight rate for Mexican Americans was 5.6 low weight births per 100 live births as compared to a rate of 5.7 for whites. Another study using a cohort of 29,415 women from the Northern California Kaiser Permanente Birth Defects Study found a low birth weight rate of 4.0 among Hispanics, most of whom were Mexican Americans, as opposed to 3.55 for whites and 12.7 for African Americans. The mean birth weights were 3.42kg for Hispanics, 3.48kg for whites, and 3.23kg for African Americans. The author of this study even noted that Mexican Americans do well despite decreased education and access to health care (Shiono, Klebanoff, Graubard, Berendes & Rhodas, 1986).

Puerto Rican infants, on the other hand, have been found to have much poorer health. For example, in 1981 the low birth weight rate for Mexican Americans was 5.6 low weight births per 100 live births, for Cubans 5.8, for Central and South Americans it was 5.7, and for whites it was 5.7. In comparison the rates for Puerto Ricans was 9.0 and for African Americans it was 12.7 (Villarreal, 1985). It has been suggested that the economic circumstances of many Puerto Ricans are such that considerations regarding socioeconomic status, access to health care, and health education and behaviors that apply to African Americans apply to Puerto Ricans as well (United States Department of Health and Human Services, 1986a). This idea can be corroborated to some extent if one examines data from the New York City Department of Health. Due to the high concentration of Hispanics living there, the New York City Department of Health collects appropriate data to report infant mortality rates for Puerto Ricans and other Hispanics in New York City. In 1984, the infant mortality rate for non-Hispanic, non-Asian whites in New York City was 10.5, while for non-Hispanic, non-Asian non-whites (i.e. African Americans) the rate was a shocking 19.8. As expected, the infant mortality rate for Puerto Ricans was also markedly elevated at 14.4, although not as high as for African Americans. Other Hispanics in New York City, as in other regions in the country, tended to do much better with infant mortality rates even lower than whites at 8.6 (New York City Department of Health, 1986).

A comparison of the 1984 New York City neonatal mortality rates shows a similar picture with that among whites of 7.7 neonatal deaths per 1000 live births and for other Hispanics 6.2, while it was 9.1 for Puerto Ricans and 12.1 for African Americans. By subtraction, the postnatal mortality rate was also obtained. This rate was only 0.6 among whites, while it was 2.2 among other Hispanics and much higher for Puerto Ricans and African Americans, at 5.3 and 7.6 respectively. These high rates among Puerto Ricans and African Americans are very disturbing and suggest that health programs in the city should make a major program goal of lowering these alarming mortality rates for Puerto Rican and African American infants (New York City Department of Health, 1986).

Cubans, like Mexican Americans, seem to have more favorable infant health data than Puerto Ricans, which is not surprising given the fact that Cubans have the best socioeconomic status of all the Hispanic groups. In 1980, the infant mortality rate among the white residents of Dade county, Florida, of whom many are Cuban (since most Cubans classify themselves as white when given a choice of black or white), was 11.0 infant deaths per 1000 live births (Ford Foundation, 1983), which was exactly the same as the national infant mortality rate for whites for that year (United States Department of Health and Human Services, 1984). As mentioned above, they also had a low birth weight rate of 5.8 low birth weights per 100 live births similar to the rate of 5.7 for whites that year. The above data then reveal that the state of Hispanic infant health varies widely depending on the Hispanic sub-group.

Maternal Factors Affecting Childbearing

As previously mentioned, birth data on Hispanics are now available for 22 states accounting for 90 percent of the Hispanic population. Two rates are commonly used in discussing births. One is the crude birth rate, which is the number of births in a given population, but this rate is partly a function of the age distribution of females in the population. For this reason, the fertility rate is often preferred because it uses only women of childbearing age (15 to 44) in the denominator and, thus, is not influenced by the age distribution of women in the population. In 1980, the crude birth rate for Hispanics was 23.5 births per 1000 people. For whites, the rate was 14.2, and for African Americans it was 22.9. This high birth rate is one of the reasons why it is estimated that by the year 2000 Hispanics will outnumber African Americans. Within the Hispanic groups, the rates varied from a high of 26.6 among Mexican Americans and 20.3 among Puerto Ricans, to a low of 9.6 for Cubans. The rate for other Hispanics was 20.0. Thus, the large increase in the Hispanic population will be due mostly to Mexican Americans, whose birth rate is higher than for African Americans, while in the next century there will be proportionately fewer Cubans if current trends persist. When one looks at the fertility rates, the ratios are still similar albeit a little less striking. For Hispanics the fertility rate overall was 95.4 births per 1000 women aged 15–44. Among the sub-groups it was 111.3 for Mexican Americans, 77.0 for Puerto Ricans, 75.3 for other Hispanics, and 41.9 for Cubans. For whites and African Americans, the fertility rates were 62.4 and 90.7 respectively (United States Department of Health and Human Services, 1985a).

The literature mentioned several factors which have been linked to low birth weight and high infant mortality rates. One of the most important factors in determining the health of the infant is that of prenatal care by the mother. Prenatal care provides screening for certain risk factors in pregnancy like diabetes and hypertension and provides an opportunity for education and guidance of the mother to be. Furthermore, it provides the social opportunity for the mother and either the father or significant other to get to know the physician and vice-versa. A good patient-physician relationship is important because it increases the tolerance to labor pain and facilitates labor and a good outcome by decreasing anxiety and fear of the unknown. It has also been pointed out that prenatal visits are especially beneficial to Hispanic women because, although they are more attached to the values of the old country and are keepers of traditions, during the prenatal period, Hispanic women are more open to change because it is for the benefit of their family, thus providing a fertile period for preventive medical education (Poma, 1987). Commonly used measures in describing prenatal care in the population include when the prenatal care was first started and also the number of prenatal care visits.

In 1981, 82 percent of all white mothers who gave birth received prenatal care in the first trimester, but among African Americans this number was only 62 percent. Hispanics have an even lower percentage, with only 60 percent of mothers receiving prenatal care in the first trimester. Breaking this figure down provides some even more surprising results. First, Puerto Ricans were the least likely to have early prenatal care, with only 54 percent of the births falling into that category. Mexican Americans had relatively lower rates of low birth weight infants, yet the percentage of mothers who received early prenatal care for this group was 60 percent, which was lower than the percentage for African Americans. The only group with a rate similar to whites was the Cubans for whom it was 80 percent. It has also been suggested that Hispanic women will often stop prenatal visits since they are feeling fine and are more used to crisis intervention than preventive medicine measures (Poma, 1987). The low rate of prenatal care among Puerto Ricans requires further discussion.

New York City vital statistics from 1978–80 data show that among Puerto Ricans who are the first generation living in New York City, the percentage of mothers receiving early prenatal care was 32.7 percent; and for those who are second generation or more Puerto Ricans in New York City, the rate was 31.7 percent. At the same time, the percentages for other Hispanics in New York City was 33.4 percent; for whites it was 66.9 percent; and for African Americans it was 34.1 percent (New York City Department of Health, 1986). Although the data among different generation Puerto Ricans living in New York City were similar, they differed significantly from the percentage of mothers who received early prenatal care in Puerto Rico, which was 60.6 percent in 1980 (Center for Disease Control, 1987).

Language barriers or cultural traits at odds with those of the system may be reasons that prevent Puerto Rican women from seeking prenatal care. Similar reasons may also cause Mexican Americans not to receive early prenatal care. One study examining this lack of prenatal care among Mexican Americans in Texas found that 52 percent of the Hispanic surnamed women in Texas prefer health care services and information delivered in Spanish (Smith & Wait, 1986). Mexican Americans have more favorable low birth weight rates as compared to Puerto Ricans despite similar underutilization of prenatal care services. It may be fruitful for studies to focus on the causes of this apparent paradox. For example, it may be that the birth weight data are inaccurate due to underreporting or that there may be some protective factors in the Mexican culture which make up for this lack of early prenatal care.

Smoking is another major factor that has been linked to a poor pregnancy outcome. Smoking among Hispanics continues to be a major health problem in the adult population. Studies using recent HHANES data show that the prevalence of smoking in men was 43.6 percent for Mexican Americans, 41.8 percent for Cubans and 41.3 percent among Puerto Ricans (Escobedo & Remington, 1989). In 1983, the prevalence of smoking for white males was 32.0 percent and 23.2 percent for black males (United States Department of Health and Human Services, 1986a). The data also showed that as compared to the general population, the decline in cigarette smoking among successive cohorts for Puerto Rican and Cuban men was slight, while Mexican Americans had a more favorable rate of decline. Among women, the prevalence of smoking was 24.5 percent for Mexican women and 23.1 for Cuban women, while Puerto Rican women had a significantly higher rate at 32.6 percent (Escobedo & Remington, 1989). Among white and black women in 1983, it was 17.2 percent and 10.7 percent respectively. More data showed that as compared to the small increases in smoking among women in the general population, successive cohorts show that the prevalence rates of smoking for Cuban and Puerto Rican women are increasing markedly (Escobedo & Remington, 1989). Thus, future smoking prevention efforts should especially target Puerto Rican and Cuban women since it seems that they are most at risk.

Another factor linked to a poor pregnancy outcome is that of drinking. Even moderate use of alcohol during pregnancy is associated with a significant decrease in birth weight. Unfortunately, data on drinking patterns of Hispanics are very limited. What is published though seems to indicate that while Hispanic men drink more than whites, women tend to drink less. The 1979 National Institute on Alcohol Abuse and Alcoholism National Survey indicates that based on self-reported data, Hispanic American males age 18 and older have higher levels of drinking and higher levels of alcohol-related problems. Other studies have also shown that Hispanic males tend to drink more often and drink more on each occasion than the general population (Caetano, 1984).

As opposed to males, Hispanic females tended to be more abstainers or light drinkers as compared to the general population (Caetano, 1987, United States Department of Health and Human Services, 1985b). The pattern of less drinking among Hispanic women also seems to be true when they become pregnant. The Kaiser Permanente study showed that in their group of Hispanic women who were pregnant, 68.8 percent of them did not drink as compared to only 45.6 percent of the whites and 60.2 percent of the African American females (Shiono, Klebanoff, Graubard, Berendes & Rhodas, 1986), but one should keep in mind that this study included only Hispanic women in Northern California. One significant factor that has been reported is that among Hispanic women there is a strong relationship between acculturation and heavy drinking. Acculturated women have five times the risk of becoming drinkers and have higher rates of frequent high maximum drinking than women who are less acculturated. This pattern of drinking especially among Hispanic acculturated women, resembling that of United States women, was independent of age, education, work status, or generational group (Caetano, 1987).

The other serious maternal lifestyle problem with effects on infants' health is that of drug addiction. While much research has been conducted on this problem, there is very little data concerning Hispanics. What data are available will be discussed later in this chapter along with factors related to the health of Hispanic youth.

Finally, two other important maternal diseases are discussed. These are diabetes and hypertension. Both of these are routinely checked for in prenatal visits to doctors because they are associated with problems during pregnancy and have adverse effects on the health of the infant. The importance of these diseases should be stressed given the fact that many Hispanic women do not receive early prenatal care. These two factors are also very important in the development of cardiovascular disease in adults, which is the leading cause of death in the United States. As a result, many studies have examined the rates of hypertension and diabetes among Hispanics.

Many studies have established the high prevalence of hypertension among African Americans. Among Hispanics however, the data are a little controversial. In a recent review of many studies of Mexican Americans, it has been concluded that the problem of hypertension among Mexican Americans in the Southwestern United States is generally not of the same magnitude reported for the United States African American population overall, although it may be substantial and greater than for whites among certain subgroups (Kumanyika, 1986). One of the studies found that among Mexican American women in Texas, the diastolic blood pressures were lower in the Mexican American women between 18–44 than in white women of similar ages.

However, another study in California found that the prevalence of hypertension was higher among younger Hispanic women than among white women. For example, the percentage of women 18–49 years with hypertension or currently taking anti-hypertensive medication was 7.6 percent as opposed to 6.4 percent for white women (Hazuda,1986).

Another factor in hypertension which needs to be discussed is that of its relationship to socioeconomic status. Similar to white women, there is a strong inverse relationship between socioeconomic status and hypertension in Hispanic women. That is, with increased socioeconomic status, there is a lower prevalence of hypertension. The rates for hypertension control in Mexican American women are similar to national figures, while Mexican American men lag far behind white men in this parameter. Some recent studies have begun to investigate hypertension among Puerto Ricans. One study on hypertension among Puerto Ricans conducted in New York City found a very disturbing rate of undiagnosed hypertension among Puerto Rican females of 46.6 percent and 66.6 percent among African American females (Barrios, Mullay, Goldstein & Munoz, 1987). A recent publication describing the prevalence of hypertension among Puerto Rican women of child bearing age found that hypertension was about 8 percent for women 18–25, 17 percent for women 25–34 and 23 percent for women 35–44 years old (Munoz, Lecca & Goldstein, 1988). Clearly, these numbers are much higher than the rates found in other studies of Mexican Americans which place the percent of women between 18–49 years old with hypertension at 7.6 percent (Kumanyika, 1986).

The other significant maternal health factor affecting pregnancy is diabetes among Hispanics. Diabetes is divided into two types. The first type is insulin dependent. A review of the literature indicated that the prevalence of insulin dependent diabetes in Hispanics is less than 5 percent. The other type of diabetes is called non-insulin. It is a major health problem among the Hispanic population and is a major cause of morbidity and mortality among adult Hispanics (Villareal, 1986). Studies have cited different prevalence rates of diabetes among Mexican Americans, but all have found it be much higher than among whites (Hazuda, 1986). The most recent data available come from the HHANES which also includes data for other Hispanic groups. This report showed that the rates of diabetes among Mexican Americans was 23.9 percent, 26.1 among Puerto Ricans and 15.8 percent among Cuban Americans as compared to rates of 12.0 percent for whites and 19.3

percent for African Americans. Thus, all Hispanic groups are at risk of diabetes.

It has also been found that, at least among Mexican Americans, the rate of diabetes varies by socioeconomic status. Studies in the southwest have shown that Hispanic women in low-income areas are four times more likely than Hispanic women in the suburbs to have diabetes (United States Department of Health and Human Services, 1985b). Since Mexican American women are much more obese than non-Hispanic whites, studies have been done to see if obesity plays a role since obesity is a major risk factor for diabetes. The report found that, indeed, obesity contributes to diabetes in Mexican American women, but does not explain entirely the excessively high rate that has been observed relative to non-Hispanic whites (Hazuda, 1986).

The Health of Hispanic Children

As mentioned earlier in discussing infant mortality, national mortality rates for Hispanics are not available. One recent study among Hispanics was able to establish mortality rates for different Hispanic groups. This study ingeniously took advantage of the fact that around 1980, the National Center for Health Statistics began to code place of birth for select countries in the Western Hemisphere on death certificates. By looking at place of birth on death certificates as well as census data, these mortality rates for Hispanics were described for those born in Mexico, Cuba and Puerto Rico (Rosenwaike, 1987). Although these foreign born Hispanics account for only 33 percent of all Hispanics in the United States and differ on various health parameters from United States born Hispanics, it nevertheless presents a breakthrough in describing national rates of mortality for Hispanics. The study included only persons five years of age or older and did not report infant mortality rates since there would be no way of knowing how many foreign-born infants were in the country that year.

Rosenwaike's study showed that in 1980, the age-adjusted crude death rate among all three major Hispanic groups, Cubans, Mexican Americans and Puerto Ricans, was lower than that for United States African Americans and whites, particularly among Mexican Americans and Cubans. This finding led the author to conclude that Hispanic migrants have retained the more favorable aspects of their original environment, thereby holding their mortality to a lower level than that generally prevailing in the United States (Rosenwaike, 1987).

In describing the health of children and youth, though, the important rate is the age-specific death rate. This rate reveals that unlike the general pattern, foreign born Hispanic children have higher death rates than other children in the United States, particularly Puerto Ricans and Cubans. The death rates among children 5–14 was 29.1 deaths per 1000 children among whites and 38.7 among African Americans. Among foreign-born Hispanic children the rate was 43.5 for those Cuban born, 40.3 for those Puerto Rican born, and 32.5 for those Mexican born (Rosenwaike, 1987). These rates would lead one to conclude that the health of Hispanic children is rather poor as compared to United States whites. What one must keep in mind, though, is that these data were only for foreign born Hispanic children in the United States who are not the majority of Hispanic children in the United States.

Most Cuban children aged 5–14 in the United States were born to parents who had left Cuba in the early 1960's when the Castro regime took power. This study examining foreign-born Hispanics, however, mostly included Cuban children who had just arrived in the late 1970's as refugees. The only conclusion that can be made about Cuban children from this study then is that it appears that the health of Cuban refugee children is rather poor as compared to other groups, but no conclusions can be made about the majority of Cuban children. It is rather unfortunate that there has really been next to nothing reported in the literature comparing the health of these two groups of Cuban children.

These mortality rates also seem to show that children born in Puerto Rico and who now live on the mainland have poorer health as compared to United States whites. Their mortality rates in fact are even higher than those of African American children who have typically been described as having very poor health when compared to white children. Mexican-born children, on the other hand, seem to have better health. While their age-specific mortality rate was higher than for whites, it was much lower than for African Americans.

Another aspect of health is nutrition. The nutrition of Hispanic children is of primary importance in the first few months of life, during which the concern is with the issues of breast feeding versus bottle feeding among Hispanics, an issue that has received some attention recently in the literature. It was not long ago when it had been recommended that mothers should bottle feed. However, with further research the advantages of breast feeding became apparent, and today the American Academy of Pediatrics recommends that breast feeding occur for the first 4–6 months of life. Health advantages from breast feeding include optimal nutrition for infant growth and development and immunological protection against allergy and infection. Studies have shown that an infant assumes a sixteen times greater risk of significant illness by two months if not breast fed. Most of the literature tends to agree that Hispanics have not participated in the dramatic resurgence in breast feeding seen among middle and upper income groups. For example, one study on infants in a Health Maintenance Organization (HMO) in Arizona found that the percentage of infants being breast fed at two months was 73 percent for whites but only 49 percent for Hispanics, most of whom were Mexican Americans (Wright, Halberg, Taussig & Group Health Medical Pediatricians, 1988). Another study in Southern California using market research techniques described how in the 1970's breast feeding along the United States border had increased among whites but had diminished slightly for Hispanics (Weller & Clairborne, 1986).

Studies in other regions of the country have reported very different data. One study of Hispanics in Florida found that the breast feeding rate among whites was only 35 percent, and that for Cubans it was even lower at 10 percent; and among Puerto Ricans in Florida it was 10 percent (Bryant, 1982). The study found that while whites typically breast-feed for several months, their Hispanic counterparts change to bottle feeding after 2–6 weeks. One factor all these studies agree on is that breast feeding among Hispanics is not as predictable as for whites. It has been found that among whites socio-demographic characteristics such as living with father, parity, and education were predictive of feeding patterns, but they were not among Hispanics. Higher education and less employment are not associated with breast-feeding in Hispanics, suggesting that the effect of ethnicity is different from that of education and employment. Other studies found that important factors in breast feeding rates among Hispanics were relatives', friends' and neighbors' influences along with the husbands'/boyfriends' attitude toward lactation (Bryant, 1982).

In terms of the overall nutrition of Hispanic children in the first few years of life, one study suggests that Hispanic children are more undernourished than African Americans or whites (Gayle, 1987). Most population estimates of malnutrition are based on prevalence estimates of poor linear growth, low length for age, and low weight for height. The study found that the low length for age prevalence among whites was 10.4%, for Hispanics 11.7 percent, and 12.0 percent for African Americans. When only children of normal birth weights were included, the rates were 7.4 percent for whites, 8.1 percent for African Americans, and 8.6 percent for Hispanics. Recent literature did not include any studies of specific nutritional deficiencies among Hispanics. It has been reported though that iron and vitamin C deficiencies have been found in higher prevalence in Hispanic infants. Hispanic children 10–12 years old have been found deficient in calcium and vitamins A and C, while girls of similar age were additionally found to be deficient in iron. Pregnant and lactating Hispanic women have been found deficient in calcium, vitamins A and C and iron (Villarreal, 1986). Another study conducted in Texas in which a cause specific infant mortality rate was presented showed that the infant mortality rate due to avitaminoses (lack of vitamins) and other nutritional deficiencies was 0.6 per 10,000 births for Mexican Americans but 0 (or low enough to be zero) for whites (Molina, 1987; Villarreal, 1986).

Another major problem in the Hispanic community which was touched upon when discussing diabetes is that of obesity. Recent HHANES data have documented the extent of this problem among Hispanic young adults (Powell, 1984). It showed that among Hispanic adults aged 20–24, the percentage of overweight men was 15.5 percent for Mexican Americans, 21.2 percent for Cubans, and 15.8 percent for Puerto Ricans. Additionally, 4.3 percent of Mexican men in that age group, 6.6 percent of Cubans, and 1.6 percent of the Puerto Rican men were found to be severely overweight. Thus, Cuban males were most at risk to be overweight. Young Hispanic women were found to have an even higher prevalence of obesity, with 21.9 percent of Mexican, 13.6 percent of Cuban and 23.6 percent of Puerto Rican women aged 20–24 being overweight. The percentage of severely overweight women in that age group was 9.0 percent for Mexican Americans, 2.9 percent for Cubans, and 10.4 percent for Puerto Ricans. Thus, Puerto Rican and Mexican women were found to be most at risk for obesity. Similar to adults, studies also seem to suggest such a problem exists among Hispanic children. One study also using body mass index and triceps skin fold reported a larger number of short but heavy children among Mexican Americans of lower socioeconomic status in Texas as compared to reference data for American children (Mascola, 1984).

The next issue to be discussed is vaccinations. Surveys using two ethnic categories (white versus all other) have found that at least 60 percent of all white children 1–4 years old had been immunized for measles, rubella, DPT (diptheria-tetanus-pertussis), polio and mumps. In contrast, over 50 percent of the children included in the all other categories had not been immunized for rubella, polio and mumps, only 52 percent had been immunized for measles, and 51.3 percent had received the DPT vaccine (United States Department of Health and Human Services, 1986a). Such hard data are not available for Hispanics as a separate group, but state data have been examined, and it was found that the four border states of California, Arizona, New Mexico, and Texas which account for 18.4 percent of the United States population and in which a significant percentage of the population are Hispanics had 43.9 percent of all the cases of measles in the United States and 32.6 percent of all cases of rubella (Villarreal, 1986).

Infections and parasitic diseases are other important factors in discussing Hispanic children's health. Results from the National Health Interview Survey (NHIS) indicated the rate of infective and parasitic conditions to be elevated among Puerto Rican children (less than 17 years old). The rates were 18.5 per 100 children for Mexican Americans, 78.2 for Puerto Ricans, 39.4 for Cubans, and 32.3 for other Hispanics. For white children it was 52.6 and for African Americans 27.8 per 100 births. One study done in South Texas found that the rate of infant mortality due to infective and parasitic diseases was 10.4 per 10,000 live births for Mexican Americans as opposed to 2.4 for whites. Further breakdowns revealed that the rates of enteritis and other diarrheal diseases (which in infants are mostly due to infections) as the cause of death was 2.3 for whites and 5.0 for Mexican Americans. For deaths due to septicemia (blood infection) the rate was 4.1 for Hispanics and 0 (or near zero) for whites (Villarreal, 1986).

It has also been found that, as in developing countries, enteritis and diarrhea were among the five leading causes of death in children in the states of Texas, Arizona, California and New Mexico (Villarreal, 1986). Another study, among Mexican immigrants in Contra Costa County in California, found that 39 percent of the immigrants had evidence of infection by pathogenic disease causing worms or protozoa. For children the prevalence of such infection was 28 percent among those 0–4 years, 62 percent among those 5–9, 36 percent among those 10–14 and 66 percent among those 15–19 years old (Arfa, 1981). It has also been suggested that, due to socioeconomic factors and overcrowding,

Hispanics are heavily affected by diseases caused by the bacteria Hemophilus influenza, which is the principal cause of meningitis and other infectious complications in infants and small children (United States Department of Health and Human Services, 1986a).

A discussion of infections among Hispanic children needs to include two diseases which have relatively low prevalence in the population but which are very serious and are found in higher rates in Hispanics. These are tuberculosis and congenital syphilis. Recent data have indicated that the rate of tuberculosis in Hispanics overall is 18.1 per 100,000 people as compared to whites in which it was only 4.5 per 100,000. Of the Hispanics, 48 percent of the cases occurred in individuals less than 35 years old, and 11 percent were in those under 15 years old. The high rate of tuberculosis among young Hispanics may be partially attributed to foreign Hispanic births, which account for about 33 percent of the Hispanic population in the United States but accounted for 42 percent of the cases among Hispanics; while only 34 percent of the cases of tuberculosis in Hispanics occurred in United States-born Hispanics; and no information was available on the other 24 percent of the cases. Furthermore, among foreign-born Hispanics, 57 percent of the cases were in people less than 35 years old, and 17 percent were in children less than 15 years old (American Medical Association, 1987).

Another serious disease among Hispanics is that of congenital syphilis which many in this country consider a disease of the past. This idea though is not accurate, as one study shows. In 1982, there were 159 cases of congenital syphilis in the country (Mascola, 1984). Of these, 50 occurred in Texas alone, and of these, 27 were to Hispanics and 23 to African Americans. It was also found that even though African Americans in Texas have seven times the rate of syphilis as Hispanics, African American women had only a two times greater risk of giving birth to a child with congenital syphilis as compared to Hispanics. Among Hispanics, part of the reason for such high rates was due to foreign-born Hispanics. Foreign-born Hispanic mothers, it was found, were three times as likely as United States-born Hispanic women to have a child infected with syphilis. It was also found that over half these cases of congenital syphilis were due to not receiving prenatal care. The high rates of infection and lack of vaccinations among Hispanic children present a major public health problem which must be addressed in the United States. The methods of preventing these infections have been known for decades and have been partially responsible for the tremendous improvement in health among children in this country. The fact that Hispanics appear to be affected to a higher degree than others in the population implies that increased efforts by the federal, state and local health authorities are needed to prevent these serious infections in Hispanic children.

In discussing the health of children, special mention should be made of one particular subgroup. Although there are very little data on the health of Puerto Rican children, one disease has been well documented in these children. Various studies have found Puerto Rican children to have high rates of asthma. It has been speculated that socioeconomic conditions, such as poor housing, are partially responsible for the high prevalence of asthma in Puerto Rican children (Irigoyen & Zambrana, 1982). The data from the NHIS also show that the rates of respiratory ailments for Puerto Rican children were much higher, at 165.1 as opposed to 100.7 for Mexican Americans, 81.1 for Cubans, 132.7 for other Hispanics, 115.0 for whites, and 89.5 for African Americans.

There are other health characteristics of Hispanic children and youth that can be categorized into those describing illness and disability and those describing utilization of health resources. In terms of days of restricted disability, both Puerto Rican and Cuban children and youth had more days of restricted activity per year, 14.2 and 14.6 respectively, as compared to 9.7 for Mexicans and 10.9 for other Hispanics, and 11.5 for white and 8.7 for African American children. When asking about limitations on activity due to chronic conditions, it was found that only Puerto Rican children were higher, with 6.2 percent of the children having such limitations as compared to 4.0 percent for whites, 3.7 percent for African Americans, 3.0 percent for Mexicans, 3.5 percent for Cubans, and 2.9 percent for other Hispanic children. The data reviewed seem to indicate that, as compared to other Hispanic subgroups, Puerto Rican children are the ones who have the poorest health (United States Department of Health and Human Services, 1984).

As far as ambulatory physician services, Mexican American children seemed least likely to see a doctor, with 2.8 visits a year. Puerto Rican children, on the other hand, averaged the highest, with 5.8 visits a year; for Cubans and other Hispanics it was 3.9 and for whites and African Americans it was 4.5 and 3.2 visits respectively. Additionally, 21 percent of all Mexican American children had no contact with a medical doctor during the year; but this was similar to 18 percent of the Puerto Ricans, 19.4 percent of other Hispanics and 23.3 percent of Cubans. For whites and African Americans, it was 21 percent and 17 percent respectively. As far as hospitalizations, Puerto Rican children were by far the most likely to be hospitalized, with 7 percent of them having been hospitalized in the last year. For Mexican Americans it was only 3.7 percent, for Cubans 5.7 percent, for other Hispanics 3.6 percent, for whites 5.4 percent and 4.8 percent for African Americans. What is hard to interpret from these utilization data is whether Mexican Americans underutilize services because they are healthier or because of decreased access to health care (United States Department of Health and Human Services, 1984).

Utilization of dental services, however, has been broken down into Hispanic categories. It seems that all Hispanic children are at risk of not seeing a dentist. Among Mexican Americans, 30.7 percent of all children ages 4–16 had never seen a dentist, for Cubans it was 33.3 percent, for Puerto Ricans it was 20.5 percent and for other Hispanics it was 28.7 percent. For whites only 9.7 percent of the children 4–16 years old had never seen a dentist while for African Americans it was similar to Hispanics at 22.3 percent. In light of such poor utilization of dental services it is reasonable to assume that Hispanics have poorer dental health than white Americans (United States Department of Health and Human Services, 1984).

It has been explained that the entry of Hispanic children into the health care system is strongly related to socioeconomic factors; and medicaid coverage in particular has a very strong impact on utilization, especially among Mexican Americans and Puerto Ricans who are least likely to have insurance. Therefore, recent medicaid cutbacks might affect these children most. Other factors cited were that for African Americans and Hispanics, it was income that was the most important contributor to children to enter the health care system, while for whites it was health characteristics. However, once entry into the health care system is achieved, subsequent visits are more likely to depend on health needs rather than socioeconomic or demographic variables (Guendelman & Schwalbe, 1986).

Acquired Immune Deficiency Syndrome

One particular disease that has become a recent major threat to the Hispanic community, and particularly to Hispanic children and youth, is Acquired Immune Deficiency Syndrome (AIDS). AIDS is a disease caused by infection with the human immune deficiency virus (HIV). The HIV virus attacks a certain type of white blood cell (T-helper lymphocytes) which normally helps protect the body from infections and diseases. As a result, the body cannot effectively protect itself from infections and diseases that people with normally functioning immune systems can. AIDS is the most serious complication that a patient with the HIV infection can get. It should be kept in mind that infection with the HIV virus does not mean that a person has AIDS. However, it is estimated that at least 55 percent of the people infected with the HIV virus will get AIDS. In terms of mortality, 85 percent of those diagnosed with AIDS before 1986 had died by the end of 1988 (Center for Disease Control, 1989).

The three main modes of transmission of the HIV virus are: (a) through sharing needles and syringes with an infected person, common among intravenous (IV) drug abusers; (b) unprotected sexual activity with infected individuals where blood, semen, or vaginal fluids are interchanged; and, (c) transmission to children from infected mothers during pregnancy, childbirth or breast-feeding. Since national surveillance for Acquired Immune Deficiency Syndrome (AIDS) began in 1981, when the epidemic was first recognized, until the end of 1988, the Center for Disease Control had received 82,764 reports of AIDS cases in the United States. Ethnic breakdown of these cases reveals that 61 percent of these occurred in whites, 24 percent in African Americans, and 15 percent in Hispanics (Center for Disease Control, 1989). In terms of cumulative incidence, AIDS is 2.7 times higher among Hispanics than among non-Hispanic whites. As of 1988, of every hundred thousand Hispanics, 58.2 of them had AIDS as compared to 21.5 per 100,000 non-Hispanic whites (National Coalition of Hispanic Health and Human Services Organizations, 1989). Since 1981, Hispanics have accounted for between 13 and 17 percent of all AIDS cases in the United States; and as the total number of AIDS cases drastically increases from year to year, it will also drastically increase in the Hispanic population (National Coalition of Hispanic Health and Human Services Organizations, 1989). In order to reverse this disproportionate share of Hispanics with AIDS, more intensified prevention messages and changes in behavior have to occur in the Hispanic communities.

One common myth about AIDS in Hispanics is that most cases result from IV drug use. In fact, only 39 percent of the cases of Hispanic AIDS are linked to IV drug use, while 43 percent of the cases are linked with homosexual contact, and 7 percent with homosexual contact and IV drug use. Furthermore, in California, Texas, and Florida almost three out of four AIDS cases among Hispanics are linked to homosexual contact (National Coalition of Hispanic Health and Human Services Organization, 1989). Therefore, it is important not to ignore homosexuality and bisexuality in AIDS prevention and education programs targeted for Hispanic communities.

Another facet of the AIDS epidemic is that of pediatric AIDS. By the end of 1985, 307 cases of AIDS had been diagnosed in children less than 13 years old (it should be kept in mind that for epidemiologic reasons anyone fourteen or older with AIDS is placed in the adult group). Even back then, experts were warning that although they make up 1 percent of the total AIDS cases they have unique clinical, social, and public health problems that required special attention (Rogers, Thomas, Staicher, Noa, Rush & Jaffe, 1987). As of the end of 1988, there were 1346 reported cases of AIDS in children less than 13 years old, with 82 percent of these children less than 5 years old, and 40 percent of the children less than one year old. Of these children with AIDS, 24 percent were white, 53 percent were African American and 23 percent were Hispanic (Center for Disease Control, 1989). It is here when one examines the incidence of pediatric AIDS that the link between AIDS and intravenous (IV) drugs becomes most important. As mentioned, AIDS is spread to the infant mostly by the mother. It is important to mention that before blood was screened for the HIV virus, transfusions were a major route of infection for children, but this is no longer the case. Thus, in an attempt to understand the relationship of AIDS in children to drugs, one has to discuss AIDS in women. As of the end of 1988, 6983 cases of AIDS in women had been reported to the CDC and, of these, 28 percent of the women were white, 52 percent were African American, and 20 percent were Hispanic, a pattern very similar to the ethnic profile of AIDS in children. Overall, 52 percent of the women with AIDS report having a history of IV drug abuse, and another 18 percent reported having sex with an IV-drug-using partner.

For Hispanic women the percentages are 54 percent and 29 percent respectively (Center for Disease Control, 1989).

In an analysis of the reported cases of pediatric AIDS until 1988, among white children, only 22 percent were due to an IV drug using mother, and 10 percent were due to the mother having sex with an IV-drug-using partner. It should be noted that a substantial number of white infants developed AIDS due to transfusions before 1985. In Hispanics, however, 50 percent of the cases involved an intravenous-drug-using mother, and another 21 percent involved an IV-drug-using partner. Thus, over 70 percent of the cases of pediatric AIDS in Hispanics can be linked exclusively to IV-drug use. This relationship to IV-drug use can also be shown by an estimate that 50 percent of the IV-drug-using women in New York City are infected with the AIDS virus and that 20 percent of the women with a partner who uses IV drugs also have the virus (Gross, 1987a). In fact, in 1987 it was estimated that 50,000, or 3 percent, of the women of child bearing age in New York City were infected with the HIV virus (Gross, 1987b).

The prognosis for infants with AIDS is even more grim than for adults. Although the virus can have an incubation period (time from infection to development of symptoms) in adults of 5 years or more, the mean incubation period in children is about 17 months. Once AIDS is diagnosed in children the median survival is 6–7 months (Rogers, Thomas, Staicher, Noa, Rush & Jaffe, 1987). Another very disturbing factor of pediatric AIDS, particularly among children of IV-drug-using mothers, is that many of these children are abandoned. Unfortunately, there is a lack of foster care homes for abandoned infants who have AIDS, and many are left to live out their lives in hospitals where they are known as border babies.

Finally, this section would not be complete without a short discussion of Hispanic youth and AIDS. There have been over 300 AIDS cases reported among teenagers, and Hispanics make up 17 percent of this group of AIDS patients. More important, there have been over 2,500 cases of AIDS reported in Hispanics between 20 and 29 years of age, and, since the virus has an incubation period which may be over five years, it can be assumed that many of these adults acquired the virus as teenagers (National Coalition of Hispanic Health and Human Services Organization, 1989). It should be a top priority for everyone to make these youth aware that the choices they make as teenagers regarding IV drug use and unprotected sexual practices can have tragic consequences in the future.

At present, the only feasible approach to the AIDS epidemic is through prevention. Education of the public, training of health and social service professionals, and personal risk reduction counseling are the only effective methods we have to curb this epidemic. An effective vaccine is not available and most likely will not be available in the next five to ten years. Likewise, drugs like AZT have been found helpful only in prolonging the life-span of patients with AIDS and, most recently, in prolonging the incubation period of those infected with the HIV virus; but a cure for AIDS does not exist. Therefore, a multifaceted prevention and risk reduction strategy is a critical public health priority.

Chemical Dependency among Hispanic Children and Youth

One of the most urgent problems confronting contemporary society is the use and abuse of drugs by elementary and secondary school students. Many inexperienced youth, still in the trial-and-error stage of adolescent life, will eat, drink, smoke or sniff almost anything that promises to make them happier and feel better. Other youths use drugs as a means of escape from the society, while others smoke, drink alcohol, or use drugs as a way to rebel against society. There is the concern of the widespread abuse of a large variety of substances among the younger Hispanic population (Frank, 1983; Preyo, 1980; Department of Health and Human Services, 1985; Velez, 1981). Drugs used by Hispanics tend to have long-term, physically and physiologically damaging effects. Heroin is the primary drug used among Hispanics whose drug use is higher than for all other ethnic groups (United States Department of Health and Public Services, 1985a, 1985b).

National surveys of drug and alcohol have been designed to focus on the general population. Consequently, there are no national data on ethnic-specific rates for drug abuse or the health consequences of drug abuse. Despite these limitations of the data, the studies that have been done suggest that drug abuse related morbidity and mortality in African Americans, Hispanics and Native Americans are greater than for the white population (United States Department of Health and Human

Services, 1985b). A significant percentage of the Hispanic population lives in inner cities. As such, they may be at a somewhat greater risk of drug abuse and its consequences. Results from the 1983 SRO study of drug abuse in New York City suggests that Hispanics have higher rates of drug use than non-Hispanic whites for marijuana, cocaine, heroin, and illicit methadone (Frank, 1983).

Multiple drug use is a problem for all minorities. Data from hospital emergency room cases and from drug abuse treatment programs indicate that Hispanics were more likely than whites to report a primary problem with heroin, cocaine, or phenocyclidine. In addition, inhalants were the most commonly reported category of other drugs used. A dramatic increase in reports of positive toxicology for cocaine was found among the Hispanic population. Between 1982 and 1984, cocaine-related deaths among Hispanics tripled, while they doubled among whites (United States Department of Health and Public Services, 1985a). It has been suggested that the prevalence of inhalant use by Hispanic youths is high. Although this drug use cannot be supported by household and high-school population surveys, a 1979 study of Mexican American children and adolescents in Los Angeles found the prevalence of inhalants to be 14 times that of the general population (Padilla, Padilla & Morales, 1979). Crack, a cheap derivation of cocaine, was one of the most used drugs in the 1980's. It is cheaper than cocaine and has the same effects, although due to its highly addictive chemical ingredients it is a very dangerous drug.

Hispanics are 2.7 times more likely to be in treatment for a drug abuse-related problem than are whites. Data indicate that of those treated for drug-related emergency room episodes, 42 percent of Hispanics as compared to 40 percent of whites administer cocaine by injection; 6 percent of Hispanics as compared to 3 percent of whites administer cocaine by smoking or free-basing. Both are more dangerous routes of administration than the intra-nasal route, and both lead to more frequent use of the drug (United States Department of Health and Human Services, 1985a).

The use of chemical substances increases the risk of accidents, suicide and homicide. It contributes to family disruption, poor academic achievement, and poor employment performance. Parents who are drug users cannot provide an environment conducive to the healthy development of their children. Child chemical users are not physically and mentally apt to live normal lives.

Mental Health Status of Hispanic Children and Youth

In the 1950's, a popular view was that Hispanics suffered less than whites from debilitating psychiatric disorders. This notion was predicated on the fact that Hispanics were underrepresented in the mental health service population. It was thus concluded that since Hispanics used fewer mental health services, they needed fewer services. These early theories, though, were not substantiated by epidemiological studies. In the late 1960's and 1970's, researchers proved these notions to be false. In fact, it was found that the prevalence of Hispanic mental illness was at least equal to or greater than that of whites. In light of their underutilization of services, this could only mean that Hispanics were receiving less help for their mental problems than other groups (Becerra, Kamo & Escobar, 1982). In terms of epidemiologic data, there still seems to be a controversy on the prevalence and incidence of psychiatric disorders among Hispanics. It should be pointed out here that just as with other health parameters, there are very little data collected on the national level regarding mental illness of Hispanics. Also, there is no equivalent of the HANES or the Health Interview Survey when discussing mental illness. Thus, the data are often much more confusing, even in the general population, but particularly so when discussing Hispanics.

The literature points out the contradictory nature of psychiatric symptoms among Mexican Americans. Studies in California using the Center for Epidemiologic Studies Depression Measure have found that the rates of depressive symptoms among Hispanics in California are about two times those of whites, but these differences were mostly attributed to socioeconomic factors. Two studies in Texas found lower psychiatric symptoms among Mexican Americans while one study found higher rates. Another study using telephone interviews of a Health Opinion Survey of measures of psychoneuroticism found that Spanish-speaking, Mexican Americans had much higher rates of these symptoms, while English-speaking Mexican Americans and whites had similar rates, but these differences disappeared when adjusted for sex, age, education and marital status (Vega, Kalody & Warkeit, 1985). Another study in California, using data from surveys, found that the prevalence of mental illness based on structured clinical interviews according to the Schedule for Afflictive Disorders and Schizophrenia-

Diagnostic Criteria was similar for whites and Mexican-Americans, 22 percent and 21 percent respectively. This study also found that a similar percentage had reported psychiatric hospitalizations, 4.4 percent for whites vs. 4.6 percent for Mexican Americans (Vernon & Roberts, 1982).

The prevalence of psychiatric disorders among Puerto Ricans, particularly women, on the other hand, has been shown to be higher than for whites or African Americans. In a review of literature, Comas-Díaz cites studies which found Puerto Ricans to have a higher incidence of psychosomatic symptoms than whites or African Americans. Puerto Rican women particularly had a higher incidence of suicidal ideation (Comas-Diaz, 1982).

In discussing mental disorders among Hispanics, though, one note of caution needs to be made: Cultural differences are absolutely critical in mental health care where misunderstandings can lead to atrocious misdiagnoses. For example, a study showing that Puerto Ricans were admitted to mental health facilities at twice the rate of whites was found to have strong implications of diagnostic distortion and bias (Moore and Pachon, 1985). Another study has also shown that Hispanic clients are consistently rated as more pathological when interviewed by English speakers as opposed to Spanish speakers (Marcos, Murray, Urcuyo & Kessdman, 1973). Thus, these studies, highlighting some of the discrepancies and difficulties involved in understanding Hispanic adult psychiatric data, should be kept in mind when considering mental health issues of Hispanic children and youth. Studies have shown, though, that when one compares the ages of patients admitted to psychiatric hospitals, Hispanics tend to be younger. One study found that 60 percent of Hispanics admitted were under 35 years of age versus 40 percent for whites and, furthermore, over one third of the Hispanics admitted were under 25 years old. These differences, though, are probably due more to the youth of the Hispanic population rather than to a higher incidence of psychiatric disorders in Hispanic youth. Another study found that half the adolescents seen at a center in a neighborhood in New York City with a heavy concentration of Hispanics had mental health related problems (Irigoyen and Zambrana, 1982).

Unfortunately, there is very little data available on the national level concerning the mental health of these children. But, despite the paucity of data, it is agreed that Hispanic children are at higher risk for mental health disorders due to the high-stress environment in which they live (Canino, 1982). A large proportion of these children come from large families of low socioeconomic status whose primary language is not English. Poverty and language barriers are common stresses that compound mental health problems of these children. The fact that a large proportion of these children live in an urban environment is also contributory. The adverse effects of high-rise housing, the anomaly of city living, and frequent change of housing increase the stress to which these children are exposed. Changes in traditional family structures such as unemployment, single parent families and the undermining of the parent's authority, which are common in families of low socioeconomic status, cause further stress in children's lives. Even school can be a stress factor in the lives of Hispanic children and youth. In those schools plagued by overpopulation, underpaid teachers, rapid teacher turnover, and unresponsive political institutions in the community, the school's supportive and growth-enhancing capacities may be seriously hindered. For many urban Hispanic children who also lack adequate family support networks, these factors may create undue stress and result in behavioral problems (Canino, 1982).

Despite the sources of stress in the lives of Hispanic children and youth, it has been noted that the connection between stress and emotional problems is not direct and immediate. Normally, there are certain protective factors in Hispanic culture to meet these stresses. Persons who are strongly integrated into socially supportive networks such as family, circles of friends, religious or other groups, and the ritual component system of Hispanics (*compadrazgo*) are better able to withstand the pressures of stress (Farber and Rogler, 1981). It is when these protective factors are deficient that the children are then at risk. Therefore, mental illness among Hispanic children and youth should be understood as an imbalance between the high level of stress these children face versus the protective factors mentioned above, which would normally be present in the lives of these children.

In light of this information, certain general recommendations have been made for the treatment of the Hispanic child and youth (Canino, 1982). First of all, after a detailed assessment of the Hispanic child's socioeconomic and ecological milieu, there should be an attempt to minimize or decrease whenever possible those stress factors directly associated with the environment. Secondly, there should be a full evaluation of the family and school to test the variables that may be impinging on the successful treatment of the child (Canino, 1982). The strengths and detrimental factors that the family and school system supply must be assessed and incorporated into the therapy. In view of the high frequency of school problems seen in this population, good psycho-educational evaluations and school placement practices may have to be offered as part of the treatment plan. Finally, the socio-cultural background, childbearing, and religious practices of the child's family along with the individual child's language, communication, and coping styles should be fully known. For example, cultural elements such as the use of folk and religious belief systems like *curanderismo, espiritismo, and santerismo,* which are still widely used among Hispanics, should be known. In fact, one study found that 24 percent of the Puerto Rican families investigated had consulted with folk-healers about their child during the past year, and many had involved the child directly in folk religious practices. Additionally, one must understand how verbal interactions, toys, motivational and temperamental factors, and discipline are interpreted in the child rearing practices of each specific Hispanic child's family (Canino, 1982).

Aside from these general recommendations, it is noted that there has not been much written about specific treatment approaches to use with Hispanic children. One of the methods that has been used with Hispanic children includes psychoanalytic-oriented psychotherapy for latency age children with difficulties such as fighting and temper tantrums; this treatment has been found to be successful when combined with special classes and environmental interventions. Group therapy has been recommended for children of multi-problem families. Family therapy emphasizing conflict resolution has also been used with Hispanic children from disorganized and disadvantaged families. One interesting approach has been that of using a therapeutic community. These communities attempt to recreate some of the protective factors lacking in the families of these children in order to help them overcome the stresses in their daily lives (Farber and Rogler, 1981).

Conclusion

Ethnical, cultural, and socioeconomic factors play an important role in the physical and mental health of individuals in the United States. Many factors such as culture heritage, socioeconomic status, social support, knowledge, attitudes and health practices interact to affect the health status of Hispanics who, due to their low socioeconomic status, different linguistic and cultural traits do not appear to be in good physical and mental condition (Anderson, 1986; Garcia, 1985; Guendelman, 1986; Perez-Stable, 1987; United States Department of Health & Human Services, 1989). Because high percentages of Hispanics are city dwellers, they are exposed to a relatively greater number of health problems including environmental hazards. Also, the unique exposure to and ways of dealing with stress and adversity may play a crucial role in Hispanic health, especially mental health. But, although there already exists some information on mental illness among Hispanic adults there is almost no information regarding children and youth. First and foremost, more data are needed on a national level to determine the varied mental health needs of children and youth of different Hispanic populations. Given the large differences in other health factors, it is not unreasonable to assume that Mexican American children in the Southwest have different mental health problems from Puerto Ricans in the Northeast and Cubans in Florida. More studies are also needed on specific treatment programs for these different children.

The use of chemical substances is a big problem in the Hispanic community. There is a need to promote the initiation and/or expansion of efforts to develop coping skills in children and adolescents, aged 9 to 15 years, including development of peer-group instruction programs in school settings, to delay or prevent the use of substances such as drugs, tobacco, and alcohol. AIDS is another big problem in the Hispanic community, which directly affects thousands of children and youth every day. An understanding of the nature and the extent of AIDS in the Hispanic community is needed, along with recognition of some cultural and socioeconomic factors that complicate education and prevention efforts. In summary, there is much to be done in finding ways to make Hispanic children and youth physically and mentally healthier.

CHAPTER 8

Hispanic Youth in the Criminal Justice System

Society tries to develop social, legal, and organizational structures that will filter out law violators and, at the same time, provide an avenue of freedom to those who are innocent. The criminal justice system is the device by which organized societies protect the security of individual interests and assure the survival of the group. There is a general consensus in the United States that ethnic and cultural considerations ought to play a part in the administration of criminal justice. Hispanics represent an increasing percentage of the inmate and youth offender population in the United States. On the offender side of the criminal justice system, Hispanics are represented in excess of their proportion in the general population. Crime statistics on Hispanics indicate that the United States jails and prisons contain a sizeable, significant, and growing Hispanic group. There are several cultural and legal reasons that force Hispanics to became legal offenders or victims of crime.

This chapter presents an overview of Hispanics in the criminal justice system, and it describes Hispanic youth delinquency and causes for the high involvement of these youth. Several recommendations to decrease Hispanic youth involvement in the criminal justice system are listed and discussed at the end of the chapter.

The United States Criminal Justice System

The criminal justice system is an instrument in the service of society that is made up of several components: law enforcement, prosecution and defense, courts, probation and correction. The criminal justice system defines criminal offenses, regulates the apprehension, charging and trial of suspected persons and identifies punishment for convicted offenders. The process of criminal justice begins when the police decide to make an arrest and ends when a person leaves the control of the criminal justice system. Criminal refers to the violation of some criminal law, and justice refers to the operations of due process as set down in the Constitution of the United States, the Bill of Rights, and state laws that specify how criminal cases are to be handled. Thus, the criminal justice process refers to the procedures and agencies used for handling people who have been accused of violating the criminal law.

American society has defined what is legal and illegal conduct. Legally defined, crime is an offense against the state punishable by fine, imprisonment, or some other penalty. The United States Constitution guarantees all persons living in the United States equal protection under the laws and due process against any deprivation of life, liberty and property. Defendants in criminal proceedings have the right to confront and cross-examine witnesses and the right to be protected against discrimination. But, the good intentions by which policies are planned and implemented in the criminal justice system are often accompanied by only a vague understanding of the nature of the population to be served. For example, Hispanics' experiences with criminal justice reflect a great diversity due to negative experiences as well as Hispanic cultural backgrounds. Referring to this diversity Sissons (1979) stated that:

> Of fundamental importance to an understanding of Hispanic culture and the Hispanic experience of criminal justice, therefore, is the fact that the Latin American nations, including to a large extent the Commonwealth of Puerto Rico, plus other former Spanish territories, such as the Philippines, are civil law countries. Thus, Hispanic people living in the United States have a legal tradition derived largely from Spanish colonial law and not from Anglo-American case law which, in turn, is derived from English common law (p. 3).

Sissons (1979) establishes the differences between civil law and common law by saying that :

> Civil law is based on the presupposition of the rationality of the human will. It is generally characterized by codification, the separation of public and private law which restricts equity in legal proceedings involving the State, and the historical acceptance of closed proceedings in which the judge plays an investigatory role.
>
> Common law, on the other hand, is rooted in the assumption that social control is dependent less upon a State-imposed rationality than upon the legal order which exists in nature. In common law traditions, the doctrine of stare corpus (precedent), the adversary system in criminal justice, habeas corpus (the right against illegal imprisonment), and trial by jury testify to a fundamental legal restriction upon the power and the authority of the State and serve to provide a contrast with civil law (pp. 3–4).

The two traditions represent different views of the place of power and authority within society and different cultural responses to social control. Civil law establishes its codes on the basis of legal principles; common law finds its principles in the complexity of the case (Sissons, 1979). Hispanic violators of the law may experience confusion when they become involved in the United States legal system. Ignorance of the United States legal system may result in violation of the law and may lead to complicated legal procedures.

Parents of Hispanic Children and Youth in the Criminal Justice System

The criminal justice system reflects a great diversity of experiences among the Hispanic populations in the United States. Mexican Americans' experience is one of conflict with United States law enforcement agencies due mainly to conquest and immigration conflicts. This experience is also shared, to a minor extent, with some of the more recent arrivals from Latin America. The Puerto Ricans' experience with the United States criminal justice system has been one of prejudice against them by law enforcement officials. Cubans, due to their status as political refugees, feel protected by the law. To some extent these experiences affect Hispanic attitudes toward the United

States criminal justice system and also affect the way they are treated by the system. Being a Hispanic increases the probability that the offender has been convicted of a drug offense or homicide, decreases the probability of being placed on probation, increases the probability of being sent to prison, and increases the probability of a longer sentence than if the offender is non-Hispanic.

The numbers and percentages of Hispanics in United States prisons have been increasing in the last two decades. These increases may reflect demographic shifts in the population as a whole as well as demographic changes such as age, socioeconomic status and place of residence. Sissons (1979) indicated that in New York State, for example, Hispanics in the correctional system were double the percentage of Hispanics in the total population of New York State.

A typical Hispanic offender is ". . . a 34-year-old Colombian or citizen of the Dominican Republic who may not have completed high school and who has received a five-year prison term for a federal narcotics violation" (Castro, 1980, Moore & Pachon, 1985, Sissons, 1979). A Puerto Rican inmate is described as ". . . a 32 year-old male who has not graduated from high school. He is most likely to be a drug offender although he might have committed other federal offenses, particularly mail theft for which he received a five-year sentence on probation, although there is a strong likelihood that his sentence was to a prison term" (Sissons, 1979, p. 59). Castro (1980) identified five basic types of Hispanic inmates:

1.   The recent immigrant or illegal alien who is usually detained on Federal warrants on drug charges. This group could also includes a small number of well-educated persons caught in narcotics trafficking.
2.   The *jíbaro* or *peón* who is usually from a rural background, and is arrested for crimes of passion, interference, public nuisance, or who may have been an unfortunate who ran into an insensitive police officer.
3.   The young, first or second generation Hispanic youth, who is usually arrested for violent crimes, drugs and property theft.
4.   The older (adult) Hispanic, who is quite expert at getting around the law, who speaks acceptable English and may earn his keep as a small king pin in a larger drug ring, small rackets, loan sharking, protection, fencing and burglary.
5.   The mentally disturbed or retarded Hispanic who is arrested for violent crimes, fratricide, rape, child molestation or public

exposure, and who actually belongs in a mental institution and requires extensive psychiatric care (99–100).

An analysis of the types of crime committed by the clients of the system reveal an increasingly high involvement in drugs, homicide, and violence by the convicted Hispanic offenders. The above description reveals that there are several types of inmates representing different groups from the Hispanic community who violate the law for several reasons. One of the most frequent offenses among Hispanics at the federal and state levels involves narcotics. Moore & Pachon (1985), indicated that Puerto Rican and Mexican American drug offenders tend also to be narcotics addicts, while Colombians and Dominicans who illegally import drugs tend not to be addicted to drugs.

Upon admission to the correctional system the Hispanic inmate is separated both physically and psychologically from the Hispanic community and culture. The temporary custody in the detention center is very difficult for the Hispanic inmate. Hispanic criminals find themselves in a cultural vacuum which is a serious threat to their mental health as well as to the structure of the family network to which they belong (Sissons, 1979).

The Hispanic community itself provides the environment for violation of law. There are more people unemployed there than in any other community; thus, this fact in itself leads to violence, and to participation in illegal activities that lead to the acquisition of some money. Possibly deprived of cultural support systems because of their family's humiliation at their imprisonment, it is not surprising that Hispanic inmates constitute a major suicide risk in the early days of their detention. However, when inmates are assigned to permanent housing in the correctional system, the Hispanic inmates are received into an Hispanic sub-culture that provides them with an immediate reference point as they socialize in the institutions. These Hispanic sub-cultures help to protect inmates from cultural isolation and from physical danger.

There are several factors that contribute to the high incidence of Hispanic offenders: socioeconomic variables, language barriers, cultural traits, and the characteristics of the system itself. For example, the socioeconomic aspects are reflected in neighborhoods of the Hispanic community that lend themselves to organized crime activity in those areas where there exists a poor economy, high unemployment, and other forms of deprivation. These communities tend to be good places for networks of illegal activity, such as drugs and illegal lotteries.

Cultural misinterpretation may result in an individual being labeled deviant, if not criminal, by the dominant culture. It may also result in negative values being attached to the external manifestations of Hispanic culture, which would lead to stereotyping (Sissons, 1979). Understanding cultural traits affects the treatment that Hispanics receive in the courts. There are often unspoken attitudes and images that need bicultural individuals. Whether citizens or noncitizens, Hispanics are entitled to due process within the legal system. Interpersonal communication patterns (to demonstrate values, respect, aggression, obedience) are important features of non-Hispanic representatives of the criminal justice system, and between Hispanics and the police and between Hispanic inmates and the prison administration.

The unfair and discriminatory law enforcement practices of police against Hispanics are also evidenced by their disproportionately higher numbers of convictions and incarcerations. In the federal system, Hispanic offenders are more likely to serve a prison term than they are to be placed on probation; but when sentenced to probation the length of the sentence is likely to be longer than that imposed on other offenders. Thus, more Hispanics than non-Hispanics are sent to prison rather than placed on probation. This fact raises serious questions about the ability of a legal system dominated by white males to the near exclusion of Hispanics to dispense to Hispanics justice free of racial and ethnic bias.

The United States criminal justice system exists in an exclusively English-speaking world, even though many of the Hispanic inmates function poorly in English or not at all. However, notwithstanding the current lack of knowledge, classifications of Hispanics in English and non-English-speaking terms are made everywhere throughout the criminal justice system. These classifications are always made routinely, informally, instantaneously and without question. But, it is a procedure that serves the Hispanic offender poorly. Classification as non-English-speaking for example, does not guarantee a Hispanic offender the services of an interpreter. The most common practice once a language deficiency is recognized is to try to locate any employee volunteer who will serve as interpreter. No inquiry is made about this interpreter's qualifications or effectiveness. The criminal justice system generally does provide for a formal determination of an English language handicap if the issue is raised before a judge in the course of a legal proceeding. But the assignment of an interpreter in a court proceeding appears to be less a matter of right or routine than of demand (Castro, 1980). The lack of language familiarity may cause Hispanic inmates some type of psychological trauma if inmates do not understand what is happening around them.

The Miranda warnings (*Miranda vs. Arizona*, 1976) are designated to protect defendants from psychological coercion and to permit them a full opportunity to exercise the privilege against self-discrimination. The Miranda warnings (1976) state that: "the accused must be adequately and effectively apprised of his rights" (p. 22). But, the standards are not met when the warnings are given orally in English to Hispanics who understand only Spanish or when the warnings are given orally in Spanish by incompetent interpreters. Printing and posting the Miranda warnings in Spanish may not satisfy the constitutional rights of those offenders who can speak but cannot read Spanish. And, as stated in earlier chapters, Hispanics show several English/Spanish language levels and characteristics.

Prisons do not provide a diversity in the range and quality of services offered to inmates who cannot comprehend English. These services do not provide for Spanish education and counseling and daily prerequisites such as religious services, medical and psychiatric care, record keeping, disciplinary hearings, family visits, commissary purchases and recreation. In cities such as New York and Los Angeles, due to the large numbers of inmates (most of them Hispanics or African Americans), jails are overcrowded and do not provide basic inmate services. Lack of Hispanic personnel affect Hispanic inmates since they do not see more Hispanic role models or individuals who may speak the same language or may share the same ethnic and cultural roots. The Hispanic inmate is surrounded primarily by white officers, the language spoken is English, and the inmate is not made familiar with criminal justice procedures.

The Hispanic offender is confronted with a criminal justice system in which, except for fellow offenders, there is virtually no Hispanic presence. Hispanics are underrepresented in the police force throughout the United States. Most police officers are middle class whites with different cultural and value systems. Observing the New York City police graduating class of December 1989, it was evident that Hispanics and African American police officers represented a very small percentage of this graduating class.

Police officers are viewed with skepticism, fear and hostility by the Hispanic community. The police, in turn, view the Hispanic community with fear, suspicion and hostility. Police are often seen as oppressors who do not understand the Hispanic culture, and lack empathy and sensitivity when reacting to what otherwise would be minor or routine situations.

Affirmative action and equal employment opportunity policies have helped to increase Hispanic personnel in the criminal justice system. In the last two decades, more Hispanic and bilingual English/Spanish personnel have been hired. But, too often, the majority of Hispanic personnel are hired on federal grants and on provisional basis, and are the first to be dropped when the funding source ends. In many instances, prison managers have additional burdens—usually these facilities are located in remote, rural areas where it is difficult to recruit professional or paraprofessional Hispanics willing to work in their facilities.

Hispanics are also underrepresented in the courts. There is gross underrepresentation of Hispanics and administrators of justice, members of the legal profession, and law students and teachers. In the federal judiciary, it was not until 1979 that, for the first time, a Puerto Rican, Jose Cabranes, was named to a Federal District Court judgeship in the mainland United States. Hispanic judges bring to the courts their familiarity with the Hispanic culture, and they are also a symbol that Hispanics are found in the system other than as defendants and help to motivate Hispanic youth to aspire to such positions and to feel that they too can achieve. Also, the courtrooms appear less intimidating when there are other Hispanic faces around, be they prosecutors, judges, court officers, defense counsel or jurors.

Hispanics are not well-represented at the prosecutorial level. It is the prosecutor's office that makes the initial determination as to whether a person will be charged with a crime and held subject to trial. It is the prosecutor who must consent to any lesser plea offered by a defendant. Too often prosecutors who come from middle class backgrounds, with little or no knowledge of life in the lower socioeconomic *barrios,* or of Hispanic culture and values, impose their notions of justice and law upon Hispanic defendants. These notions are generally insensitive as to the defendants' needs or mores. The prevailing trend is toward long, mandatory jail terms instead of probation and rehabilitation programs. A prosecutor familiar with Hispanic customs and culture can often deal with what might otherwise be a miscarriage of justice, as many incidents before the court are generally the result of misunderstandings and family-related situations.

Hispanic youth and their parents perceive that the legal process is unfair. Hispanics perceived that when compared to whites: (a) if detained by a law enforcement officer, they stand a greater chance of being arrested; (b) if arrested, they stand a greater chance of being prosecuted, (c) if prosecuted, they stand a greater chance of being convicted; (d) if convicted, they stand a greater chance of receiving a disproportionately longer sentence; (e) if sentenced, they stand a greater chance of being denied parole. Many Hispanic offenders do not see any hope once they are out of prison: they must face a disintegrated family situation, no employment possibilities, inadequate skills or education, poor living conditions and discrimination. They face a future of shame, guilt, substance abuse, and more crime.

Hispanic Youth Delinquency

As a child enters adolescence, major biological changes occur. At this time, the beginning of an awareness of sexuality occurs involving certain muscular and physiological changes as well as the development of more complex interrelationships with members of the opposite sex. The complexity of these changes puts adolescents in a state of uncertainty about their appearance and ability to manage their new social responsibilities. The crisis of adolescence brings adolescents together in tight knit peer groups which supply comfort, understanding and information.

The drives toward achievement and peer acceptance intensify during this period. Adolescents often express strong preferences for personal freedom and autonomy as they begin to test newly acquired identities. Adolescence is often a time of ambivalence in which one strives for personal autonomy along with the need to belong and as the desire to be grown up conflicts with a wish to revert to more childlike and dependent behavior. It is a time when youngsters are most prone to social suggestion and seek peer affiliations to learn appropriate and, sometimes, inappropriate social behavior. Most adults find it easy to remember at least one occasion during their youth when they committed some act solely on a dare.

The adolescent peer group provides a setting in which the adolescent can experiment with forbidden commodities, such as tobacco, alcohol and drugs, or engage in other such negative behavior without scrutiny. For most youngsters, this experimentation produces no harmful effects; but, for a few, these experiments may seriously interfere with normal physical and social development. What is crucial here is not how to prevent unacceptable behavior in adolescents but, rather, how to structure the adult response to this behavior so that the child will be protected from unnecessary early negative labeling or social responses that embitter the young person for life. Whether the subject is drug abuse, adolescent sex, or youthful misbehavior, official response to such behavior should strengthen the possibilities for positive child development by minimizing negative sanctions.

Juvenile delinquency traditionally has been used as a catch-all phrase for any anti-social behavior committed by youth. A juvenile delinquent, according to the Family Court Act of 1962, is a person over the age of seven and under the age of sixteen who has committed an act that constitutes a crime and requires supervision, treatment or confinement. The concept of a special tribunal to handle young people accused of criminal violations grew out of the social reform movement of the nineteenth century. The basic concept behind the juvenile court was that children were not to be treated as criminals. The juvenile court was conceived as something of a hybrid in the judicial system. Its function was not merely to determine whether a juvenile had committed a particular act, but, more importantly, to emphasize the parents' involvement and role in the process. A child was not accused of a crime, and adjudication as a delinquent was to carry with it none of the disqualifying stigma of criminal conviction. Judicial records of the juvenile courts were not available to the public or the press, and juvenile court hearings were to be conducted in private. The aim was to delve into the child's background and design a treatment plan likely to help the child become a responsible member of society. Broad statutes were added to give juvenile courts jurisdiction over youths involved in a wide range of activity. The juvenile reformers wanted to attack what they considered the depravity of urban life, and they wanted to control such activities through the institution of the juvenile court. Although there are variations from state to state, most statutory definitions of delinquency include: (a) acts which would be criminal if committed by adults, (b) violations of town, county or municipal ordinances, and (c) various acts that are proscribed only for children, such as curfew violations, truancy from school and violations of alcohol and tobacco restrictions.

Since 1960, the federal government has been directly involved with juvenile delinquency primarily in response to the public's concern over the increasing rates of youth crime. In 1961, the Juvenile Delinquency and Youth Offenses Control Act was created to prevent and control juvenile delinquency. It was modified in 1968 to provide federal funds to states to strengthen their juvenile justice efforts. But it was not until 1974 that the Juvenile Justice and Delinquency Prevention Act was passed to support the Department of Justice's role in juvenile delinquency. Although in principle the separation of youthful offenders from adult offenders appears to be a good legal strategy, the general conclusion is that the courts are not living up to the high hopes of its founders; they have not been providing the special treatment and rehabilitation, which in theory, they are expected to give.

The Hispanic population is young, which means that there is a high number of young Hispanics who are likely to violate the rules and laws of United States society. The focus of delinquency and youth violence is more likely to be in an urban, low-socioeconomic neighborhood with its lack of recreation and job opportunities for youth. The criminal violence of Hispanic youth has many of its roots in the demographic realities: deteriorating physical features of the urban environment, accompanying social and psychological forces, sub-cultural traditions of lawlessness in the barrio, and models of violence diffused through every day American life. A significant proportion of Hispanic youth offenders are from broken homes, from single parent families, or from homes in which parents work long hours and are unable to provide adequate parental supervision. Another group consists of children who have been raised in foster homes or reformatories with no parental guidance or role models.

Most youthful offenders are male, and there is a disproportionate representation of African Americans and Hispanics. Data on Hispanic youth under the age of 16 in the juvenile system indicated that African American and Hispanic youths are by far the largest number of American juvenile delinquents. Hispanic children and youth are identified in large numbers as being perpetrators of delinquent and criminal behavior. They are overrepresented in the juvenile system as well as in the criminal justice system. Each year, more youths are arrested for violent crimes—homicides, assault, rape, and robbery than any other crimes. Most Hispanic juvenile delinquents live in environments conducive to perpetuating their behaviors. Some of the youth delinquency is related to gang activities, especially as they relate to robbery and burglary.

The age of the perpetrator and nature of the offense usually determine whether the case will be processed through the juvenile or criminal system. The age varies from state to state, and the judge has the authority to transfer the perpetrator from juvenile to adult court depending on the nature of the crime or a previous criminal record. The most often given reasons for juvenile delinquency have to do with: (a) poor school attendance and lack of achievement, (b) negative self-attitudes, fears and pregnancy (c) peer pressure, (d) family conflict, and (e) drug or alcohol abuse. It should be noted that while the above list establishes reasonable patterns which certainly may cause juvenile delinquency, this list in no way can be considered all inclusive.

Hispanic youth offenders show a variety of language characteristics. The literature indicates that Hispanic youth's language may be divided into three groups. The first group is composed of youthful offenders who speak English fairly well. However, their ability to read and write English is far below acceptable standards. This group of youths may demonstrate some conversational knowledge of Spanish, but no knowledge of Spanish reading or writing either. The second group represents Hispanic youthful offenders who cannot communicate in English, but demonstrate proficiency in Spanish. They can read and write Spanish with different levels of proficiency. The third group shows limitations in both languages, although, if tested they demonstrate more strength in one language than the other. Difficulties with the English language may cause frustrations to Hispanic youth and may become a factor contributing to juvenile delinquency. Although this theory has not been discussed in the literature, it makes sense to think that when students are frustrated with school, they drop out of school; they cannot find jobs; and they become involved with the life of the streets where they become perpetrators of crime. As mentioned in chapter 5, lack of proficiency in English is one of the factors leading to school desertion.

The youth's family plays an important role in the prevention of the youth's delinquency. Parents with self-defined cultural values may be successful with their children. Anderson & Rodriguez (1984) stated that:

> . . . the parents' degree of identification with Hispanic culture could influence how children are socialized and the values they instill. Hispanic-oriented parents may be more likely to emphasize loyalty to the family and unquestioning respect for parents. Children from traditionally-oriented families may have more attachment to an interaction with their families, and thus, fewer bonds to delinquent peers. Ethnic pride may act as a protector against delinquency by increasing adolescents' self-esteem which has been associated with low delinquency (p. 4).

Parents who are able to monitor and discipline their children's behavior are more successful at preventing or limiting delinquency by their consistency in supervising their children's behavior and by instilling more family cohesiveness (Anderson & Rodriguez, 1984). Also, unacculturated families may lack knowledge of accepted behavioral norms in the United States, and, thus, will be less likely to adequately socialize their children, thereby affecting the strength of family and school bonds.

Causes for Hispanic Youth's Juvenile Delinquency

Authorities (Anderson & Rodriguez, 1984, Castro, 1980, Edelman, 1984, Sissons, 1979) have identified causes of illegal behavior by Hispanic youth. Most authorities indicate that the family, social, economic, educational and environmental factors are the main contributors to Hispanic youth's illegal behavior. Inadequate recreation facilities, overcrowded and poor housing conditions, low educational attainment, unemployment, and lack of opportunities in the urban environment are forces associated with juvenile delinquency. For the Hispanic youth these forces provide the background for explaining Hispanic youth's delinquency in terms of disparities between American definitions of success internalized by all social classes and the restricted opportunities of Hispanic youth to achieve these goals. The following factors have been mentioned in the literature as contributing to youthful delinquency.

Family Organization and Values

It is a well-established fact that the family is the primary agent for the social control of conduct. Family structure and values may influence an individual's tendency toward criminality in a variety of ways. Some authorities (Anderson & Rodriguez 1984, Edelman, 1984) have suggested that delinquents often have parents characterized by drunkenness or criminality, ineffective household management, economic difficulties and low self-respect. Family disorganization, resulting from desertion, the death of a parent or other important family figure, and extreme tension preceding divorce are often significant factors in the increasing rates of delinquency. A high proportion of delinquents is found to be illegitimate, and studies indicate that the backgrounds of habitual criminals frequently include an abnormal amount of parental marital discord. Multiple family problems, especially in families that are very large and headed by parents of poor health with low and irregular incomes, are also frequently felt to generate criminal behaviors. Family disciplinary policies may be either too lax or too strict, causing young people to commit crimes. Delinquents often indicate that their families are not concerned about their welfare. General disciplinary practices were more erratic and physical punishment more frequent for youthful delinquents than for non-youthful ones.

Housing

Dilapidated housing, inadequate sanitary facilities, and overcrowding contribute to youthful delinquency. Inadequate housing is usually accompanied by inadequate recreational and park facilities, a lack of community services, unrepaired streets and sidewalks and infrequent garbage collection, poor sanitation and resulting health problems. Youth from low socioeconomic groups grow up on streets littered with trash, discarded liquor bottles, sleeping drunks, narcotics addicts, and prostitutes. Home life is characterized by crowded sleeping arrangements, inadequate plumbing and sanitary facilities, falling plaster, rats, roaches and a shifting group of relatives housed in incredibly few rooms. There is little to hold a youth close to this kind of home, and the parents often lose control of their activities. These housing characteristics lead youth away from developing a sense of respect for personal possessions and respect for the property of others.

Employment

There is a relationship between unemployment and crime. One of the largest ethnic groups today are unemployed Hispanic youth, a group that is vulnerable to becoming criminal offenders. Lack of employment opportunities contributes to juvenile delinquency. Hispanic youth look for employment, but, due to their lack of academic preparation, or lack of educational attainment, or employer discrimination, few of them are hired. This continuous search for jobs and the inability in finding them creates in these youth a sense of anger against society and its institutions. This anger is demonstrated in illegal behavior that in many cases may lead to criminal conduct. And, even if they find jobs, Hispanics are the last to be hired and the first to be laid off due to lack of training, language difficulties, and poor educational attainment.

School Attainment

The link between school failure and delinquency is not completely known, but there is some evidence that those youths who fail in the educational system contribute disproportionately to the delinquency rates. One estimate is that the incidence of delinquency among dropouts is much higher than among youths who stay in school. There is considerable evidence that delinquency and criminal behavior first become visible to society in the school setting. Large numbers of repeat offenders have been found to have had unhappy school careers and truancy records. Hispanic youth go to schools in which the teachers, the curriculum, and the school organization often do not relate to them, causing them to avoid school, falling involuntarily into the trap of committing mild to severe crimes.

One theory suggests that the delinquency of working class youth is a response to disappointing experiences in school, especially in high school, where the delinquents are unable to meet the qualifications for social achievement in an essentially middle-class oriented school. Low-socioeconomic Hispanic youth will become delinquent because they are required by modern society to pursue certain goals of the dominant culture, such as money and other status symbols, but are not given the opportunity to acquire them because of poor educational facilities, poor housing, poor job opportunities, or other discriminatory factors. The current prevailing trend is to postulate a degree of ambivalence about middle class and lower class values and to suggest that the delinquent has difficulty understanding what values to adhere to.

Urban Living

Hispanic adolescents living in inner-city areas are at greater risk of engaging in delinquency than adolescents living in less urban areas (Anderson & Rodriguez, 1984). Urban living releases the individual from community restraints more easily than in tradition-bound environments and, thereby, provides greater opportunity for deviance. Urban social life is impersonalized and formally controlled, meaning that regulatory orders of conduct are often directed by distant bureaucrats. The police are often strangers carrying out their duties in an alien sub-community and among an anonymous set of subjects. Metropolitan areas with mass populations, many commercial establishments, and highly visible wealth provide more frequent opportunities for theft than do other places. Victims are depersonalized, property is insured, and consumer goods are vividly displayed and portable. Edelman (1984), in a study of delinquency and delinquency avoidance in the South Bronx in New York City, found that the interrelated problems of violence, fear of violence, and the carrying of weapons are more pronounced than in most other settings and, consequently, play a particular role in causing delinquency.

The youth of the lower class are the most vulnerable to status deprivation, to alienation, and to perceived disparities between what they want and what they are likely to get (Anderson & Rodriguez, 1984, Edelman, 1984). To be poor and Hispanic, to want what the society claims and shows, to see illegitimate and often violent methods of obtaining those things, and to see others using these means successfully and with impunity is to be burdened with an enormous set of influences that pull many Hispanic youths toward crime and delinquency.

Violence in the Mass Media

Violence is a pervasive theme in the mass media. This force shapes the values and forms the mentality of many American youths. Advertisements, availability of guns, and violent television programs and films contribute to youth violence. These media presentations may cause violence and may well affect the behavior of adolescents as they are molded by the socializing process.

Other Factors

Other factors not discussed are Hispanics as victims of illegal behavior and the treatment Hispanic youth are subjected to once they are found guilty of a crime. Hispanic children are also victims of crimes. Crime victims include the poor, the elderly, the members of ethnic minorities and the residents of decaying urban neighborhoods. Violent crimes tend to occur within relatively fixed socioeconomic and socio-cultural groups who are victims of a society that commits crimes without considering against whom the crime is committed. They are also victims of an arbitrary allocation of police resources that provides inadequate protection to members of the Hispanic community.

Recommendations to Prevent Hispanic Juvenile Delinquency

Hispanic juvenile delinquency is a complex issue. Although there are many indications of the participation of Hispanic children and youth in the criminal justice system and the factors that contribute to Hispanic youth's illegal actions, little is being done to prevent Hispanic youth from continuing to commit illegal actions. Authorities question if the juvenile delinquency system is preventing or decreasing Hispanic youth's delinquency rates. The literature reviewed indicates that, in many instances, the criminal juvenile system's prevention programs are not designed to work with the social, economic, cultural, and linguistic diversity of the Hispanic youth population. In many instances, these prevention programs are geared to middle class youth. Also, most of the personnel in leadership positions do not relate to the Hispanic population. Thus, the following recommendations are made for improving the conditions of Hispanic youth in the United States criminal justice system with the purpose of decreasing their involvement as youthful offenders.

Recommendation 1: The federal government cannot ignore the fact that it is a partner in local and state efforts to improve the quantity and quality of law enforcement and to increase the responsiveness of law enforcement agencies to the concerns of all citizens, particularly Hispanic citizens. There is a general recognition that agencies should employ more Hispanics in both law enforcement and treatment capacities. In part, the government must respond to the need for bilingual law enforcement and treatment personnel who can increase the efficiency of the agencies and function as cultural advocates for bewildered Spanish-speaking clients.

There is a need to provide a Hispanic presence in prisons and correctional facilities, a climate, created either by people or resources, which is sufficiently congenial to establish a better rapport between youth offenders and the rest of the staff. Hispanic youthful offenders will benefit from posted bilingual rules and regulations that will also contribute to more understanding among the offenders, their family visitors, and security personnel assigned to these areas. If the language or languages of the youthful offenders are used in the facility, they may serve to convey a sense of cooperation rather than a hostile atmosphere.

Efforts must be made to let qualified Hispanics know of job openings in the criminal justice system and job placement offices. Since many Hispanics are not educationally prepared to apply for these positions, there is a need for pre-hiring training programs to prepare special workshops for helping Hispanics in preparing their applications or resumes. Hispanics also need training in exam preparation and in tips for passing the required exams.

Recommendation 2: Hispanic youth's language shows variations. The judicial system needs to provide services to the three language groups described in the previous section. English classes should be provided for non-English-speaking offenders and for those who are limited in English. The better prepared Hispanic youth leave the legal facility, the better for the government and society at large since those youth can integrate into the society and become useful citizens. Mandatory bilingual education services need to be provided at the facility for non-English speakers. Once these youth offenders leave the facility, they can leave with an adequate command of English, thus improving their job or educational opportunities.

There is also the need for Hispanic cultural and ethnic awareness courses for non-Hispanic staff members of the criminal justice system. This training may include information on cultural and linguistic characteristics of the Hispanic community, appropriate non-verbal behavior of Hispanics and common linguistic expressions used by Hispanic youth. This training may help in bridging the gap between the Hispanic inmate or youth offender and the non-Hispanic officer.

Recommendation 3: Official programs to prevent juvenile delinquency should increase support for projects aimed at improving the capability of ethnic and racial minority-youth-serving agencies and organizations to plan, develop and implement programs that prevent and control crime and delinquency in Hispanic communities. Prevention programs are effective and, in the long run, cost effective. The criminal justice system is an expensive one, while prevention programs can help a large group of individuals for life. Prevention programs are needed at all levels, especially during childhood and early adolescence. Hispanic youth need more school and job incentives as well as programs to help youth and parents/guardians improve family relationships and interactions. Prevention cannot start once youths have committed a crime. It needs to start early to prevent Hispanic juvenile delinquency.

Recommendation 4: Youth offenders' education is a prime concern. The need exists for a range of courses tailored for Hispanic inmates and youth offenders to include: (a) English as a second language (b) literacy development/basic adult education, (c) high school equivalency in Spanish or English (d) vocational classes, and (e) college level courses in English and Spanish. Educational programs must be a required component in each of the facilities. Teaching personnel with training in criminal justice needs to be hired to work with youth offenders. Tests, certificates and diplomas need to be part of this educational program.

Recommendation 5: The Hispanic inmate population has increased considerably. It is important to determine the reasons for it through research and the extent to which this increase may be a product of demographic changes or practices by the police and courts, and the extent to which it is a genuine reflection of increasing Hispanic crime rates. This research needs to identify recommendations for preventing crimes, especially among Hispanics.

Recommendation 6: There is a need to identify more support systems for incarcerated Hispanic offenders and their families, especially if there are children and youth involved, such as counseling and financial support. There is no doubt that the family of the Hispanic offender suffers a great deal. This suffering is related to humiliation of the immediate relatives and friends, the absence of the offender from the home, the lack of income, and the routine of visiting the offender with all its psychological consequences. The present criminal justice system provides very little support to the family. In many instances, the children of the family feel frustrated and ashamed and begin to demonstrate abnormal behavior. The children stop attending school regularly and, in some cases, become youthful offenders themselves. But, if support systems are offered, there is a probability that family suffering may be ameliorated.

Recommendation 7: Hispanics and Hispanic youth have a high involvement in drug related offenses. It has been found that a large percent of Hispanics are accused and convicted of selling or using drugs. Causes of their involvement include the socioeconomic level of the environment, the easy acquisition of money with all the luxuries it involves, peer pressure, and the adult role models. Although these causes are known, very little is being done to prevent drug selling and use. Prevention programs must include the participation of the family and the school together as one unit to develop in the youth a sense of danger and health risks that are more profound than the mere financial benefits. There is a need to identify causes of this involvement and to establish appropriate prevention programs.

In summary, delinquency is more likely to be reduced by increasing the rewards for conventional behavior through increased job and educational opportunities than by increasing the sanctions for illegal behavior. Long range social reconstruction programs need to be planned to have the greatest impact on reducing the criminal violence and offenses of Hispanic youth. These programs include more employment and re-training, greatly improved education, teaching curricula more consciously emphasizing non-violent values, educational projects conveying non-violent methods of child rearing to parents, new decisions in making roles for the young, community participation programs designed to give Hispanic youth opportunities for legitimate success, policies aimed at reducing the social stimuli to youthful violence, and advocating for stronger gun controls and a more sensitive approach to the problems of drug abuse.

Conclusion

Hispanic presence in the United States criminal justice system is increasing. Parents of Hispanic youth are convicted of drug-related offenses, theft, homicide or violence. Once the offenders are admitted to the correctional facility, they are socially, linguistically and culturally isolated from their world, and the prisons, rather than reforming them, contribute to harden the offender's desire against becoming a useful citizen. Jails, with their lack of educational, bilingual, and counseling services make it harder for Hispanic offenders to start a new life.

The criminal justice system needs to evaluate the services it provides to Hispanic inmates, not only to incarcerate them for a prescribed number of months or years, but to help them once they are back on the streets to avoid violating the law again.

Juvenile delinquency among Hispanic youth is a concern for policy makers and the society at large. It is acknowledged that antisocial behavior does exist among a significant number of youth; however, very little is being done to investigate the community conditions contributing to delinquent behavior. During adolescence, children are either taught and encouraged to conform to accepted behavior or there begins a process of cynicism and alienation that may lead to delinquency and possible adult criminal careers. Toward the end of puberty, these youths begin to see their social role and either start feeling good or disillusioned about themselves. Family members and school personnel can offer support and encouragement during difficult periods for youth. Negative peer influences can be countered by loving parental attention. But the family cannot be expected to work miracles in the case of children who have begun to be labeled failures in school or in work situations. The cohesion of the family is often strained by pressures to meet basic living needs, resulting in the inability of the family members to solve problems and conflicts. In other words, decreasing Hispanic youth delinquency requires the cooperation of the family, the school, and governmental social and legal agencies as well as private agencies and organizations.

CHAPTER 9

Labor Force Participation
of Hispanic Youth

Hispanics are a sizable and growing part of the United States population; thus, they represent an increasing proportion of the nation's labor force and an important human resource. For Hispanic workers, the changes in the nation's demography and economy during the 1990's represent both a great risk and a great opportunity (Escutia & Prieto, 1986; Johnston & Parker, 1987; Marshall, Brings & King, 1984). Predictions up to the year 2000 indicate that with fewer new young workers entering the workforce, employers will need to offer jobs and training to those they have traditionally ignored. At the same time, the types of jobs being created by the economy will demand more sophisticated skills than the jobs that exist today. As the society becomes more complex, the amount of education and knowledge needed to make a productive contribution to the economy becomes greater. In general, and with the exception of the Cubans and refugees from Central America, Hispanics have migrated to the United States for economic reasons. They have come to the United States to work in whatever jobs have been available to them, and not dependent upon education and high level job skills. But, Hispanics have encountered various obstacles to employment due, in part, to low educational attainment, lack of technical occupational skills, language problems and discrimination.

Information about Hispanics' employment and Hispanic youths' employment is not readily available, since there is a scarcity of studies examining all the different ethnic Hispanic groups. Data on the labor market status of Hispanics were not collected regularly by the federal government until 1973. There are no comprehensive studies available on Hispanic youth employment, and only a few studies have specifically addressed the employment situations of Hispanics. Thus, generalizations are based on a few studies of Hispanic youth employment; the extrapolation of findings are from studies of minority workers in general, of whom Hispanics form one of the groups. For example, most of the studies examined male Mexican American or Puerto Rican workers; however, studies of other Hispanic groups and Hispanic females are very scarce. Since differences exist among Hispanics, not only by ethnic group, but by sex, the numbers of employment studies of Hispanics do not uniformly represent all Hispanics in the United States by ethnic group or sex. A discussion of Hispanic employment issues requires recognition of the diversity and differences of Hispanic groups. The discussion of Hispanics' employment also needs to address reasons for Hispanics' unemployment and underemployment among the different subgroups. This chapter presents a summary of the employment status of the parents of Hispanic youth as well as Hispanic youth employment and unemployment. The chapter ends with recommendations for the improvement of employment conditions for Hispanic youth.

Employment Status of Parents of Hispanic Children and Youth

By almost every measure of employment, labor force participation, earnings, and education, Hispanics suffer much greater disadvantages than whites. Comparisons with African Americans and whites reveal that in several ways Hispanics in the work force were better off than African Americans, but worse off than whites. Hispanic men are more likely to be unemployed or seeking work than any other American men, 79 percent versus 74 percent, although only about 71 percent of Puerto Rican and other Hispanic males are in the labor force (Bureau of the Census, 1988d; Valdivieso & Davis, 1988). Cubans, Central, and South Americans are better placed in the work force than Mexicans and Puerto Ricans. The labor force participation rate measures the percentage of those persons aged 16 and over who are either employed or actively seeking employment. Hispanics are younger than non-Hispanics, and are more likely to leave school early and join the labor force. In 1988, Hispanics made up 7 percent of the United States labor force. The Hispanic share is likely to increase as the non-Hispanic population ages and the number of working-aged Hispanics continues to grow (Valdivieso & Davis, 1988). In 1985, there were 7.5 million Hispanics in the labor force, accounting for 6.7 percent of the labor force; and they are projected to account for 8 to 10 percent by 1995. The growth rate of the Hispanic community tends to indicate that the labor market supply will have a significant percentage of Hispanic workers.

The following chart summarizes information of the 1988 Census comparing the employment status of Hispanics with non-Hispanics by type of employment:

The Employment Status of Hispanics Compared to non-Hispanics by Type of Employment.

Employment	Hisp. Men	Non-Hisp. Men	Hisp. Wom	Non-Hisp. Wom
Managerial and professional specialty.	13.0	27.3	15.7	25.9
Technical, sales and administrative.	15.4	20.3	41.1	45.3
Service occupations.	14.8	9.0	21.7	17.4
Farming, forestry, and fishing.	8.2	3.7	1.5	0.9
Precision, production craft and repair.	20.5	19.4	3.5	2.2
Operators, fabricators and laborers.	28.1	20.3	16.6	8.3

Source: Bureau of the Census, *The Hispanic Population in the United States; March 1988.*

In 1988, only 28 percent of Hispanic men were in the upper-level managerial, technical and administrative categories compared to 48 percent of non-Hispanic men. Cuban men are an exception: 51 percent held higher-status positions. The above data indicate that the more skill or education the job requires the smaller the percent of Hispanics employed in that particular occupation. Hispanics are overrepresented in the occupational category of operators, fabricators and laborers. Most Hispanics in this occupational category are employed as machine operators and assemblers. Hispanics are also overrepresented in farming and related occupations. Hispanics are somewhat overrepresented in service occupations, but to a lesser extent than

African Americans. Although more than 50 percent of the jobs of Hispanics are machine operators or service workers, these are also the lowest paid occupations. Not only are Hispanics overrepresented in low-paying, semi-skilled jobs, but they work in economic sectors vulnerable to cyclical unemployment, and in some industries, like manufacturing, that are threatened with a long time decline.

In 1988, Hispanics made up only 7 percent of the United States civilian force. Because of their relatively low educational levels, language barriers, and prejudice, Hispanics tend to enter poorly paid jobs with little chance of advancement. The National Commission for Employment Policy (1982) conducted an analysis of available data on the labor market position of Hispanic Americans. The Commission found that:

1. Hispanic-Americans were worse off in the labor market than was the non-Hispanic, white population.
2. A lack of fluency in English is the major source of the labor market difficulties of all subgroups.
3. A low level of education is the second major reason for Hispanics' poor labor market experience.
4. Discrimination in the labor market further contributes to their weak position (p. 2).

Hispanics and other minorities make up a small share of the labor force (National Employment of Fall Employment, 1987). As in the distribution of the Hispanic population, Mexican American parents are the largest single group in the labor force; Cubans and South and Central Americans are the smallest. These data do not mean that Cubans are less able to work; rather, they indicate that they are represented less since they are a small number in the total Hispanic population. In a summary of the U.S. Bureau of Labor Statistics from 1983, Johnston and Parker (1987) presented the following table:

African Americans and Hispanics are Much Less Successful in the Labor Market (1983)

	Ethnic Group		
	White	African American	Hispanic
Labor Force Participation	64.3	61.5	63.8
Unemployment Rate	8.4	19.5	13.7
Median Weekly Family Employment	$487	$348	$366
Percent Below Poverty	12.1	35.7	28.4
Median Years of Schooling	12.8	12.5	12.1

Cited by Johnston & Parker, 1987, p. 90.

Source: Bureau of the Census, *The Hispanic Population in the United States;* March 1988.

Although Hispanics remain underrepresented in the more skilled, higher-paying occupations, their status, as a group, has shown some improvement since 1973, though more for women than for men.

Data on Hispanic subgroups indicate large differences in labor force participation for both men and women. Mexican American men have the highest labor force participation rate among Hispanic men, and Puerto Ricans have the lowest. Cuban women have the highest rate among Hispanic women; they are more likely to be in the labor force than are white women, and almost as likely as African American women (Escutia & Prieto, 1986). Puerto Rican women have much lower participation rates than other Hispanic women. About half of all Hispanic women are in the labor force, compared to fewer than two in five Puerto Rican women. Regardless of ethnicity, employed Hispanics are concentrated in occupations that are low paying, low skilled, and experience high rates of unemployment. Hispanic women are highly concentrated in the lowest-paying jobs, a large percentage of them in clerical positions. Labor force participation rates for Hispanic women increased from 48 percent in 1982 to 52 percent in 1988 (Bureau of the Census, 1988d). For non-Hispanic women, the rates rose from 52 percent to 56 percent. The participation rates for Hispanic men declined from 81 percent in 1982 to 79 percent in 1988 and from 75 percent to 74 percent for non-Hispanics (Bureau of the Census, 1988d). Hispanic workers earn the lowest wages in the labor market. Hispanic women earn much less, about 53 percent, than white women (Escutia & Prieto, 1986). The proportion of Hispanic women in the labor force has grown. This increase among Hispanic women is consistent with the trend of non-Hispanic women.

The National Commission for Employment Policy (1982) indicated that the experiences of Hispanics in the job market differ from those of African Americans and whites as follows:

1.   The rate of participation in the labor force among Hispanic men is as high as those of whites and above that of African Americans. Hispanics and white women have about the same rate of participation, which is below that of African American women. Hispanic youth participate in the job market at a rate below that of whites but above that of African Americans.
2.   The unemployment rates of Hispanic men, women and youth are above those of whites, but below those of African Americans.
3.   Hispanics are more likely to be in blue-collar jobs than either whites or African Americans.
4.   Hispanic men earn less per hour than African American or white men; all groups of women earn less than men; and Hispanic women earn less than men; and Hispanic women earn the least per hour among women (p. 10).

Another factor to consider in this discussion is that the United States labor force is not proportionately balanced, with Hispanics at the bottom, many of them marginally employed or underemployed. Hispanic youth, especially those living in urban areas, are also affected by this disproportionate amount of unemployment or under employment. The United States economy is becoming increasingly technological; however, Hispanics are not holding high-technological skills jobs in proportion to the population. Thus, marked improvements will be required to meet the demands of a technological employment market. The discussion below does not take into consideration this disproportion of the United States labor force market; rather, it presents only an overview of the status of Hispanics in the labor force without considering external forces that may have affected their status. Johnston and Parker (1987) indicated that: "If every child who reaches the age of seventeen between now and the year 2000 could read sophisticated materials, write clearly, speak articulately, and do some complex problems requiring algebra and statistics, the American economy could easily approach or exceed the four percent growth of the boom scenario" (p. 116).

Hispanic children are twice as likely as white children to have no parent employed. Hispanic women, and Puerto Ricans in particular, are less likely to be working than other women. Only 51 percent of female

Hispanics and 40 percent of Puerto Rican women were in the labor force in 1988, compared to 56 percent of non-Hispanic women (Johnston and Parker, 1987; Valdivieso & Davis, 1988). Married-couple families account for only 70 percent of all Hispanic families, compared to 80 percent of non-Hispanic families. Nearly one-quarter, or 23 percent, are headed by an unmarried or separated woman, while 16 percent of non-Hispanic families are female headed. A whopping 44 percent of Puerto Rican families are headed by females, double the Hispanic and almost triple the non-Hispanic average (Andrade, 1983; Orum, 1986; Valdivieso & Davis, 1988).

The Hispanic share, however, is likely to increase as the non-Hispanic population ages and the number of working age Hispanics continues to grow. Hispanic men, in fact, are more likely to be employed or seeking work than other American men, 79 percent versus 74 percent, although only about 71 percent of Puerto Rican and other Hispanic males are in the labor force (Valdivieso and Davis, 1988).

A 1984 Ford Foundation Report says that important social, economic and political consequences may also follow from the fact that as more whites reach social security age, their support will depend on social security taxes paid by an increasingly Hispanic and African American work force. Thus, Hispanic youth employment is another challenge for those interested in improving the conditions of Hispanics in the United States.

Johnston and Parker (1987) indicated that between 1985 and 2000 there is the prediction of changes in the structure of the United States economy. Employment and output in goods production will continue to decline. By the year 2000, manufacturing will employ fewer workers than it does today, and only 14 percent of all U. S. employees will work in manufacturing industries. There will be a decline of goods production and a shift to service jobs. They indicated that by the year 2000 the American workforce will be shaped by five demographic factors:

1. The population and the workforce will grow more slowly than at any time since the 1930's.
2. The average age of the population and the workforce will rise, and the pool of young workers entering the labor market will shrink.
3. More women will enter the workforce, although the rate of increase will taper off.

4. Minorities will be a larger share of new entrants into the labor force.
5. Immigrants will represent the largest share of the increase in the population and the workforce since the First World War (pp. 75–76).

If the policies and employment patterns of the present continue, it is likely that the demographic opportunity of the 1990's will be missed and that, by the year 2000, the problem of Hispanic unemployment will worsen, and without substantial adjustments, African Americans and Hispanics will have a smaller fraction of the jobs in the year 2000 than they have today, while their share of those seeking work will have risen (Escutia & Prieto, 1986; Johnston & Parker, 1987; Valdivieso & Davis, 1988).

Factors Affecting Employment Opportunities for Hispanic Youth

Youth employment is likely to affect Hispanics and African Americans disproportionately, as it has in the past. The literature tends to indicate that there are several factors that have affected the employment of Hispanics. These are, among others: low educational attainment, lack of work experience, lack of English competence, unfamiliarity with the environment, lack of technical or skilled training, and discrimination. Many Hispanics cannot qualify either for employment or skills training, by virtue of their educational attainment, language barriers, lack of work experience, and unfamiliarity with the work environments and patterns of the mainland. Of the above factors, those barriers that have had the greatest effect are low educational attainment, a very low school completion rate, and a very high incidence of poverty. The literature has repeatedly identified several causal factors of the high unemployment rate of Hispanic youth. Some of those are: racial prejudice and discrimination, location in poverty areas, the business cycle, education and training inadequacies, population growth, the increased supply of white youths and adult women in competition for unskilled, entry-level jobs, and the declining numbers of entry-level jobs in the central cities (Croipps, 1980; Escutia & Prieto, 1986, Johnson, 1985, Johnston & Parker, 1987, Roth, 1984).

Education and training are the primary systems by which the human capital of a nation is preserved and increased. Thus, education affects an individual's labor market status. It has already been mentioned that Hispanics have a lower educational attainment level than non-Hispanics. A disproportionately high percentage of Hispanic youth leave high school without a diploma. Low educational attainment compounds part of the employment difficulties of Hispanics; it is the most important barrier to success in the labor market for Hispanics. Although the government has sponsored employment and training programs for low-income youth to improve their economic status, in reality, their educational attainment has not improved the situation for Hispanics as a whole. Between 1990 and the year 2000, a majority of all new jobs will require post-secondary education. The least skilled jobs will require a command of reading, computing, and thinking that was once necessary only for the professions (Ford Foundation, 1984, Johnston & Parker, 1987, National Commission on Secondary Schooling for Hispanics, 1984).

Recent literature tends to indicate that there is a relationship between language and employment of Hispanics. Studies such as those by Gould, MacManus & Welch (1982) and Stolzenberg (1982) suggest that limited English is possibly one of the primary reasons for the income differential between Hispanic and white workers. De la Zerda & Hooper (1979) interviewed employers to find out their reactions to accents of Mexican American males. They found that standard English speakers were considered favorably for supervisory positions, and accented speakers were favored for semiskilled jobs. Fluency in both languages seems to be an employment asset, although studies were not found to corroborate this observation. It is not knowledge or retention of Spanish that affects Hispanic youth employment, but, rather, the knowledge of the English language. Stolzenberg's study (1982) found that English language ability has a large effect on the earning potential of Hispanic men, except, perhaps, in Florida.

Poverty among Hispanic youth is an important factor in seeking a job. With large families, low incomes and a high proportion of single-parent families, the success of a significant proportion of Hispanic youth is at risk. Hispanic low-income youth employment is more unfavorable than that of youth of higher economic classes. Low paying jobs are usually not found in poor neighborhoods. Low income youth are likely to reside in poor neighborhoods where jobs are not readily available. Many of these youths do not have the transportation necessary to commute to places where good-paying jobs are to be found. And, even if they could afford the transportation, Hispanic youth are not always welcomed in some of these places of employment.

Many Hispanic youth lack work experience, and this lack of experience affects their opportunities to get a job. Success in job hunting is very much dependent on information about available positions. Family and friends in middle class communities are good sources for obtaining information about employment. But, in the Hispanic community, low socioeconomic environments limit information about job openings and restrict contact with the job market. Hispanic youth are largely confined to their own neighborhood, where there are few new plants and business offices. Informal information on jobs is generally sought, and little use is made of state employment services.

There is not an effective market for juvenile labor. The teenaged youth of poor families desperately need after school jobs, but the demand for their services, for such things as babysitting, grass cutting, and snow shoveling, lies largely in the middle and upper-income neighborhoods. If Hispanic youth have worked before, they have been in jobs not related to the pool of jobs available. Santos (1977) found that the effect of job experience on occupational levels for Hispanic workers may be due to inadequate labor market information and that the first job often becomes a career.

The reasons behind youth's desire to work vary. Some youth are interested in working to get personal items, while others seek career or skill training in their jobs; and others may need to work to help defray family expenses. But, one thing is clear: Hispanic youth want to work. However, they do not have the skills to look for a job nor they have the awareness of how to move from job to job for greater mobility and opportunity.

Discrimination in the labor market is difficult to measure. Employment discrimination can be manifested in relation to language or ethnic origin. Hispanics are penalized more in the work force because of their lack of fluent English than are non-Hispanics with an equivalent lack of fluency. For example, Hispanic men who speak English, but not well, are in occupations with lower annual earnings than otherwise-capable Hispanics who do speak English well (Johnston & Parker, 1987, Santos, 1977, De la Zerda & Hooper, 1979).

Hispanic Youth Employment

Hispanic youth employment reflects various tendencies and characteristics. There is an increasing number of Hispanic high school students who are studying and working at the same time. Another group of Hispanic youth are entering the labor force. And, there is another group of Hispanic youth who are unemployed. Some Hispanic youth in the labor force are protected from the financial consequences of unemployment by family income. In addition, because completion of schooling is probably more important for future success in the labor market than initial work experience, the problem of teenage unemployment solves itself in most instances as teenagers mature into young adults. For a substantial proportion of youth, employment represents an important source of income.

Many Hispanic families are poor and their youth seek work in order to help them financially to cope with family expenses. In general, Hispanics seek work to help defray family expenses or to support themselves. Slightly over half of the youth seek part-time work, particularly those who were aged 16–17, and are likely to be enrolled in school. Older, out of school youth look for full-time jobs.

The employment status of Hispanics aged 16–21 overall is not as favorable as that of whites and only slightly more favorable than that of African Americans (Johnson, 1985, Roth, 1984). Among Hispanics, the employment situation varied by group, sex, age, school enrollment status, poverty status, and place of birth. For example, teenagers in 1979 comprised about 10 percent of the Hispanic labor force and 25 percent of all unemployed Hispanics (United States Department of Labor, 1981).

Age and graduation from high school, nevertheless, improve the employment status of all youth; but the relative position of Hispanic youth continues to fall below that of whites, and females trail other women; the gap, however, drops considerably for high school students and is eliminated among college students. Increasing education should bring a greater number of Hispanic women into the work force (Calabrese, 1988, Escutia & Prieto, 1986, Johnston & Parker, 1987, Valdivieso & Davis, 1988). Puerto Ricans and Mexican Americans suffer the most disadvantaged status. Employment is not as readily available for Hispanic high school students. As in the case of all youth, the prospect of obtaining a more favorable employment situation appears to increase with age for Hispanics. In general, older youth experience an increase in opportunities to get a job and a decline in their unemployment rate (Calabrese, 1988, Escutia & Prieto, 1986, Johnson, 1985, Johnston & Parker, 1987, Valdivieso & Davis, 1988). High school graduates not enrolled in college had a proportionately high employment ratio, reflecting Hispanic youth's shift from high school to work responsibilities.

Labor market difficulties of Hispanic youth are also compounded by a high proportion of dropouts. Most male high school dropouts are in the labor force, although Hispanics participated less than white or African American dropouts. Among school dropouts, Hispanic males had the most difficulty in finding work. One possible explanation of the relatively lower employment rates of Hispanic male dropouts is that local industries located in the region where Hispanics reside may not require high school graduation as a condition of employment, and other adult individuals with no high school diploma will fit into these positions. Another reason is that industries are moving away from the central cities or poor neighborhoods.

Moreover, differences in employment status appear among Hispanic females. Hispanic females have had an unfavorable employment status. Hispanic female labor force participation is not uniform across Hispanic groups. White, Cuban, female employment relates to those of whites; Puerto Rican females have had one of the most unfavorable employment situations of any youth group in the decade of the 1980's. Declining employment conditions in the Northeast, where the majority of Puerto Ricans reside, could account for this unfavorable employment situation (National Council of La Raza, 1986b). For Hispanic females, efforts to improve their employment and economic status will be compounded by the presence of children. Many young Hispanic women would like to seek a job, but cannot since they are raising a child, sometimes alone. In general, females participated in the labor force less than males and had poorer employment situations. Hispanic female graduates, however, had the lowest unemployment rate of all the Hispanic sub-groups. Hispanic male, high school graduates, on the other hand, while faring much better than African Americans, are not without their own problems. Their employment rate is substantially lower than that of whites (Johnston & Parker, 1987, Escutia & Prieto, 1986, Roth, 1984).

The employment of youth, especially ethnic minorities, has been on the agenda of the federal and state governments for several decades.

For Hispanic youth, the government represents a major source of employment. In 1946, under the Employment Act, the federal government assumed the responsibility of providing and maintaining full employment opportunities for individuals who were unable to find work. This act was more a policy declaration than a provision to decrease unemployment in the United States. It was in the 1960's that legislative programs were enacted to create a system of employment and training to assist the unemployed to find work (Marshall, Brings & King, 1984). The first base of federal employment and training legislation was the Manpower Development and Training Act (MDTA), a centralized program enacted in 1962. It emphasized vocational training for workers displaced by automatization. In 1964, categorical employment and training programs for low-income youth and adults were initiated as a part of the federal anti-poverty legislation, the Economic Opportunity Act (EOA). These programs were modified several times. Hispanics represented 12.0 percent of employment and training program participants between 1968 and 1973 (National Council of la Raza, 1989a). Congress replaced these employment and training efforts with the Comprehensive Employment and Training Act (CETA), which was designated to consolidate federally supported employment activities and to establish a single administrative framework.

Programs to address the needs of youth were a major focus of the Comprehensive Employment and Training Act (CETA). By 1978, amendments had been enacted to provide for increased accountability, strengthened targeting of the disadvantaged, greatly increased private sector involvement, and a major youth component. These programs were major employers of minority youth, especially Hispanics and African Americans. While these programs provided Hispanic youth with a first job experience, with income, and with alternatives to street life, there is little evidence to suggest that they provided the training, the experience, or the skills these young people needed to improve their future employment prospects, their future earnings, or their access to jobs in the primary labor market (Ford Foundation, 1982). Many of the CETA programs lacked effective mechanisms for transition to unsubsidized jobs in the private or public sector. Hispanics, especially Mexican Americans and Puerto Ricans, were more likely than other youth to participate in government-sponsored programs to obtain job training. The most Hispanics and other youth received from participating in government-sponsored employment and training programs were subsidized jobs, receiving job counseling, skills training, basic educational skills, medicare services and transportation. In 1979, the government sponsored about one-fifth of the jobs held by minority school students. Industry, retail trade, and manufacturing provided the most jobs for males; and more Hispanic males than other youth, particularly the foreign born, held manufacturing jobs.

When President Reagan took office in 1981, a new approach to employment and training was launched. It called for the elimination of public service "jobs" programs, decreased federal funding levels for employment and training programs, increased emphasis on the private sector, and increased emphasis on the performance of the programs. The Job Training Partnership Act (JTPA) replaced CETA in 1982. It was designed as a decentralized program with most decision making delegated to the states and to local Private Industry Councils (PICS). JTPA's target groups were the same as for CETA: low-income and long-term unemployed adults and youth (National Council of La Raza, 1989a).

Hispanic participation in JTPA has been lower than in the previous programs. All Hispanic sub-groups are underrepresented, especially Hispanic men. JTPA is not effective in reaching Hispanic dropouts either. In 1988, Hispanics comprised 11 percent of the eligible population of youth dropouts, but 14 percent of those who successfully completed JTPA (National Council of La Raza, 1989b). However, Hispanic dropouts are still underrepresented by more than one third, a proportion of eligible adults and youth who are not served by JTPA (National Council of La Raza, 1989b). Youths are overrepresented in the JTPA program, however, two of every three JTPA youth participants are either currently enrolled in school or are high school graduates.

While sizeable groups of Hispanics are limited English proficient (LEP), Hispanics and other LEP groups comprise less than five percent of JTPA enrollments; and three percent of those who complete training indicated that JTPA is providing minimal service to school dropouts with LEP proficiency (National Council of La Raza, 1989a).

The occupations sought by employed youth vary by race and, particularly, by sex. In a 1979 study, Santos (1985) found that "half the jobs sought by males were broadly distributed to include service, as laborers, operatives, and craft persons. Clerical and service occupations comprised over half the jobs desired by unemployed females; and the third most sought-after occupation was sales work" (63). Most employed Hispanic male youth held jobs as service workers, operatives and laborers, or they worked in crafts. Cubans were the least likely to work in service occupations. Clerical work provided the majority of the jobs for Hispanic youth. Other occupations include services, sales and operatives. Certain industries such as fast foods, that hire considerable numbers of youth, are more likely to be located away from central cities or poor neighborhoods.

Hispanic Youth Unemployment

Hispanics face severe, continuing unemployment and underemployment. Unemployment among Hispanics is usually 60 percent higher than that of white Americans. The unemployment rate has been consistently higher for Puerto Ricans, whose employment rate approaches the African American rate, and lowest for Cubans, whose employment rate only slightly exceeds that of whites (Escutia & Prieto, 1986). In 1988, the unemployment rate for Hispanics was 8.5 percent compared to 5.8 percent for non-Hispanics. Among the Hispanic sub-groups, unemployment causes social and economic damage, increased crime, and mental disorders (Bureau of the Census, 1988a). Young people experience the highest incidence of unemployment of any group in the labor force. The Bureau of Labor Statistics defines an unemployed person as one who did not work during the survey week but who was available for work and had actively sought a job within thirty days. There are three indexes for analyzing patterns of youth unemployment: unemployment rate, the labor-force participation rate, and the employment-to-population ratio. People not looking for work are not considered unemployed; students and others actively seeking part-time or full-time work are. Hispanic youth experience higher unemployment, lower wages, and more involuntary part-time work than others of their age cohort during their adult years. These youngsters reflect a mismatch between the skills of available workers and the requirements of available jobs. Unemployment has causes both on the demand side (an inadequate number of jobs) and on the supply side (a pool of workers lacking the education, skills, and or attitudes required by employers (Garcia, 1981; Johnson, 1985; Johnston & Parker, 1987; Roth, 1984; Santos, 1985).

Poorly educated minority youth—especially dropouts—living in central cities constitute the core of the problem of youth unemployment. Some of the obstacles that youth face are: low skill levels, limited education, inadequate work experience, discrimination, and poor information about the labor market (Ford Foundation, 1983, National Council of La Raza, 1989a, Roth, 1984, Santos, 1977, Stolzenberg, 1982). In 1979, two fifths of unemployed Mexican Americans and Puerto Ricans were dropouts (Santos, 1985). Female Hispanic dropouts participated very little in the labor force and had high unemployment rates. In 1979, only 25 percent of Hispanic female dropouts held jobs in comparison to 40 percent of whites. According to Santos (1985), three of every ten youth aged 16–21 do not have, or are not actively seeking, a job. About 75 percent of those out of the labor force were enrolled in either high school or college, but the remaining 25 percent neither attended school, held a job, nor looked for work. Of the labor force, Hispanics and African Americans are more likely than whites not to be in school. Among the Hispanic groups, nearly half of the Puerto Ricans are not in school, and the vast majority of these youths are dropouts. At the other extreme, Cuban youth who are out of the labor force are more likely to be in school.

From the 1979 study *The National Longitudinal Survey of Youth Labor Market Experience*, Santos (1985) found that Puerto Ricans were the least likely to be in the labor force and their employment/population ratio closely resembled that of African Americans. Female college students participate more in the labor force and have higher employment ratios than male college students. Hispanic college females were just as likely as other women to participate in the work force.

Functional illiteracy is a cause of unemployment for youth as well as adults. A 1980 study concluded that 7.2 million young people, 28 percent of the total young-adult population, were reading below the eighth-grade level (Office of the Assistant Secretary of Defense, 1982). The population of illiterates is further swelled by the increasing percentage of youths who drop out of school each year. Many of these youths were unable to read a help-wanted ad or to fill out a job application. This situation is still the same at the end of the decade, and the future tends to indicate that it is not going to change soon.

Attitudes toward work among the unemployed are an important consideration in developing employment opportunities. Hispanic females, for example, refuse more often than other youth to wash dishes or perform cleaning work (Santos, 1985). Foreign-born Hispanic males are, however, more willing to work at subminimal wages than other youth. Apparently, these youth will work in jobs other youths have refused.

Recommendations for the Improvement of Hispanic Youth Employment

Hispanics will soon become the majority of entry-level workers in some metropolitan areas. The decade of the 1980's did not bring better employment opportunities for Hispanics. The economic outlook for Hispanic youth is not encouraging. The employment needs of Hispanic youth require careful attention. Hispanics are not educationally and career prepared to target the job market. Most Hispanics relied on manufacturing and other related industries which are rapidly losing their international competitiveness. However, new industries are requiring workers with high levels of technical, computer, and communication skills. These requirements are diametrically opposed to the salient features of Hispanic workers: young, increasing in numbers, low school completion rates and job dependency on assembly, operative, and service work, but with a willingness to work and obtain education and skills training (Santos, 1985). Too many Hispanics are entering factories to work as operatives with dim prospects for occupational mobility. Policies need to be developed to broaden opportunities for Hispanic youth to be represented in all business and commercial activities.

The evidence suggests that the youth-employment picture is likely to worsen in the coming years and that school dropouts will be the group most adversely affected, since they are not prepared for the transformation of the labor market, which is highly technological, resulting in serious dislocations both for current workers and for new entrants to the labor force. The complex interconnections among employment, education, literacy, cultural values, income, living environment, and family responsibility need complex solutions: The choices are not simply between on the job training and basic skills remediation programs for teenagers, but include investments in child care and pregnancy prevention. The following recommendations serve as suggested guidelines in developing public and private policies to improve the labor force conditions of Hispanic youth.

1. There is a need to create employment opportunities for Hispanic
    youth. The causes of youth unemployment are complex. There is a
    need to match Hispanic youth employment needs to economic and
    employment policies. The federal and state governments need to
    develop a favorable employment climate for Hispanics to increase
    the employability of Hispanic youth. There may be a need to look
    at those sectors with high levels of Hispanic youth unemployment
    in order to develop programs to employ Hispanic youth. Other
    programs are needed to better prepare the youths with educational
    and communication skills training; train them in technological and
    computerized programs; and improve their job search techniques.
    These programs need to look at the positive attributes of Hispanic
    youth toward work, look at their economic and family needs, and
    raise the participation of young Hispanic women in the labor force
    (Croipps, 1980).

    Private employers have a new and more extensive role to play
    in the development of their workforces. Not only are they critically
    affected by the quality of the workers, but employees are among
    the most knowledgeable designers and implementers of cost-
    effective, technology-based training programs. The employers
    would have to design new employment strategies to target, prepare,
    and employ more Hispanics, especially Hispanic youth.

2. There is a need to create a high level of youth employment for high
    school students. A very small percentage of Hispanic high school
    students work during the school year compared to a high
    percentage of whites. Hispanic youth cannot find jobs during the
    year in spite of having a need to work. This policy requires the
    involvement of both public and private sectors to provide more
    jobs, and, if possible, near the Hispanic communities where these
    unemployed youth reside.

3. There is a need for matching restrictive institutional practices to
    Hispanic youths' characteristics. Today, youth employment is
    restricted by institutional laws which specify a minimum wage,
    educational level, United States citizenship, or residency,
    apprenticeship experience, English language competency, and skill
    competency (Santos, 1985). Many of these restrictions prevent
    Hispanic youth who need the work to help their family and to
    support themselves from obtaining work. Many Hispanic youth are

over the employment age of 14; but they are dropouts, non-English speakers, or are not legal citizens or residents. Consequently, as Santos (1985) says "the relationship between job performance and employment requirements like high school completion, language proficiency, or the citizenship requirement needs to be ascertained to protect against discriminatory barriers to Hispanic youth" (p. 162).

4. Although education is not a panacea for unemployment, it is one of the best indicators of employment success. The lack of educational preparedness is of increasing concern to business, industry, and government, particularly in light of the structural changes in the economy that require greater skills for entry-level employment. The growing mismatch between the skills new jobs require and the skills Hispanics acquire calls for increased education and cooperation between the private and public sectors. Among youth aged 16–21, Hispanics are twice as likely as whites to be high school dropouts. Youth who fail to complete high school represent a large proportion of unemployed Hispanics. A significant number of Hispanic youth drop out of school for economic reasons—home responsibilities, good job offers, or other financial difficulties. Jobs have become more sophisticated and demanding. Job demands require an emphasis on basic skills, training, and employment assistance for Hispanics, all of which have been pursued with limited success over the past several decades. These investments will be needed, not only to insure that employers have a qualified workforce in the years after 2000, but, finally, to guarantee the equality of opportunity (Escutia & Prieto, 1986, Ford Foundation, 1984, Johnston & Parker, 1987).

5. There is a need to prepare more bilingual Hispanic individuals to fill the needs of both business and government for literate English/Spanish bilingual professionals, especially in trade and diplomatic jobs (Valdivieso & Davis, 1988). There will be a pool of over 300-million Spanish-speaking consumers in Latin America by the year 2000. Companies in foreign markets recognize that bilingual professionals provide a competitive advantage. Hispanic youth, due to their bilingual background, represent a realistic trainable group for these jobs.

A significant number of Hispanic youth are raised in households where Spanish is spoken and is the primary medium of communication. Although that in itself is not a limitation if English is also spoken, in many cases, this is not the case. Whether or not limited English usage is the foremost employment obstacle as stated by the National Commission for Employment Policy (1982) is far from clear. Santos (1985) suggests that limited-English proficiency is a major problem among foreign-born Hispanics, but not among United States-born Hispanics. Since language development is beneficial to everyone, language improvement efforts should be incorporated into measures to increase employment among Hispanics. But, as Santos (1985) states "language could well represent an artificial job barrier, or a way to discriminate by employers" (p. 165).

6.   Schools and training agencies need to train Hispanic youngsters to compete for jobs in computers, data processing, communication areas, and for jobs requiring basic computation and writing skills. Schools cannot do the job alone, but schools need to find ways to identify partnerships with industry and other employment sources. New relationships need to be developed with business and educational institutions, along with the Hispanic philanthropic community to plan and develop the structure of new partnerships and training models. These three groups need to address such issues as (a) developing basic literacy skills of dropouts and other high-risk youth parallel with the requirements of the new technological job market, (b) promoting private partnerships that address the training needs of high-risk and dropout youth, and (c) developing and supporting studies on youth and the labor market and alternative forms of employment. One of the difficulties of some well-intentioned employment programs is that they are implemented without testing to see if they can work with the intended population.

7.   Hispanic youth need more knowledge of the labor market and effective job search methods and techniques. Hispanic youth have less knowledge of the world of work than do whites. Improved information about occupations could help Hispanics make wise career decisions (Santos, 1985).

In summary, it is fair to say that Hispanic people are at a serious disadvantage in the labor market due to, among other factors, lower educational attainment, lack of knowledge of labor markets, difficulty in English, and employer and union discrimination.

Conclusion

Hispanics represent a growing proportion of the United States labor force, and they are a youthful population in an aging society. One of the most important barriers to success in the labor market for Hispanics is their low level of educational attainment. The complex interconnections among employment, education, literacy, cultural values, income, living environment and family responsibility need complex solutions. The choices are not simply between on the job training and basic skills remediation programs for teenagers, but need to include investments in child care programs and pregnancy prevention.

Underemployment and unemployment have been big problems in the Hispanic community. Federal, state and local employment initiatives and training have the potential to help overcome these problems by providing education, training, and job preparation services to Hispanics in need of job-related assistance.

What are needed are responsible policies by the federal government that recognize and effectively address the educational crisis faced by Hispanics. To enable Hispanics to fully participate in the United States economy, investment in partnerships, which include the public, private and community sectors must develop. Hispanics in the labor force are a critical human resource whose talents must be tapped to maximize their participation in the United States labor force.

CHAPTER 10

Hispanic Youth in Institutions of Higher Education

From the point of view of individual and national welfare, higher education is one of the most important services in the United States. Higher education is a natural process of investigation and learning. The purposes of higher education are threefold: students' growth and development, the expansion and refinement of knowledge, and the social impact on the community and the country as a whole. The benefits of higher education are of several sorts and are related both to individual users and to society as a whole. Throughout history, advanced education has been a doorway, although not an exclusive one, to a world of intellectual and aesthetic appreciation and a path to privileged occupations. It opens doors and enhances the quality of life as a result of higher paying and higher status occupations. Higher education raises the educational level of a society and it serves to raise productivity of that society's labor force in a manner that adds to the economic returns of all factors of production. Higher education is, thus, a significant vehicle by which a minority group may benefit from expanded opportunities and advance into the mainstream in America's socioeconomic system.

In this chapter higher education includes many sub-categories of institutions beyond the high school such as colleges, universities and community colleges. The liberal arts colleges comprise several divisions such as humanities, social, natural, and physical sciences. The primary objective of the liberal arts is the competence of the individual in a specialization. Universities, on the other hand, are intellectual in nature and are places in which substantial knowledge and research have been accumulated. The community college is an invention of the twentieth century that prepares students for technical work or for further education at a more advanced level in a college or university.

This chapter discusses higher education as it relates to Hispanic youth in the United States. Major issues are: access to institutions of higher education, Hispanic representation at the student, faculty and administrative levels, and the status of the Hispanic youth's retention and graduation.

Factors Affecting Hispanic Youth's Access to Institutions of Higher Education

The success of the U. S. higher education system in meeting the needs of Hispanic students can be best measured by how many Hispanics get into college (enrollment), how many stay in college (retention), how many achieve the baccalaureate degree (graduation), and how many complete graduate and professional degrees. Since the 1970's, colleges and universities in the United States have seen more Hispanic faces in their campuses and Hispanic students' access is greater. Access is the ability of students to enroll in post-secondary institutions of higher education and the ability of institutions through their policies and practices to serve diverse populations.

During the period from the early colonial days to the present, there has been an evolution in the American philosophy of what higher education should be and the clientele it should serve. Until 1940, higher education was mostly for the elite; only the rich and the individuals belonging to privileged social classes were allowed to attend institutions of higher education. During the decade of the 1960's, the egalitarian philosophy advocating universal access to higher education was popularized in the United States, forcing the creation of revolutionary concepts such as open doors, equal educational opportunities, and affirmative action. This new vision of the role of and participation in higher education opened new doors to low socioeconomic and minority groups in the United States. Hispanics, being the second minority group in the United States, have participated in this egalitarian movement. In the last 30 years, the federal and state governments and Hispanic advocacy groups have made tremendous efforts to promote access to Hispanics in institutions of post-secondary education. However, underrepresentation continues to be the defining characteristic of Hispanics in higher education (American Council on Education, 1989). In 1976, 36 percent of Hispanic high school graduates went to college, while in 1986, only 29 percent of Hispanics went to college (Massachusetts Institute of Technology, 1990). According to the American Council on Education (1989): "Hispanics enrolled in college dropped by a sizeable margin between 1976 and 1988 . . . the proportion of 18–24 year old, low-income Hispanic high school graduates enrolled in college fell by 10 percentage points, from 50.4 percent in 1976 to 35.3 percent in 1988" (p. 5). Hispanic students have neither attained access into a broad range of institutions nor dramatically increased their numbers throughout the system (American Council on Education, 1989; Baratz-Snowden & Duran, 1987; Cardenas, Robledo & Waggoner, 1988; Olivas, 1981; Orum, 1986). In 1987, proportionally fewer Hispanics participated in higher education than either whites or African Americans—17 percent versus 29 percent and 20 percent (American Council on Education, 1989). The racial/ethnic minority share of enrollment has remained relatively stable. For example, in 1976, the enrollment of Hispanics in institutions of higher education was 2.4 percent, while in 1982 it was only 3.0 percent (Olivas, 1986; United States Department of Education, 1984). Comparing the gains of a decade of Hispanics in higher education indicates that from 1970 to 1984, full-time Hispanic undergraduate students increased only 2.1 percent of the total to 3.5 percent. Olivas indicated that "even more dramatic is the decline of the percentage of Hispanic high school graduates attending college, from 35.4 percent in 1975 to 29.0 percent in 1980" (p. 2). A smaller proportion of Hispanic high school graduates go to college than do white high school graduates, and those proportions have actually been declining since 1976. In 1976, 37 percent of Hispanic high school graduates went on to college, while in 1986, only 29 percent went to college (Massachusetts Institute of Technology, 1990). From 1986 to 1988, higher percentages of white high school graduates enrolled in college, while the college-going rates of Hispanic high school graduates remained disproportionately low, thus widening the long-standing gap between whites and Hispanics (American Council on Education, 1989).

Knowledge of the characteristics of Hispanics and of the diversity of their characteristics may be useful in determining what factors limit Hispanic access to college. Several factors influence the choice of a post secondary institution: high school grades, college entrance examination scores, available financial resources, willingness and availability to live away from home, career goals, types of program offerings sought, and experiences of family and friends. Prior to becoming college candidates, Hispanic high school students are subject to school, home and community experiences that profoundly affect chances for college candidacy. Duran (1983) indicated that within the high school context preceding application for college, there is a need to understand how the college aspirations of Hispanic students are determined and what academic, counseling, and high school institutional factors affect the chances that Hispanics will decide to apply to college. Factors such as the economic needs of students' families, the expectations of parents about their children's education, high school counselors, college orientation and the socio-cultural influence of students' communities and peer networks affect Hispanic decisions and choices for college candidacy. The socio-cultural background of Hispanics, including value orientation and language background, also exerts an influence on students' decisions to plan for college candidacy. A combination of these factors contributes to the fact that Hispanic students are more likely to attend community colleges and are more likely to attend school on a part-time basis than are their non-Hispanic peers (American Council on Education, 1985; Astin, 1982; Cardenas, Robledo & Waggoner, 1988; Lee, 1985; Massachusetts Institute of Technology, 1990).

Duran (1983) mentioned a list of personal factors generated by Payan, Flores, Paterson, Romero & Warren (1982) affecting Hispanic education. These are: (a) proficiency in Spanish and English, (b) academic preparation for college, (c) students' financial needs and personal needs related to family responsibility, (d) personal characteristics arising from migration, (e) students' general acculturation to United States life and the social value systems of students, and (f) age and maturity of students. As this list indicates, there are several factors that impede Hispanic youth's access to college. Among Hispanics, it is common to see a combination of more than one factor that does not allow Hispanic youth to apply to or be accepted by an institution of higher education. One of the most crucial factors is lack of educational background and educational credentials. The fact that Hispanics differ among themselves and differ overall from other United States people in many ways has a significant relationship to educational attainment and access to college.

Elementary and secondary schools are graduating a significant number of Hispanic students with insufficient credentials to qualify for study in highly selective colleges. The Testing Program of the College Entrance Examination Board uses the Scholastic Aptitude Test (SAT), the Test of Standard Written English (TSWE), and about 13 separate achievement tests in various areas of scholastic undergraduate training to evaluate students' preparation for college. When the tests are administered, students also fill out a background and educational aspiration questionnaire. The SAT test is composed of two sections: the verbal section and the mathematics section. Both sections are intended to measure developed ability in use of language and in simple mathematical reasoning as might be expected of students in undergraduate college course work. Colleges vary in the importance they place on candidates' academic achievement and college aptitude test scores. Almost all selective four-year institutions rely heavily on high school grades or rank in high school class and college aptitude test scores as primary evidence of candidates' preparation for the academic demands of college. In general, Hispanic students do not do well in these tests. In 1989, the combined SAT verbal and mathematics scores for white students were 22 percent higher than scores of Puerto Rican students and 15 percent higher than scores of Mexican American students (Massachusetts Institute of Technology, 1990). Duran (1983) indicated that under the assumption that the admission test scores of Hispanics are valid indicators of students' college aptitude, one is led to the inescapable conclusion that Hispanic college candidates are not as well-prepared academically for college work as white students. There have been several explanations for Hispanic students' lack of educational credentials for college, one of them being the lack of their participation in successful schools and successful high school programs (American Council on Education, 1985; Brown et al., 1985; Gandara, 1986; Oslin, 1982). Hispanic youth's schools are not the best equipped to provide them with a variety of preparatory courses to take and pass the College Entrance Examination tests.

There has been a decrease in the number of Hispanics taking the standardized college entrance tests. Although 52 percent of Hispanic high school seniors in 1980 indicated that they planned to attend college in the next year, only 28 percent of those students had taken the SAT (United States Department of Education, 1980, 1982). The low percentages of Hispanics taking the SAT may be partly due to the fact that community colleges, where Hispanic post-secondary students are concentrated, often do not require such tests (Orum, 1988; Ramist & Albeiter, 1984). The Hispanic youth who do take the SAT generally have scores which are substantially lower than those of white students. These low test scores limit the opportunity of Hispanics at private, highly selective universities and at public four-year universities. Also, as of 1985, nearly 30 states had increased their undergraduate admissions criteria for public colleges and universities. These changes include increased high school curricular requirements or higher SAT test scores. Many colleges plan to increase the use of tests for entry to highly specialized fields. Since Hispanics do not perform as well as whites and Asian Americans on standardized tests, and tend to graduate from high school with lower grade point averages and take fewer college-preparatory courses, it is expected that Hispanic college enrollment will be negatively affected (American Council on Education, 1989).

Hispanics tended to earn lower grades in high school than did non-Hispanic white students. Among the Hispanics who aspired to go to college and who took the Scholastic Aptitude Test in 1983 differences were noted in the high school-grade point average of whites versus Mexican Americans and Puerto Ricans residing in the United States (Ramist & Albeiter, 1984). These differences indicate that Hispanics are less likely than whites to meet high school grade standards for admission to highly selective colleges. In 1984, only 41.7 percent of Hispanic 18 to 19 year old high school graduates were enrolled in some type of post-secondary education, as compared to 54.9 percent of white graduates in the same age group. Hispanic college attendance rates for high school graduates were significantly lower than those for African American high school graduates under age 18 (45 percent and 61.5 percent respectively but were higher for students 18 to 21 [United States Department of Education, 1984]). Research findings from the National Longitudinal Study of the High School Class of 1972 suggested that Hispanics overall were not achieving at the same level in high school as were non-Hispanics, affecting their access to institutions of higher education (Brown et al., 1985).

There is also a variety in the areas of high school study. Duran (1983) and Ramist and Albeiter (1984) found differences in the number of courses in mathematics and English. Students who are candidates for the most selective colleges are likely to show a more intensive background in English and mathematics than are other college candidates. The same is the case in years of study spent by students in foreign languages, biological sciences, and social studies (Duran, 1983). Hispanic high school students in the United States are deriving less academic preparation for college than are students in other groups. This evidence is based on the lower high school grades and lower achievement tests scores of Hispanics relative to white students. Hispanic high school students manifested lower achievement in course areas that are critical to college preparation.

The same differences can be seen in college admission test scores. Ramist and Albeiter (1984) data suggest that in 1983 Hispanics seeking enrollment to selective colleges showed less college aptitude than white non-Hispanic college candidates, again based on the premise of different high school educational experiences. For example, they found that Hispanics who indicated that English was not their best or primary language earned lower scores in the SAT than other Hispanics. These students received lower SAT scores than did white non-Hispanics who indicated that English was their best language. Thus, a factor that affects Hispanic youth's access is limited familiarity with the English language. The language background of Hispanic youth has an effect on school achievement (Bennet, 1988; Cummins, 1984; Diaz, 1983; Krashen & Biber, 1988; Matute-Bianchi, 1986; Pifer, 1979). The direct effect is that children who are less familiar with English than other children profit less from instruction in English due to less proficiency in English. Hispanic students' academic preparation for college may be limited in a number of ways by the lack of compatibility between the students' language background and the language environment of high school and later on college. Astin and Burciaga (1981) concluded that "Chicanos who scored high on the verbal subtest of the SAT tended to make good grades in college. Thus, language proficiency seems especially important to the college performance of Chicanos" (p. 631).

Access to higher education is also limited by the high dropout rate at the high school level, making the pool of Hispanic candidates less than any other group. The high proportion of Hispanics who leave secondary school without receiving a high school diploma dramatically affects the number of Hispanics eligible to pursue a post-secondary education. Hispanic high school completion rates are substantially below those for white students. Approximately one-half of the Hispanic youth leave high school without a diploma and, thus, are not eligible to apply for post-secondary education. The Hispanic eligibility pool is further reduced by the fact that three fourths of Hispanic high school seniors have not completed a college-preparatory high school curriculum (Orum, 1986). Even those who graduate with a college preparatory background are less likely than white students to be eligible for and competitive enough to be admitted to four-year colleges. The educational disadvantage of Hispanics at the elementary and secondary levels, particularly the small number of Hispanic high school graduates in proportion to the general population, results in significantly lower representation in institutions of post-secondary education.

Another factor affecting access and participation of Hispanics is the constantly declining resources resulting in the shrinking of available financial aid. The availability of student financial aid and the perception that resources are not available are often critical factors in the post-secondary decisions of low-income students. Hispanics in general suffered a loss with respect to the share of student financial aid received between 1978 and 1983. This situation is particularly true for Hispanics at two-year public colleges where aid declined 13.6 percent (Lee, 1985). On the other hand, whatever aid is available often becomes unavailable due to the lack of familiarity of non-traditional students with bureaucratic processes. Hispanic students do accept no for an answer. In many instances, they give up at the first answer that they receive that financial aid is not available. In other occasions, they perceive that financial aid is not available for them due to their low test scores and general average.

Another factor affecting Hispanic access to college is the poor quality of classroom interactions for Hispanic high school students. Teachers may have lower academic expectations of and lower social esteem for Hispanics than of other high school students. If this is so, teachers may not stimulate and motivate students to excel, but, rather, to accept traditional education (Orum, 1986; Payan et al., 1982; Steinberg, Blende & Chan, 1984). Hispanic students are sometimes seen by school personnel as individuals headed for failure, and schools are content to ask students to do the minimum, and not to challenge them. Thus, these students do not try hard and accept passing grades without trying to be the best students in the school and to get the best grades.

Another variable affecting Hispanic youth college attainment is the lack of a home environment conducive to study. In some instances, Hispanic youth have not been raised in a home environment conducive to learning. Sometimes the parents are not aware of the need for raising children surrounded by books and having good role models. Children who do not visit the community library with their parents or children who never saw their parents reading a book have difficulties in making the transition to college.

The steady waning of Latin American study programs is another indicator of the shrinking of Hispanic studies courses in several colleges in the United States. The college guidelines clearly support the maintenance of traditional departments and programs over their newer counterparts. Ethnic studies and special support academic programs have been eliminated or reduced. For example, in the colleges in New York City, six of the 17 existing Puerto Rican Study programs and departments have been closed and many of the surviving departments have languished as faculty and administrative lines were cut.

The above factors mentioned are indicators of the failure of the educational system to educate and provide successful educational experiences to Hispanic youth to facilitate their access to institutions of higher education.

Hispanic Participation in Institutions of Higher Education

Hispanics believe in the value of a college education, and, in general, they are interested in sending their children to institutions of higher education. However, this educational dream does not always come true for the majority of Hispanic parents. Equality of educational opportunity is not always practiced, although the literature disseminated by colleges and universities across the United States constantly mentions equal educational opportunities for all citizens (Tucker & Gray, 1980). There is also a general belief that the lack of money ought not to be a barrier to participate in institutions of higher education. During the 1960's, and in the midst of the Civil Rights Movement, Hispanics forcefully demanded full participation in American society. The right to an equal education in the schools and access to higher education were key demands. Many public institutions across the nation began to respond to the educational demands of minority groups and developed open admissions policies. For example, at CUNY, a public institution in New York City, Puerto Rican and African American students, community pressures, and student occupation of several colleges led the CUNY Board of Trustees to approve an open admissions policy, which guaranteed entry to all New York City students with a high school diploma, regardless of their school average. The board also yielded to student demands for the creation of Puerto Rican Studies programs and agreed to establish a bilingual college, Eugenio Maria de Hostos Community College, to serve the predominantly Puerto Rican population of the South Bronx.

Open admissions represented an important step in the Hispanic struggle for access to institutions of higher education. Although open admissions has contributed to more minorities attending college, minorities are still a small percentage of the college student population. Overall minority enrollment in higher education was about 14 percent of the total in 1986, for the roughly 25 percent minority representation in the total college-age population (Massachusetts Institute of Technology, 1990). Still, in 1986, Hispanics constituted only 8.2 percent of the graduate student body at CUNY, New York City (Rodriguez-Fraticelli, 1989).

Hispanic faculty and Hispanic administrators have not shown the growth one would have expected from affirmative action programs and governmental efforts to increase Hispanic participation in higher education. Most institutions of higher education provide admission to students based on a standard or criterion of performance, according to institutional philosophy and policy. Admissions may be open, restrictive, or a combination of the two. Measurable criteria can include such things as standardized tests scores, high school or undergraduate grade point averages, high school rank, as well as any combination of these and other objective and subjective factors. Hispanic youth's participation in institutions of higher education may depend on the degree of how well-prepared they are to fulfill the above admission requirements, as well as how ready institutions of higher education are to admit Hispanic students.

Hispanic students account for a very small proportion of the full-time students enrolled in higher education programs. It is true that Hispanics in general increased their participation in the 1970's, but they are still underenrolled in undergraduate, graduate, and professional studies. Orum (1986) cited data from the 1980 High School and Beyond Study that show that:

1.   Only 47.9 percent of Hispanic seniors applied for admission to one or more colleges, compared to 62.7 percent of African Americans, and 64.6 percent of whites. In contrast to the application strategies of most African Americans and white

youth who reported applying to several schools to increase their chances of acceptance, most Hispanic seniors indicated that they had applied to only one school.

2. Fully 52.7 percent of Hispanic students expecting to go to college plan to attend a two-year college, compared to 39.5 percent of African Americans and 47.0 percent of whites.

3. More Hispanics than African Americans or white students who planned to attend college planned to attend on a part time-basis. Some 44.2 percent of Hispanics intended to attend college part time, compared to 32.6 percent of African Americans and 34.1 percent of whites (p. 37).

Hispanic Students' Representation

Hispanic youth are not well represented in higher education. The general public perception is that Hispanic enrollment has greatly increased, but, in reality, neither affirmative action programs nor governmental efforts have met these perceptions (Astin, 1982; Duran, 1983; Olivas, 1982; Orum, 1986). The High School and Beyond study of 1980 showed that six years later, white students had earned bachelor's degrees at three times the rate of Hispanic students. As Orum (1986) noted, while the number of Hispanic students attending college between 1975 and 1980 remained steady, these students as a percentage of Hispanic high school graduates dropped markedly. Orum stated that:

Hispanic college enrollment as a percentage of Hispanic high school graduates declined from 35.4 percent in 1975 to 29.9 percent in 1980. Hispanic college enrollment as a percentage of the 18 to 24 year-old Hispanic population declined from 20.4 percent in 1976 to 16.1 in 1980. In 1983, there were approximately 134,000 Hispanic students 18 to 19 years old enrolled in college, which represents a decrease in the percentage of high school graduates enrolled in college from 49.8 percent in 1980 to 46.5 percent in 1983 (p. 39).

Available data show that Hispanics generally enroll in college at much lower rates than do white college students (Lee, 1985, United States Department of Education, 1988). Data from the Current Population Survey of 1984 showed that Hispanic 18 to 19 year olds comprised only 4.7 percent of post-secondary enrollments, compared to

88.6 percent for whites and 9.2 percent for African Americans. Higher education for Hispanics has become higher education according to race and class. Most Hispanics have enrolled in community colleges due to the resistance of four year colleges to re-examine and re-structure admission policies and practices (Duran, 1983). Thus, Hispanics are concentrated at the less prestigious and less well-funded institutions. Hispanics are twice as likely as whites to attend two-year colleges and half as likely to attend universities (Lee, 1985; Olivas, 1982; Orum, 1986). In 1984, only 23 percent of white full-time students attended two year colleges, while 42 percent of Hispanic students attended these institutions (Olivas, 1986). This misdistribution of Hispanics within the system indicates that a large group of Hispanic students seeking a full time, traditional experience are doing so in institutions for commuter or part-time students.

Although two year institutions have increased Hispanic access and have played a major role in higher education for Hispanics, these institutions suffer from the inherent problems of student transfers, part time faculty, commuter programs and funding patterns. Hispanic students are concentrated in fewer than two percent of the more than 3100 collegiate institutions in the country, and in institutions that do not have historical missions to serve Hispanic students (Lee, 1985, Olivas, 1986). There are only 18 Hispanic majority colleges in the mainland United States and, of these, only 3 were established with the specific purpose of serving the educational needs of Hispanic students. Orum(1986) cited data indicating that just 58 of the 3,306 institutions of higher education in the continental United States enrolled 29.5 percent of all Hispanic students who were enrolled in institutions of higher education in the fall of 1984.

The transition from two to four year institutions does not seem to be frequent among Hispanics. For example, in 1982, the University of Texas at Austin enrolled only 510 Hispanic students as undergraduate transfers, and these comprised only 8.7 percent of the total transfers. In general, while in 1976, twenty-one percent of all Hispanic students enrolled in two-year institutions transferred to four-year colleges, in 1979, only 15 percent did so (United States House of Representatives Hearings, 1983). Although some students who enroll in two-year colleges do transfer to four-year institutions and complete bachelor's degrees, students enrolled in two-year colleges are less likely to complete four-year degrees (Astin, 1984).

Although there are no data to identify the reasons why Hispanics go to two-year institutions rather than four-year colleges, one can theorize that: (a) students assume that attending four-year institutions requires at least twice as much financial resources as are needed to attend a community college, (b) once enrolled in a community college the transition is made difficult given the lack of counseling regarding courses eligible for transfer and the admission standards, (c) students often weigh their decision to transfer against criteria related to proximity and employment possibilities.

Hispanic students who do pursue higher education are the least likely to be enrolled in universities. Of those Hispanic students enrolled in institutions of higher education in 1980, only 13 percent were enrolled in universities, compared to 25 percent of whites and 14.2 of African Americans (Lee, 1985; Orum, 1986; United States Department of Education, 1984).

Current data indicate that Hispanic students are most likely to be enrolled in public institutions. In 1980, 86.1 percent of Hispanic college students were attending public institutions compared to 77.8 percent of whites and 79.1 of African Americans (United States Department of Education, 1982).

Hispanic students are not well-represented across college disciplines. Hispanics are underrepresented in the areas of mathematics, science and engineering. Of the more than 73,000 baccalaureates awarded in engineering in 1986, just six percent went to non-Asian minority students; of the more than 16,000 mathematics degrees, just seven went to minorities; in the physical sciences, only seven degrees were awarded to minorities (Massachusetts Institute of Technology, 1990).

Faculty and Administration Representation

Hispanics have not entered American institutions of higher education in any significant fashion. Current data on Hispanic post-secondary faculty and administration report little progress in achieving proportional representation. Hispanic youth do not see too many Hispanics in faculty or administrative positions in institutions of post-secondary education in spite of affirmative action regulations. By 1972, the year affirmative action in higher education was initiated, Hispanic faculties were non-existent in institutions of secondary education. For example, at that time there were 1500 faculty members who could be identified as Mexican American; and of these, 600 were at community colleges (Washington & Harvey, 1989). The number of Hispanic faculty members increased until 1976, then began to level off or declined. Between 1977 and 1984, national faculty representation for Hispanics dropped from about 1.7 percent to 1.4 percent (Washington & Harvey, 1989).

By 1985, only 1.4 percent of all faculty of institutions of higher education were Hispanic, including faculty in Spanish and bilingual education departments (Olivas, 1986). Tenure track Hispanic faculty are even fewer in number, since many Hispanics are employed in special programs which do not provide for tenured track positions or important policy making decisions. There is a shortage of bilingual counselors and advisers who can assist Hispanic students at the college level. Non-discrimination in higher education in employing and promoting faculty and administration has been grossly inadequate in meeting the equality of opportunity for Hispanics. Federal involvement in the enforcement of affirmative action policies in higher education began with the filing of a complaint against the entire academic community by the Women's Equality Action League (WEAL) in 1970. The complaint charged higher education with an "industry wide" pattern of sex discrimination. Under an executive order issued by President Lyndon B. Johnson in 1965, there was a requirement that all federal contracts include clauses agreeing not to discriminate against any employee or applicant for employment because of race, color, religion, or national origin. A non-discrimination provision on the basis of sex was added to the requirement in 1968 (Olivas, 1986). However, Hispanics are at the lower end of the scale of the full-time faculty ranks, most of them clustered as instructors and lecturers; few of them are hired as distinguished professors or full professors.

Hispanics have not controlled the political or organizational structures of education; rather, they have been held in subordinate positions by post-secondary institutions. The leadership in institutions of post-secondary education is non-Hispanic. By 1985, there were 6 Hispanic four-year college presidents, and 20 two-year college presidents in the mainland United States. There are very few Hispanic college trustees or post-secondary coordinating boards or commissioners of education. Olivas (1986) indicated that a survey of two-year college trustees revealed that only .6 percent were Hispanic, while a study of post-secondary coordinating boards found 1.1 percent of the commissioners to be Hispanic. These are the individuals who establish educational policy for institutions of higher education. Neither sector has been particularly responsive to the concerns of Hispanic parents or students and does not have knowledge of Hispanic students' academic and intellectual characteristics and needs. Search committees are the standard tool for screening and interviewing candidates for all these leadership positions. Their composition and working strategies are important in choosing committee members and in the identification of criteria to select qualified and ethnically representative individuals. As Washington & Harvey (1989) said: "Affirmative action offices reflect the mission and purpose of their institutions. They work to set goals rather than respond to the timeliness and goals set by others" (p. 2).

One reason for the limited amount of Hispanic faculty is that the prevailing policy of seniority and tenure rights was favored over affirmative action as the basis for laying off and firing faculty. The elimination of ethnic studies programs reduced the presence of Hispanic faculty members. In the City University of New York system, the Puerto Rican instructional faculty decreased from 2.4 percent to 2.3 percent between 1975 and 1986 (Rodriguez-Fraticelli, 1989). The reduction was felt especially among full-time faculty. Whereas in 1975, there were 303 full-time Puerto Rican professors, by 1986 their number had dropped to 165, a 45.5 percent decline (Rodriguez-Fraticelli, 1989). Hispanic faculty members are found mostly in community colleges. For example, by 1986, 29 percent of the City University of New York's total Puerto Rican teaching force was located at Hostos Community College.

In summary, Hispanic students as well as Hispanic faculty members are underrepresented at the college level. This underrepresentation is worsening with the years. There is no bright future in the decade of the 1990's unless affirmative action practices are again reinforced and practiced in all institutions, especially in four-year colleges and universities.

College Retention and Graduation Rate
of Hispanic Youth

Retaining enrolled students until graduation is one of the goals of institutions of higher education. The closer the relationship between a student's needs and abilities and the standards and strengths of the college, the higher are the chances that a student will graduate. The two measures of Hispanic participation in higher education are the number of students who enroll and stay in college and those who actually complete degree programs at the various levels of the post-secondary educational system. Hispanics suffer considerable losses among those staying in college and in those graduating from college. Hispanics are also underrepresented when comparing numbers enrolled to degrees earned. Hispanic college performance has become part of the so called revolving door syndrome. Many Hispanics are more likely than other college students to drop out. Brown et al. (1985) reported that over half of the Hispanics who entered college in 1972 had dropped out within four years, compared with one-third of whites. Hispanics have the lowest rate of graduation, even after allowing seven and up to eleven years after high school to complete college. The percentage of Hispanic undergraduates in 1986 (5.3) was almost double the percentage of degrees granted to Hispanics (2.7 percent). The American Council on Education (1989) stated that: "Hispanic students represented 3.2 percent of graduate school enrollment in 1986" (p. 10). As of 1984, only 3.2 percent of Hispanics over 29 were college graduates (United States Department of Education, 1984). The college completion rates for white non-Hispanics was more than three times higher than that of Hispanics (Astin, 1984). Overall, this rate is 59 percent for whites, 42 percent for African Americans, and 31.3 percent for Hispanics (Astin, 1984). Degree data for 1980–81 indicate an increase to only 4.2 percent of the associate degrees, 2.3 percent of bachelor's degrees, 2.1 percent of master's degrees, and 1.4 percent of the doctoral degrees (Brown et al., 1985). The 1986–87 college degree attainments indicate similar Hispanic attainment rates: 2.7 percent of baccalaureates, 2.4 percent of master degrees and 2.2 percent of doctoral degrees (American Council on Education, 1989, United States Department of Education, 1988). Though high school completion and college attendance are on the rise, very few Hispanics manage to complete baccalaureate programs in the traditional four-year period. City University of New York has been marked over the years by the tendency to not graduate the majority of students who enter the system. In City University of New York colleges, the graduation rate in 1984 for regular senior college students, after seven years, was 36.4. In community colleges the projected graduation rate for regular students was 25.7 percent (Rodriguez-Fraticelli, 1989). Given these figures, there can be no doubt that the degree attainment rate is low for Hispanic students, especially for Puerto Ricans.

The American Council on Education (1989) stated that despite this underrepresentation, Hispanics have registered increases in the number of degrees earned between 1986 and 1987, although these increases are mostly seen in Hispanic women. They mentioned that:

> However, women again accounted for a large segment of the gains. Overall increases in the number of degrees awarded to Hispanics between 1976 and 1987 were as follows: 50.3 percent at the bachelor's level, 32.9 percent at the master's level and 90.1 percent at the first-professional level. During the same period, Hispanic women were granted 1.5 times the number of bachelor's and master's degrees as in 1976, and quadruple the number of first-professional degrees. From 1978 to 1988, the number of doctorate degrees earned by Hispanics also rose by 25.6 percent, with Hispanic women receiving 75 percent more Ph.D.'s in 1988 (p. 10).

College completion rates also vary by state. Hispanics in the ten states where most Hispanics reside have substantially lower college graduation rates than whites in all states and lower rates than African Americans in every state but Florida. College graduation rates for Hispanics were lowest in Illinois (5.9), California (6.1), and Texas (6.8). The highest Hispanic graduation rates were in Florida (13.8), reflecting the higher educational status of Cubans (United States Department of Education, 1984).

Educators in institutions of higher education raise the question of why some Hispanics graduate from college and others do not. There are several factors that affect Hispanic participation in institutions of secondary education. High school performance is a good predictor of Hispanic college success. Duran (1983) qualified this conclusion by saying that data showed that persistence in school, expectations about schooling success, background measures of parental education, and socioeconomic status are meaningfully related to predictions of

Hispanic performance during the first two years of college and also are predictors of Hispanics' successful completion of college.

Conclusion

Accessibility to higher education is more than just the mere availability of colleges and universities. It entails the recruitment efforts expended by institutions in order to achieve a representative diverse student population. Accessibility also encompasses the academic standards that determine the admission and subsequent enrollment of student clientele. It is also the development of programs and special services that are relevant and useful in restricting attention to retaining and graduating students. But, higher education in United States continues to be distributed unequally, with Hispanics receiving the worst share. Hopes for significant educational progress have not been realized, and current trends suggest that Hispanic youth are not participating in higher education as expected. Hispanics are not attending and graduating from college in significant numbers.

Changes and modifications are necessary to improve Hispanics' access to institutions of post-secondary education. Hispanics' attitudes toward college need to be more positive. Hispanics need to realize that they can attend and graduate from college, that financial aid will be available, and that they have the academic aptitude to do college work. Once the Hispanic youth's self-image toward college is enhanced, they will find the channels to enroll in colleges. Hispanic students need better elementary and secondary preparation. Students need a mastery approach to learning. In schools using such an approach, all children will master the basic curriculum, at their own pace, and will be provided with the materials and resources needed to succeed. This approach will give Hispanic students a sense of success. Successful students seldom drop out of school. Hispanic students will stay in school, and many more will go on to college. Virtually all students are capable of mastering a core curriculum that will provide them with the option of post-secondary education.

A significant number of Hispanic youth are limited in the English language. These are often students with proficiency and mastery of basic skills in Spanish. Yet, colleges across the United States insist on the demonstration of mastery of English as a prerequisite of college admission. In fact, the assumption is that they cannot be accepted into the regular college curriculum until they can speak, read and write English as well as the other fluent college students. And, if accepted, they are placed in remedial classes which, in many instances, carry no credit, although remedial students pay the same tuition as do regular students. The result of these programs is the limited amount of students who are able to finish the college degree in a regular amount of time. Limited-English-proficient students need to be part of the regular curriculum. More bilingual college programs are needed to provide students not only with the opportunity to take a few courses in Spanish and English as a second language; but programs are needed that provide students with the majority of the courses taught in English and Spanish. In these programs, the objective is to prepare individuals with enough skills in the subject areas using a bilingual approach.

Public schools and universities should be partners in developing strategies for getting more Hispanic youths into higher education. University personnel must reach down into the schools to work and motivate the students who will form the college classes a few years later. Mentoring programs, counseling programs, and tutoring programs help students to feel that someone believes in them and thinks that they are capable of doing college work. Professors of education, sociology, public policy, and related disciplines should teach at least once a week in the public schools to share with students information about college life and the academic benefits of a college degree. A college education must become a real and tangible possibility to Hispanic children and youth.

Finally, college education has become very costly for many students, especially for Hispanics. The concern about debt and the reluctance of some students and families to incur those debts inhibit the education of many Hispanic youth. Qualified Hispanic students who cannot afford to pay, and have been admitted to a private or state college, should receive fee waivers and not only costly loans, grants, or aid. States need to recognize that the social and economic returns of education to society more than pay back society's initial investment.

CHAPTER 11

The Future of Hispanic Children and Youth in the United States

On October 16, 1978, *Time* magazine printed an article "Hispanic Americans: Soon The Biggest Minority." The article alluded to the 1960's being the African American power decade and to the 1980's being the decade of the Hispanics. Certainly, by 1989 the number of Hispanics in the United States reached 19 million and continues to grow with the projection being between 23 and 27 million by the year 2000. The growing Hispanic population presents challenges to United States policy makers in nearly every area, but, most urgently, in education, labor, socioeconomic development and social programs. Hispanics with their relatively high fertility and immigration rates are producing a significant and growing part of today's relatively small cohort of children on whom the burden of an aging American society is going to be exceedingly heavy. It is important to ask whether this country can continue to afford treating any portion of its children and youth as expendable.

The future of Hispanic children and youth depends on how the adult population of whites, African Americans, Asians and Hispanics, among others, contribute to their well-being. Hispanic children's and youth's development as well as their future require a holistic approach involving a wide range of professionals, parents, private and public agencies and Hispanic leaders working together for their children and youth. Effective programs must be based on a clear understanding of the Hispanic children's and youth's unique place in today's United States society—their history, their social, cultural, and linguistic characteristics, and their needs. The challenges and opportunities that such a youthful, rapidly growing and diverse population possesses for society are profound. The complex problems created by the interconnections among employment, education, literacy, cultural values, income, living environment and family responsibility require complex solutions. Johnston & Parker (1987) state the problem as follows: "The choices are not simply between on-the-job training, basic skills remediation programs for teenagers, but any investments in child care, pregnancy prevention, welfare reform, big brother programs and other possible interventions" (p. 115).

There are variables that contribute to the success or failure of Hispanic children and youth. It is important to reduce popular misconceptions about Hispanics and make known their cultural, economic and social contributions to society. American institutions do not understand the fact that although Hispanics share common characteristics, in many ways they are different and unique. Hispanic children are significantly affected by public and private institutions and are vulnerable to them. The society at large needs to be educated about the status, concerns and contributions of Hispanic Americans. For example, many American institutions such as schools, support agencies, health and criminal justice systems, and institutions of higher education presume that Hispanic children and youth are a homogeneous group, particularly if they are poor. Also, the lives of Hispanics living in the United States have been complicated by racial prejudice, by the language barrier, and by their isolation into segregated neighborhoods and schools, locking many of them into low-level, marginal jobs. This chapter outlines specific steps that need to be implemented to provide for the progress and development of Hispanic children and youth.

Authorities such as Valdivieso and Davis (1988), Johnston & Parker (1987), Moore & Pachon (1985) and Wilson (1987), among others, describing the trends of Hispanics in the 1990's, have come to the following conclusions: (a) the Hispanic population will continue to grow more rapidly than the United States population as a whole over the next decade, comprising over 10 percent of the United States population. (b) Hispanic children and youth will constitute about 16 percent of both the school aged-children and of those 18 to 24 years old. (c) After two decades of low fertility the United States may begin to experience labor shortages during the 1990's because fewer young Americans will be entering the labor force. (d) The overall socioeconomic status of Hispanics will remain low. These statements summarize the projected condition of Hispanics in the 1990's and serve as the foundation for the recommendations that follow.

Improvement of the Socioeconomic Conditions of Hispanic Children and Youth

Hispanic children and youth want to become active participants in the economic, social and political institutions of the United States without abandoning their language and cultural characteristics that mean so much to them. The socioeconomic conditions of Hispanic children and youth are inadequate, especially in the Mexican, Puerto Rican and Dominican origin populations. Poverty is one of the characteristics of a significant number of these children. Valdivieso & Davis (1988) indicated that "poverty rates are likely to persist among Hispanics in the 1990's. Actions to curb the high poverty levels must deal primarily with: a) education and job training, b) discrimination in hiring and promotion, and c) access to welfare programs by the Hispanic poor, especially single-parent families" (p. 8). Large proportions of children are growing up with inadequate housing, clothing, health care and educational opportunities. As adults they will scarcely be in a position to compete in modern society. To improve the employment opportunities in order to improve the socioeconomic level of Hispanics, especially their children and youth, the following steps are recommended:

1. Develop the basic literacy skills of dropouts and other high-risk youth through the development of appropriate and realistic programs that take into consideration their cultural, linguistic and educational characteristics. When basic skills instruction is followed by appropriate training or employment experience, Hispanic children and youth achieve substantial lifetime gains in earnings (Banks, 1982; Brown et al., 1985; Ford Foundation, 1983; Orum, 1988; & Treviño, 1986).

2. Promote public/private partnerships that address the training of youth. There is a need to design and implement effective employment programs involving business organizations, governments, training institutions, schools and community organizations. Jobs need to be available to Hispanics, and Hispanics need to possess the skills necessary for the job (Ford Foundation, 1983; Garcia, 1981; Johnston & Parker, 1987).

3. Improve the economic reinforcement provided by the home to children. Hispanic homes need to be places of financial and social reinforcement and encouragement. In many instances, children are

raised in homes where there are no working adults, and all are socially dependent. There is a need for parents to show their children the dignity and rewards of being employed. Children who are raised in homes where parents work, where there is a salary, tend to be successful workers and productive citizens. Parents can motivate their children to be future workers by placing value on education and in getting a degree and having a career. Homes must share with the schools and the society expectations for the child. There is a need to extensively present Hispanic role models to Hispanic children and youth.

But poverty is not the only focus of the discussion of Hispanic children, which reduces differences to social class variation. Their educational status needs to be improved, too.

Improvement of Educational Conditions of Hispanic Children and Youth

Still, it is in education that the gap in achievement between Hispanics and other groups, extending from preschool through graduate training, is the widest. The 1980's was cited as the decade of educational reform, a time when national attention was focused on the improvement of schools. This reform has yet to address the separate and unequal context that American schools offer their Hispanic students who have not been the beneficiaries of policies which have sought to increase academic and graduation standards, improve curriculum offerings, reduce teacher/student ratios, and provide effective classrooms and schools. Rather, the increasing segregation of Hispanic students in central cities has contributed to limiting access to successful English language development programs, college preparatory and advanced placement curriculum (Arias, 1986; New York State Education Department, 1988c; Steinberg, Blende & Chan, 1984; and Strother, 1986). The isolation of Hispanic students from access to the benefits of American public schooling poses a great threat to the ideal for equal educational opportunity.

There has been some progress in the educational development of Hispanic children and youth. Since 1985, Hispanics have made significant gains on scores on the Scholastic Aptitude Tests, one of the traditional measures of academic success. Hispanic students' high school and college attainment levels in 1988 were at all-time highs. About 51 percent of Hispanics aged 25 and over completed four years of high school and/or some college in 1987 and 1988, the highest percent ever recorded (Bureau of the Census, 1988d). Still, it is in education where ethnic differences are more marked. But, the report notes that, despite these improvements, the proportion of non-Hispanics completing high school (78 percent) and college (21 percent) remained higher than that of Hispanics. Hispanics are behind in educational achievement from pre-school through the college level.

The schools must work for better ways to motivate Hispanic students and engage them to stay in school. Schools must identify the specific needs of and approaches that best serve Hispanic students and other ethnic-minority students. Schools need to create a climate of excellence, demanding a great deal from the students and involving parents to also contribute to their children's success.

There is a need to reduce overcrowded schools and increase resource allocations to predominantly minority schools. The literature on successful schools indicates that the teacher/student ratio is an important indicator of success. Teachers need the classroom flexibility to provide small group and individualized instruction to students. Teachers need opportunities to meet their children's parents or guardians and to have positive interactions with them. Schools serving Hispanic students need necessary resources, materials, and programs directed at their particular and unique needs.

Schools and parents need to improve students' self-concepts. The development of Hispanic children's self-concepts is essential to social and academic success. Hispanic children need to have the conviction that they can, with the necessary effort, succeed in doing school work and excel in those areas in which they have talent.

Recommendations have been made to decrease dropouts among Hispanics. Solving the dropout problem is a tremendous challenge, and it is among the top priorities of educators and elected officials at every level throughout the country. Programs of early intervention may help in preventing drop outs among Hispanic youth. Early childhood education prevention programs may be one of the solutions to the dropout problem. Pre-kindergarten schooling for Hispanics is recommended to reduce the gap between them and other children over time. Hispanic children, beginning at an early age, need to be enrolled in quality nursery and kindergarten programs. For those children who come from Spanish-speaking homes, both languages need to be used, with an emphasis on oral Spanish and English language development, and with a special focus on building concepts and vocabulary. The cost of early childhood education will pale next to the savings in welfare and criminal justice costs. The literature lists specific recommendations to decrease high school dropout rates. These recommendations are:

1. Strong parental involvement and parent education programs. Many parents have been conditioned to accept lower quality. Many are convinced by educators that their children must be trained for vocational pursuits. These parents seldom confront the school, primarily because they have been socialized to accept the school's authority. One way to alter this situation is to train minority parents assertively to confront the school organization with legitimized demands for equal education. Schools must genuinely desire to involve parents and not simply pay lip service to the concept of parental involvement. To plan effectively for parent involvement, it becomes critical for schools to begin to engage in real dialogue with parents, to listen to their needs and concerns, and to have the resources to respond to them. It will also require a redefinition of what parent involvement means and include reaching out to parents and sharing the educational program with the community at large.

2. Schools should consider the idea of creating "Parent Centers" that would have flexible hours and allow parents to participate at their convenience. Such centers could help parents to negotiate the school system, provide other social services, serve as the advocate for improved parent-school relationships, offer parenting skills training, and other programs identified as needed by parents. To help develop adult education programs that could be offered on site to parents, center staff members should be bilingual and able to recognize the cultural backgrounds of parents.

3. Intensive in-service training for teachers focused on increasing the level of awareness of cultural and socioeconomic differences among students. Presently, school personnel are not prepared to work with Hispanic children and youth. School personnel do not all understand the diversity among Hispanics in terms of language, culture, family structure, and organization, among others, and, in many instances, the school's curriculum and teaching approaches do not reflect this diversity. Schools need to recognize that when students' languages and cultures are incorporated into school programs they are significant contributors to academic success. Schools should "add" to students linguistic and cultural knowledge rather than eliminating their native language and cultural identity.

4. Student leadership forums and similar personal development programs designed to enhance students' self-confidence and leadership skills. Students at all levels need to develop a sense of wanting to improve, and a realization that they can. Leadership forums can provide this important ingredient to children and youth. This initiative can be developed with work-related programs that will enable students to remain in school while working. These programs usually relate elements of the academic or vocational curriculum to actual work experience to encourage students to recognize the important relationship between occupational success and schooling. Intensive cooperative efforts should be initiated with local community agencies, churches, civic organizations, clubs, and other appropriate organizations to provide tutorial, personal development, and counseling services to dropout-prone youth and their families. Some of these approaches can also include community internships and cooperative learning programs for at-risk or highly-at-risk students. Counseling approaches are recommended to these students who experience low self-esteem, alienation from school and family, or behavior problems. Hispanic students who experience academic failure may also display low self-esteem or negative attitudes toward language, school, and the mainstream culture. These programs address personal problems common to at-risk students as well as their need for academic and personal direction.

5. Tutorial approaches to reduce or prevent school dropouts. In tutorial programs, students receive individual instruction to enhance their academic achievement and motivate them to remain in school (National Clearinghouse for Bilingual Education, 1989b). One example of a successful tutoring program is found in the Valued Youth Partnership program in San Antonio, Texas, developed by the Intercultural Development Research Association (IDRA), in which high school students are trained to tutor junior high school at-risk students several hours a week. The key change agents for promoting academic success on the part of Hispanic children and youth must be skillful, dedicated teachers who represent children and youth, who actually believe they can and will learn if properly taught, and who understand the types of homes and cultures from which the children come. Such teachers do not survive and develop unless they have educational leaders who believe the same things (Sherman, Celebuski, Fink, Levine & St. John, 1987). Specifically, recommendations to improve

students' attendance and graduation at the college level include alternative programs for students who do not perform well in traditional school programs. Programs in which native language support classes in the content area and intensive instruction in English are provided to students before they transfer to regular high schools are listed as alternative programs. For example, Duran (1986) recommended that in order to improve Hispanic students' access to college there is a need to conduct research on the procedures for guiding admissions staff interpretation of Hispanics' high school grade information and admission tests scores. The following factors may be reviewed: (a) Candidates' language background and English language proficiency. (b) Candidates' exposure to schooling in Spanish and academic achievement in Spanish content. (c) High educational aspirations and high achievement motivation that are coupled with lower high school grades and admission tests scores than expected. (d) Higher than expected high school grades or admission test scores given the parents' educational background and income. (e) The presence of financial and other obligations of the family during high school coupled with higher than expected high school grades and admission test scores.

In summary, there is much that needs to be done by policy makers and educators to improve the educational status of Hispanic children and youth in the United States. Several approaches to dropout prevention have been implemented in the United States, some of them with varying degree of success. These approaches include early childhood education, tutorial programs, counseling programs, alternative curriculums and work-related programs.

Improvement of Community and Parental Support for Hispanic Children and Youth

Community and parent involvement are critically important in the future of Hispanic children and youth. It has been found that the most successful schools are those that have strong, enduring links to the communities they serve, and that successful students have parents who are willing and able to become partners in teaching and learning. Hispanic leaders must do more of what they are doing to help schools and social agencies to better serve their children. Parents play a significant role in their children's well-being. They can model positive attitudes and values to reinforce the school's goals. Programs are motivators. Parents are program supporters when they engage in advocacy activities at the local, state and national levels. Parents can be involved in maintaining and improving program quality through direct contact with local communities and educational organizations. Parents can lobby the city and the school administration to initiate, maintain or extend programs that benefit their children. Parents can lobby legislators in local, regional and national governments to secure legislation that will promote socioeconomic and educational opportunities for them and their children. Alliances and collaborations among schools, business and community organizations, and parents' organizations coupled with incentives for Hispanic children's and youth's development are also important factors. Work partnership programs also strengthen these ties. Partnerships with businesses need support beyond just having jobs built into them to include social service, mentoring and school-based support.

Information and collaboration need to be shared within all of these partnerships. Across organizations, coordination must also entail evaluation of all these efforts to ensure the continued social, economic, and educational improvements in the conditions of the Hispanic children and youth.

Development of a Sense of Social Cohesion and Belonging

One of the greatest risks to our society is that so many young Hispanic children and youth do not feel that they have a real stake in the society's well-being. They lack social cohesion—a sense of being an integral and important part of the larger society. This lack of social cohesion may be reflected in the Hispanic economic and political participation, and the society's recognition of the value and validity of different cultures (Hayes-Bautista, Schink, Werner & Chapa, 1984).

Parents, schools, and political organizations can contribute to building social cohesion by teaching necessary survival, academic, and life skills and by preparing children and youth to succeed in all aspects of life and work. Hispanics do not participate fully in the political process and often feel that decisions are made at their expense. The apparent Hispanic political apathy is a reflection of their belief that their vote and their involvement do not count or would not change their socioeconomic and educational status. This attitude needs to be changed. But it can be changed only through their active involvement in all aspects of the society, especially in their political involvement.

Hispanic children and youth need to be motivated to feel that they also contribute to the United States society's well-being: a sense of being an integral and important part of the larger society and, subsequently, some obligation to participate in it. The school, the parents, and the local community play key roles in this social cohesion. Educators and schools can contribute to this social cohesion by: a) teaching necessary academic and life skills and by preparing students to succeed in all aspects of life and work, b) teaching students to know how to participate in the political process, c) demonstrating the value of different cultures that enables all cultural groups to be included in the societal whole, rather than excluded because they do not conform to a majority culture or are perceived as not being the right culture.

Recommendation for Federal, State and Local Initiatives

There is a need for inspiring Hispanic political representation so that the voices representing Hispanics needs and the creation of social, economic and educational programs to benefit Hispanics may have a receptive forum in Congress. The Hispanic political presence in Congress will depend on the number of Hispanics who register and vote. There is a need to duplicate the role of organizations such as the National Association of Latino Elected and Appointed Officials (NALEO), the National Council of La Raza, that have contributed to the recent increase of Hispanic voters and legal residents to become citizens, and the Office of the Commonwealth of Puerto Rico in New York in increasing Hispanic voters. Hispanic women have played a key role in becoming more involved in social, educational issues. Today's younger Hispanic females register and vote at higher rates than their male counterparts.

Hispanics are especially vulnerable to restrictive federal policies in education, employment and health. For example, attempts to reduce or eliminate bilingual education programs will negatively affect language-minority children, especially those Hispanic children who are already more likely to drop out of school and likely to leave at an earlier age than white or African American children. Reducing access to bilingual education will increase rather than prevent this trend. The minimal federal support that literacy programs receive negatively affects Hispanics who have the highest rate of illiteracy of any group in the country.

In summary, Hispanic children and youth need specific attention to their needs. Such efforts are needed as: (a) focusing on the Hispanic children's and youth's ethnic/racial, linguistic and cultural differences, for the purpose of helping them to cope and live in a society that promotes uniformity and conformity and does not value pluralism; (b) accepting the idea that diversity does not necessarily mean inferiority. These children are an asset to the United States in terms of their bilingualism and biculturalism. Thus, interested institutions need to look at and build on their strengths.

Conclusion

Hispanics constitute a large pool of potentially productive citizens and workers. Hispanics form a sizeable proportion of the United States labor force. However, the social, economic, and educational deficiencies of Hispanics pose problems in terms of unemployment and poverty unless appropriate action is taken. Who is responsible is the question posed in a position paper published by Quest International (1987). The authors answer the question of responsibility by saying:

> These barriers will not fall until the issue of institutional change—producing good schools for all students—is addressed in a creative and positive way. Good schools reach out to parents and build bridges with their communities and their constituents. They respect the language and culture of their communities. They respect parents as the primary educators of their children, regardless of their race, ethnicity, or social class. They are orderly, civilized places where the expectations of all students are high-expectations supported both by the faculty and the community.
>
> Local Hispanic leadership groups must be involved, networks must be built to support parents in their demands for good schools, and, where appropriate, parents must be provided with the kinds of skills and knowledge they will need in order to become effective advocates on their children's behalf (p. 10).

Hispanics themselves need to have a greater knowledge and understanding of their economic, social and political situations and of the roots of their disadvantage, along with the development of the infrastructure that will increase their participation in mainstream society. Every Hispanic adult needs to make an effort to improve the socioeconomic, educational, physical and mental health of Hispanic children and youth.

But, Hispanic children have been stereotyped as "newcomers" and as children concerned with only two issues: immigration and educational attainment, especially as it is related to bilingual education. There is a need to provide adequate information on the full range of Hispanic children's concerns, on the status of children in our population, and their contributions to American life.

There is a need to increase communication between African Americans and Hispanics, perhaps to build a national agenda, since there is tension between both groups and this tension affects the communication of Hispanic and African American children. There is also the need to establish more positive communication with the other racial/ethnic groups in American society, to build a sense of cooperation and sharing among all groups. In the long run, everyone is responsible for the well-being of Hispanic children and youth in the United States.

CHAPTER 12

Advocacy for Hispanic Children and Youth:
A Resource Guide

There are numerous agencies, organizations and associations in the public and private sectors which have as one of their objectives the advocacy of Hispanic children and youth to promote their social, economic, and educational development. The objective of this chapter is to highlight these organizations, emphasizing their advocacy role for children and youth. This chapter is divided in two parts. Part one identifies organizations that have received national recognition for, among other things, promoting the well-being of Hispanic children and youth. The following is a selective list of these agencies:

Aspira of America Inc.
Congressional Hispanic Caucus Institute Inc.
Cuban American Legal Defense and Education Fund (CALDEF)
Cuban American National Council
Intercultural Development Research Associates
Institute for Puerto Rican Policy
League of United Latin American Citizens (LULAC)
Mexican-American Legal Defense and Educational Fund (MALDEF)
National Association for Bilingual Education (NABE)
National Association of Latino Elected and Appointed Officials (NALEO)
National Coalition of Hispanic Health and Human Services Organization (COSSMHO)
National Council of La Raza

| National Hispanic Scholarship Fund (NHSF) | Puerto Rican Legal Defense and Education Fund (PRLDEF) |
| National Puerto Rican Forum | |

The second part of the chapter presents a selective list of organizations, associations or agencies that have contributed directly or indirectly to Hispanic development. Most of these organizations are housed in local communities and serve several ethnic and age groups. The objective of the list, which in no way is a list of all the available Hispanic organizations and agencies in the United States, is to serve as a resource guide to readers. The listing of these agencies, organizations or associations is grouped by topical areas which reflect the content discussed throughout this book. These topics are:

Child, Youth, and Family Advocacy (Adoption, foster care, public assistance and child welfare)
Education (Language, elementary and secondary education and higher education)
Health (AIDS, drugs, pregnancy and mental health)
Immigration
Youth Labor

Selected Organizational Profiles

Aspira Association, Inc.
(1112 16th Street, N.W. Suite 340, Washington, D.C. 20036; 202 835-3600)

Organization, Scope and Structure
The ASPIRA Association, Inc. is a national non-profit organization serving Puerto Rican and other Latino youth through leadership development and education. Its ten offices are located in five states, Puerto Rico, and the District of Columbia. ASPIRA is the oldest and largest Hispanic youth organization in the country, serving over 13,000 youth annually with a combined staff of 220.

ASPIRA's central mission is to advance the socioeconomic development of the Latino community. To fulfill that mission, it has worked for 28 years to provide more than 165,000 youth with the emotional, intellectual, and practical resources they need to remain in school and contribute to their community. At the same time, Aspira has endeavored to bring about change in the environmental conditions that limit young people's development. ASPIRA uses an integrated model known as the ASPIRA Process. Unlike many programs that focus on a youth's problems, the ASPIRA Process is an enrichment model based on the belief that our youth can succeed and that collective effort can bring about positive change. The ASPIRA Process means working directly with students and parents in their communities to develop self-confidence, leadership skills, educational achievement, and a dedication to the improvement of their community.

ASPIRA has local Associate offices in the Bronx and Brooklyn, New York; Carolina, Puerto Rico; Chicago, Illinois; Newark, Jersey City, Trenton, Camden, and Paterson, New Jersey; Philadelphia, Pennsylvania; and Dade County, Florida. These Associates, along with ASPIRA's broader network of over 2,000 community-based organizations, local and national policy makers, and corporate representatives, receive information and assistance from ASPIRA's Washington, D. C. National Office.

Advocacy/Socio-educational Activities

Aspira has identified three major goals designed to prepare Hispanic youth: to develop the leadership potential of Hispanic youth, to motivate and assist Hispanic youth in their educational development, and to increase the access of Hispanic youth to quality education and leadership training. The National Office works on short- and long-range strategic planning for the Association, facilitates expansion of services, ensures quality programs, and promotes coordination and communication within the Association. To this end, the office develops and administers national programs, including:

1. The ASPIRA Public Policy Leadership Program, which brings together 90 students per year in six sites to study public policy and work with local and national policy makers in community service internships.
2. The Aspira National Health Careers Program, which has for nearly two decades provided over 1000 high school and college students per year with exposure to role models, information on health professions, internship opportunities, individual counseling, and academic and financial support.

3. The Hispanic Community Mobilization for Dropout Prevention project, which provides Latino parents in ten major cities with practical information and assistance in implementing strategies to help improve their children's performance in school.
4. Research and development programs to increase the access of Latino students to quality educational opportunities through publication of research and development of relations with policy makers who affect the Hispanic community.
5. Studies on dropout prevention to document reasons why Hispanics are dropping out at such a high rate and developing guidelines for dropout prevention policy development.

Congressional Hispanic Caucus Institute, Inc.
(504 C Street NE, Washington, D.C. 20002; 202 543-1771)

Organization, Scope and Structure
The Congressional Hispanic Caucus Institute, Inc., is a nonprofit, nonpartisan organization founded by the Hispanic Members of Congress to provide young Hispanic students with an opportunity to learn about the function and operation of the United States political system.

Advocacy/Socio-educational Activities
The Institute serves as a clearinghouse for educational programs available throughout the country. Through its fellowship and internship programs the Institute offers leadership training to our community's future leaders. The Institute also highlights the contribution of Hispanic Americans to the betterment of the Hispanic community and United States mainstream society.

Cuban-American Legal Defense and Education Fund (CALDEF)
(2119 S. Webster Street, Fort Wayne, IN 46804, 219 745-5421)

Organization, Scope and Structure
Cuban-American Legal Defense and Education Fund is a nonprofit organization funded by corporate and public contributions, established to help Cuban-Americans and other Hispanics gain equal treatment and equal opportunity in the fields of education, employment, housing, politics, and justice.

Advocacy/Socio-educational Activities
This organization strives to end negative stereotyping of Hispanics and to educate the public about the plight of Latin Americans.

Cuban American National Council
(300 SW 12th Avenue, Third Floor, Miami, Florida 33130-2038, 305 642-3484)

Organization, Scope and Structure
The Cuban American National Council is a private non-profit agency established to identify the economic, social, and educational needs of Cuban Americans and other minorities, and to assist them in their adjustment to American society. Created in 1972, the Cuban American National Council was the first national organization primarily concerned with the improvement of the quality of life of Cuban Americans.

The Cuban American National Council conducts research and policy analysis on issues affecting Cubans in the United States, and provides education, employment and other services to Cuban Americans, and the disadvantaged. The Cuban American National Council initiates economic expansion through community development, and promotes special programs and events in the fields of leadership development, dropout prevention, and multi-ethnic cooperation.

In addition to administering a network of services, the Cuban American National Council develops cooperative relationships with Hispanics, minority and majority groups in order to benefit the entire community.

Advocacy/Socio-educational Activities
Among the Cuban American National Council activities are:
1. Dropout prevention and multi-ethnic cooperation among high school students in Dade County.
2. Little Havana Institute (LHI) and Hialeah Institute (HI) are alternative schools for students at risk.
3. The Computer Literacy Project, Saludos, and Who am I? are three of the innovative in-school programs. The Computer Literacy Project and Saludos, both funded by Dade Community Foundation, promote writing and computer skills, and entrepreneurial skills respectively, through the publication of a student-produced newsletter and a student-operated greeting card business.

4. Summer Internship Program, sponsored by Philip Morris, provides summer internships to Cuban American college students in Miami, New York and Los Angeles.
5. Education for Jobs, funded by the South Florida Employment & Training Consortium, prepares high school dropouts ages 16 to 21 for the world of work. The program provides remedial education classes in preparation for the GED test, and job training leading to employment.

Intercultural Development Research Associates (IDRA)
(5835 Callaghan Road, Suite 350, San Antonio, Texas 78228; 512 684-8180)

Organization, Scope and Structure
Intercultural Development Research Association is a non-profit research and public education organization dedicated to the principle that all children are entitled to an equal educational opportunity. Since its inception in Texas in 1973, IDRA has worked toward eliminating the obstacles that minority, economically disadvantaged, and limited-English-speaking students encounter in schools. IDRA works to promote educational success for students by its involvement in the areas of research, curriculum and materials development, training and technique assistance, and information dissemination.

Advocacy/Socio-educational Issues
Intercultural Development Research Associates objectives includes:
1. Research, Development and Evaluation. Includes research on effective schooling, bilingual education and language programs, technological applications in education, school finance, student assessment and minimum competency testing.
2. Curriculum Development and Dissemination. IDRA follows the process from conceptualization through design and final production of instructional materials.
3. Parent and Community Involvement. Recognizing that parents play a vital role in their children's education, IDRA assists districts in planning programs, developing materials, conducting training, and evaluating community involvement efforts.
4. Dropout Prevention and Recovery. The Center for the Prevention and Recovery of Dropouts at IDRA functions as a clearinghouse of information on such issues as the magnitude of the problem, the cost

of early school leaving, and mechanisms for school/community responses to the problem.

Institute for Puerto Rican Policy
(286 Fifth Avenue, Suite 805, New York, NY 10001-4512; 212 564-1045)

Organization, Scope and Structure

Established in 1982 as a non-partisan and non-profit organization, the Institute for Puerto Rican Policy's work is predicated on an agenda of research, advocacy, and networking. This triple agenda is stimulated by an effort to develop innovative strategies to overcome the many complex problems afflicting the Puerto Rican community in New York City. The Institute is governed by a Board of Directors with members in Puerto Rico and throughout the nation. Angelo Falcon is the Institute's president. The institute publishes studies, a newsletter, "Dialog", and a data note series. It sponsors the National Puerto Rican Policy Network which includes 1500 members. Studies include voter registration and trends among Puerto Ricans and other Hispanics, employment, government policies, and the role of the news media. As the challenges facing the Puerto Rican community in the 1990's continue to grow in magnitude and complexity, the Institute for Puerto Rican Policy will continue to help the community confront them creatively and aggressively.

Advocacy/Socio-educational Activities

The Institute has conducted studies in the areas of Puerto Rican and Hispanic political participation, voter registration trends, election analyses, state and city government employment policies, media coverage of communities, and Hispanic organizations. The Institute's research program starts from the principle that research findings are irrelevant unless applied to concrete goals and objectives. To carry out the advocacy component of its agenda, the Institute makes use of the media and other organizations as platforms to disseminate and publicize its findings, as well as community groups to develop cooperative strategies aimed at social and political change beneficial to the Puerto Rican community and New York City as a whole.

Supporting the research and advocacy components of the Institute are its networking activities. At their center is the Institute-sponsored National Puerto Rican Policy Network, an information-sharing network of over 1,500 professionals and community activists from 24 states, Washington, D. C., and Puerto Rico. These three elements—research, advocacy and networking—and a commitment to increase private and public sector responsiveness to Puerto Rican and Hispanic community needs are the foundations of the Institute for Puerto Rican Policy.

League of United Latin American Citizens (LULAC)
(400 First Street, NW, Suite 721, Washington, DC 20001, 202 628-8516)

Organization, Scope and Structure
With approximately 115,000 members throughout the United States, LULAC is the oldest and largest Hispanic organization in the country. Today it continues to pursue its original purpose of uniting the efforts of civic groups to assist underprivileged and unrepresented Hispanic Americans.

Advocacy/Socio-educational Activities
It provides direct services as well as research on virtually all social, political, and economic issues facing Hispanics. LULAC has trained and found jobs for thousands of Hispanics; has built housing for thousands more; has provided scholarship aid to Hispanic students; has launched programs for youth, women, and the elderly; and has reached out in cooperative alliance with corporate America and other organizations.

Mexican-American Legal Defense and Educational Fund (MALDEF)
(634 S. Spring Street, 11th Floor, Los Angeles, CA 90014, 213 629-2512)

Organization, Scope and Structure
The Mexican-American Legal Defense and Educational Fund was founded in San Antonio, Texas in 1968. It is a national, non-profit organization whose principal objective is to promote and protect the civil rights of Hispanics living in the United States. Throughout the years, MALDEF has been at the forefront of civil rights litigation, setting precedents in many cases and establishing new systems to elect officials, hire employees and educate our children. Today, MALDEF

continues to expand opportunities for Hispanics, allowing them to become full, productive members of our society.

With a national office in Los Angeles, and regional offices in Chicago, San Antonio, San Francisco, and Washington, D. C., MALDEF concentrates on building an awareness among Hispanics of their heritage and issues that affect their lives. It has recognized the need for removing the obstacles preventing Hispanics from actively participating in American society. Those efforts, whether they be class action litigation, community education, or leadership training, have allowed the organization to work within the country's infrastructure to create beneficial solutions.

Advocacy/Socio-educational Activities

Mexican-American Legal Defense & Educational Fund's specific program areas are: education, employment, political access, immigration, and leadership. It administers the Law School Scholarship Program for Mexican-Americans. MALDEF objectives include the following programs:

1. The Education Program ensures equal educational opportunities for Hispanics by gaining equal allocation of school district resources and by maintaining programs that assist students with limited-English-speaking abilities and curb the high Hispanic dropout rate. It also opens the doors to higher education by increasing post-secondary opportunities for Hispanics and eliminating unfair testing.

2. The Employment Program expands job opportunities for Hispanics by eliminating barriers that prevent Hispanics from being hired and from moving into the management ranks, protecting the rights of Hispanic employees under the new immigration law, and challenging English-only rules in the work-place.

3. The Political Access Program enhances Hispanic participation and influence in the political process by replacing discriminatory election systems with those that better serve the Hispanic community and by eliminating voter registration practices that prevent Hispanics from voting.

4. The Immigrants' Rights Program protects the civil rights of Hispanic Americans and the immigrant poor by monitoring the effects of the new immigration law in the work-place and the schools, and by informing the immigrant communities of their rights and responsibilities under the law.

National Association for Bilingual Education (NABE)
(Union Center Plaza, 810 First Street, NE, 3rd Floor, Washington, DC
20002-4205, 202 898-1829)

Organization, Scope and Structure

The National Association for Bilingual Education (NABE) is a
broad-based association founded in 1975 to address the educational
needs of language-minority children, youth and adults. NABE is a non-
profit organization supported by annual dues. An association of
educators, parents, business people, college and university,
paraprofessionals, and other interested individuals with the common
goal of promoting bilingual education for linguistic minority
populations, this organization holds as one of its first priorities the
training of bilingual instructors, administrators, and other personnel.
Members work to improve educational opportunities for language-
minority populations and for all learners in the United States. NABE
members are united by the belief that language pluralism and bilingual
competence in English and other languages benefits the nation and all
its citizens.

Advocacy/Socio-educational Activities

The historical concern of NABE's founders for educational equity
for limited-English-proficient (LEP) learners and other members of
language-minority populations has led to the establishment of the
following goals: (a) ensuring that language-minority students have
equal opportunities for learning the English language and for academic
success; (b) involving language-minority parents in the process of
schooling and in public policy decisions affecting them and their
children; (c) identifying and publicizing exemplary bilingual education
programs; (d) promoting and publishing scholarly research in the fields
of language education and multicultural education; (e) coordinating the
compilation and dissemination of the evidence and knowledge which
supports bilingual education; (f) increasing public understanding of the
importance of language and culture in the education process; and (g)
fostering the establishment of national language policies which meet
the needs of a pluralistic society in an era of global interdependence.
These broad goals are augmented on a yearly basis by the Executive
Board of NABE through the adoption of specific objectives which
guide the work of the organization for the year. One of NABE's
primary goals is to publicize quality bilingual curricula in educational

programs serving all languages and to inform the public of the necessity of such programs.

National Association of Latino Elected and Appointed Officials (NALEO)
(708 G Street, SE, Washington, DC 20003; 202 546-2536)

Organization, Scope and Structure

NALEO is a nonpartisan, non-profit civic affairs research organization concerned with a broad range of issues affecting the Hispanic community, including children in poverty, federal employment of Hispanics, citizenship, and amnesty. NALEO uses the strengths, resources and leadership of Hispanic elected and appointed officials to initiate public policies responsive to the Hispanic community. Its membership includes influential representatives of the Hispanic community—members of Congress, state representatives, mayors and school board members. NALEO is open to all individuals who support non-partisan advocacy on behalf of more than 20 million United States Hispanics. NALEO publications include: *Annual Roster of Hispanic Elected Officials, NALEO National Report*, a free quarterly newsletter and *NALEO Naturalization*, also a free quarterly; and *NALEO Green Sheet.*

Advocacy/Socio-educational Activities

Among the activities carried out by NALEO are:

1. Citizenship projects to increase naturalization rates. Strategies include citizenship workshops, a clearinghouse of citizenship materials, advocacy on behalf of the legal permanent resident, and a toll-free citizenship hot line.
2. Surveys to help change the prevailing stereotypes about Hispanics.
3. Census data involvement—a full count project ensuring that Hispanics are fully counted in the Census.
4. Work with NALEO-elected officials and supporters to fight the negative English-only campaign.
5. Provide information, research and technical assistance to formulate appropriate policies and programs emanating from the AIDS epidemic.

NALEO informs Hispanic voters on issues affecting the Hispanic community and registers Hispanic voters. It maintains a clearinghouse on citizenship materials.

National Coalition of Hispanic Health & Human Services Organizations (COSSMHO)
(1030-15th Street, NW, Suite 1053, Washington, DC 20005; 202 371-2100)

Organization, Scope and Structure
    COSSMHO is a national coalition of organizations and individuals concerned with improving health and social services for Hispanics. Now thirteen years old, COSSMHO has become a multi-disciplinary, cross-cultural (Mexican American, Puerto Rican, and Hispanic American), national membership network involving more than 508 agencies and organizations. It conducts research and functions as an advocate for Hispanic health and social services needs. COSSMHO activities include the publication of *COSSMHO Reporter*, and *COSSMHO AIDS Update*, published monthly.

Advocacy/Socio-educational Activities
    Working jointly with local Hispanic-serving agencies that conduct program operations, culture-specific services and training are provided to Hispanic families, youth, children, and the elderly. An example is Concerned Parents, a national demonstration project developed in 1983, targeted at five sites (Boston, Albuquerque, Los Angeles, Miami, and San Antonio). Parents and extended family members were organized and trained as major prevention resources in reducing the incidence and prevalence of adolescent pregnancy, sexual activity, and associated health and social risks. COSSMHO's Project Hope, operating at eight sites (New Mexico, New Jersey, Arizona, Connecticut, Texas, Nevada, California, and Utah), assists community-based agencies in developing and implementing model programs for runaways and for physically/sexually abused youth. As part of its community child abuse prevention strategy, the La Familia Counseling Center in Sacramento, California, produced a group of bilingual materials. The items included a videotape and study guide for service providers to aid them in understanding the cultural considerations that could affect Hispanic families impacted by child abuse, and *The Child Abuse Bilingual Services Directory*.
    The organization's most recent activities include programs for nationwide Hispanic AIDS education and the establishment of a consortium to encourage research on Hispanic health issues. Materials

for non-Hispanic health providers working in Hispanic communities are currently being field tested.

National Council of La Raza
(810 First St. N. E., Suite 300, Washington, D. C. 20002-4205; 202 289-1380)

Organization, Scope and Structure
A non-profit, tax-exempt organization incorporated in Arizona in 1968, the Council serves as an advocate for Hispanic Americans and as a national umbrella organization for about 100 formal affiliates, and community-based groups which serve 32 states, Puerto Rico, and the District of Columbia, and for other local Hispanic organizations nationwide. The Council is governed by a 29-member Board of Directors who reflect the varied Hispanic population in terms of subgroups and regional representation, and half the elected Board members represent Council affiliates or other constituencies. Raul Yzaguire, the Council's President and Chief Executive Officer, has provided staff leadership since 1974. The Council receives ongoing advice and assistance from its Corporate Advisory Council (CAC), which includes senior executives and liaison staff from 15 major corporations who work with the Council and its network on a variety of cooperative efforts, from education and community health projects to visibility and fund raising. The council works extensively in coalitions with other Hispanic, minority, and mainstream organizations both on specific issues such as education or housing and on broader-scope efforts.

Advocacy/Socio-educational Activities
The National Council of La Raza has played a major role in immigration reform, efforts to increase opportunities for Hispanics to become English-literate, prepared major analyses of Hispanic demographics, education and employment status, focused attention on the growing population of Hispanic elderly, and provided an Hispanic perspective on civil rights enforcement issues such as fair housing. It provides applied research, policy analysis, advocacy on behalf of all Hispanic Americans, and technical assistance and support to Hispanic organizations and officials. La Raza has developed and tested five innovative approaches to improve the educational status of Hispanics,

three of which are designed to address the need of "at-risk" school-aged children. They are:

1. The establishing of after-school and summer academies (such as the Academia del Pueblo) and supplemental educational assistance to prevent academic failure and grade retention of elementary school children.
2. Educational programs (such as Project Success) designed to improve high school completion of junior and senior high school students.
3. Educational and counseling programs (such as Project Second Chance) for Hispanic dropouts.

National Hispanic Scholarship Fund (NHSF)
(P. O. Box 748, San Francisco, CA 94101; 415 892-9971)

Organization, Scope and Structure
The purpose of National Hispanic Scholarship Fund (NHSF) is to assist Hispanic American students in completing their higher education. The National Hispanic Scholarship Fund provides scholarships for undergraduate and graduate students of Hispanic background. Applicants must be United States citizens or permanent residents of the United States who have Mexican American, Puerto Rican, Cuban, Caribbean, Central American, or South American heritage and who attend a college in the United States.

Advocacy/Socio-educational Activities
NHSF has awarded more than $6.4 million in scholarships to over 9,600 National Hispanic Scholarship Fund Scholars. NHSF scholarships are available on a competitive basis to undergraduate and graduate Hispanic students.

National Puerto Rican Forum
(31 East 32nd St., New York, NY 10016; 212 685-2311)

Organization, Scope and Structure
The Forum is a national organization with offices in six states serving Puerto Ricans who reside on the mainland. The national headquarters is located in New York City, with branch offices in Hartford, Connecticut, Cleveland, Ohio, Chicago, Illinois, Miami, Florida and Philadelphia, Pennsylvania.

Advocacy/Socio-educational Activities

The Forum offers a variety of employment and training programs, advocacy for local Hispanic communities, representation before hearings and local manpower councils, and research. Its goal is to ensure that public funds legislated for the programs are distributed according to the proportionate representation of local ethnic eligibles and used as mandated to assist disadvantaged Hispanics.

Other services of the Forum include the provision of business development and expansion by ethnic entrepreneurs and placement of professionals. The Career Skills Job Placement Program conducts outreach and enrichment of eligible applicants, job development and job placement.

Puerto Rican Legal Defense and Education Fund (PRLDEF)
(99 Hudson Street, 14th Floor, New York, NY 10013; 212 219-3360)

Organization, Scope and Structure

Puerto Rican Legal Defense and Education Fund was created in 1972 to protect and further the rights of Puerto Ricans and other Hispanics. It is a non-profit organization that challenges discrimination in housing, education, employment, health, and political participation. PRLDEF's efforts are carried out through two major programs: legal advocacy and legal education assistance.

Some of PRLDEF's accomplishments include: (a) expanding employment opportunities for Puerto Ricans and other minorities in the New York City Police, Fire and Sanitation departments; (b) establishing bilingual education programs for thousands of Latino and other non-English-speaking children in the school systems of New York and other cities; (c) creating greater public and private housing opportunities for Puerto Rican and other Latinos in the Northeast and Midwest; and (d) increasing Latino voter participation and empowerment in New York, New Jersey and Pennsylvania. PRLDEF is expanding its legal services and developing means to publicize its services more widely.

Advocacy/Socio-educational Activities

PRLDEF has helped Puerto Ricans and other Hispanics by guaranteeing bilingual and special education and political participation as well as remedies for discriminatory housing and employment practices. PRLDEF offers the following programs:

1. The Legal Education and Training Division. It ensures future equality by increasing the number of Latino and other minority students entering the legal profession. The work in this division falls into the categories of admission counseling and professional development.
2. Admissions and counseling. PRLDEF offers the following services: educating students about their choice of law schools; helping students develop successful applications through personal essay workshops as well as LSAT and GAPSFAS courses; hosting a Law Day so that applicants can meet admissions officers from law schools around the country; and awarding limited financial aid for qualified students.
3. Professional development. The Legal Education and Training Division provides law students and young lawyers with legal work experience through internships in addition to other job listings maintained in its job bank.
4. Placement service for Hispanic lawyers. It offers advice and financial assistance to Hispanics considering entering the legal field. Its programs offer recruitment and orientation of law students, scholarships and financial aid, and summer internships. A pilot mentor program pairs current law students with recent graduates for support and assistance.

Organizational Directory

Child, Youth and Family Advocacy

Arawak Consulting Corporation
210 East 86th St.
New York, NY 10028
(212) 737-9685

Aspira of New York, Inc.
332 East 149th Street
Bronx, NY 10451
(212) 292-2690

Asociaciones Dominicanas, Inc.
142 West 42nd Street
New York, NY 10036
(242) 202-4500

Casa del Pueblo
1459 Columbia Road, NW
Washington, DC 20009
(202) 332-1082

Casita Maria
928 Simpson Street
Bronx, NY 10459
(212) 589-2230

CEDEN Family Resource Center
1631 East Second Street
Building A-B, Austin, Texas
78702

Centro de la Comunidad
109 Blinman St.
New London, CT 06320
(203) 442-4463

Chicanos Por La Causa, Inc.
112 East Buckeye Road
Phoenix, AZ 85034
(602) 257-0700

Circulo de la Hispanidad
54 West Park Ave.
Long Beach, NY 11561
(516) 889-3831

Coalition of Cuban Professionals
742 S. E. 8th Street
Suite 205
Miami, FL 33135
(305) 858-3433

Coalition of Florida Farmworkers
Organizations (COFFO)
P.O. Box 326
Homestead, FL 33090
(305) 246-0357

Committee for Hispanic Children
and Families, Inc
140 West 22nd St., Suite 302
New York, NY 10011
(212) 206-1090

Connecticut Association for
United Spanish Action, Inc.
(C.A.U.S.A.)
3580 Main Street
Hartford, Connecticut 06106
(203) 549-4046

Cuban National Planning Council
(CNPC)
300 S. W. 12th Avenue, 3rd.
Floor
Miami, FL 33130
(305) 642-3484

District of Columbia Commission
on Latino Community
Development
(CLCD)
1801 Belmont Road, NW
Washington, DC 20009
(202) 673-6772

Family Focus West Town
1450 Chicago Avenue
Chicago, Illinois 606622

Family Resource Coalition
230 North Michigan Avenue
Chicago, Illinois 60601

Florida Commission on Hispanic
Affairs
Executive Office of the
Governor, The Capitol

Tallahassee, Fl 32399-0001
(904) 579-9000

Foundation for the Advancement
of Hispanic Americans
P.O. Box 66012
Washington, DC 20035
(202) 866-1578

Greater Washington Ibero-
American Chamber of Commerce
1000 T. Jefferson Street, NW
Washington, DC 20007
(202) 737-2676

Hacer, The Hispanic Women's
Center
611 Broadway
New York, N.Y. 10012
(212) 254-1444

Hispanic Advocacy and Resource
Center
1170 Broadway, Suite 805
New York, NY 10001
(212) 410-4220

Hispanic Affairs and Resource
Center
15 Main Street
Asbury Park, New Jersey 07712
(201) 774-3282

Hispanic Information Center
270 Passaic St.
Passaic, New Jersey 07055
(201) 779-7022

Hispanic Multipurpose Service
Center
45 East 21 St.
Paterson, New Jersey 07504
(201) 684-3320

Hispanic Policy Development
Project (HPDP)
250 Park Avenue South
New York, NY 10003
(212) 529-9323

Hispanic Women's Council of
California
5803 E. Beverly Boulevard
Los Angeles, CA 90022
(213) 725-1657

Hispanic Youth Action Center
815 Penbroke St.
Bridgeport, Connecticut 06608
(203) 576-8381

Hispanic Youth Organization
2312 Mickle Street
Camden, New Jersey 08105
(609) 964-4802

Hunt's Point Multi-Service
Center
630 Jackson Ave.
Bronx, NY 10451
(212) 993-3000

Institute for Puerto Rican Policy
Network
286 Fifth Avenue, Suite 804-5
New York, N.Y. 10001-4512
(212) 564-1075

IPRUS Institute
c/o Culturelink
220 E. 23rd. Street Suite 505
New York, NY 10010-4606
(212) 725-2240

Kansas Advisory Committee on
Hispanic Affairs (KACHA)
1309 S. W. Topeka Boulevard
Topeka, KS 66612-1894
(913) 296-3465

Ladies Committee for Puerto
Rican Culture
494 Hopkinson Ave.
Brooklyn, NY 11212
(718) 345-4775

Latin American Research and
Service Agency (LARASA)
899 Logan Street, Suite 400
Denver, CO 80203
(303) 839-8300

Latino Institute
228 S. Wabash Street, 6th Floor
Chicago, IL 60604
(312) 663-3603

Latino Issues Forum (LIF)
1535 Mission Street
San Francisco, CA 94103
(415) 552-3152

Latino Organization Atlantic City
417 Atlantic Ave.
Atlantic City, New Jersey 08401
(609) 348-5877

Latino Youth Development, Inc.
155 Ominor St.
New Haven, Connecticut 06519
(203) 776-3649

Maryland Commission on
Hispanic Affairs
Saratoga Street Center
Office 254
311 W. Saratoga Street
Baltimore, MD 21201
(301) 333-2532

Mexican & American Foundation
1446 Front Street, Suite 203
San Diego, CA 92101
(619) 232-1010

Mexican-American Women's
National Association (MANA)
1201-16th Street, NW, Suite 230
Washington, DC 20036
(202) 822-7888

National Alliance of Spanish-
Speaking People for Equality
(NASSPE)
1701-16th Street, NW, Suite 601
Washington, DC 20009
(202) 234-8198

National Association of Latino
Elected Officials
708 G Street, S.E.
Washington, DC 20003
(202) 546-2536

National Concilio of America
41 Sutter Street, Suite 1067
San Francisco, CA 94104
(415) 550-0785

National Conference of Puerto
Rican Women (NACOPRW)
5 Thomas Circle, NW
Washington, DC 20005
(202) 387-4716

National Hispanic Institute
P.O. Box 220
Maxwell, TX 78656
(512) 357-6137

National Latinas Caucus (NLC)
853 Broadway, 5th Floor
New York, NY 10003
(212) 673-7320

National Puerto Rican Coalition
1700 K Street, N.W., #500
Washington, DC 20006
(202) 223-3915

National Puerto Rican Forum, Inc
159 Washington St.
Hartford, Connecticut 06106
(203) 247-3227

National Puerto Rican Forum, Inc
31 E. 32nd Street, 4th Floor
New York, NY 10016
(212) 685-2311

National Puerto Rican-Hispanic
Voter Participation Project, Inc.
6 North 186th St.
Brooklyn, NY 11211
(718) 787-3910

Nevada Hispanic Services, Inc.
190 E. Liberty Street
P.O. Box 11735
Reno, NV 89501
(702) 786-6003

New Jersey Office of Hispanic
Affairs
Department of Community
Affairs
101 S. Broad Street
Trenton, NJ 08625
(609) 984-3223

New York State Governor's
Office for Hispanic Affairs
Executive Chamber
2 World Trade Center, Suite
5777
New York, NY 10047
(212) 587-2266

Office of Hispanic Affairs
92 Bassett Highway
Dover, New Jersey 07801
(201) 366-4770

Office of Hispanic Affairs
163 Prospect St.
Passaic, New Jersey 07055
(201) 473-2303

Ohio Commission on Spanish
Speaking Affairs
77S. High Street, 18th Floor
Columbus, OH 43266-0323
(614) 466-8333

Oregon Commission on Hispanic
Affairs
695 Summer Street, NE
Salem, OR 97310
(503) 373-7397

Oregon Council for Hispanic
Advancement (OCHA)
621 S. W. Morrison, Suite 729
Portland, OR 97205
(503) 228-4131

Pennsylvania Governor's
Advisory Commission on Latino
Affairs
Forum Building, Room 379-80
Harrisburg, PA 17120
(717) 783-3877

Plaza Family Support Center
4018 City Terrace Drive
Los Angeles, CA 90063

Program Inc.
304 Park Avenue South
Suite 312
New York, NY 10010
(212) 982-1677

Puerto Rican Association for
Community Organization
392 Manila Ave.
Jersey City, NJ 07302
(201) 963-8282

Puerto Rican Association for
Human Development
100 First St.
Perth Amboy, New Jersey 08861
(201) 442-1081

Puerto Rican Congress of New
Jersey
515 S. Broad Street
Trenton, NJ 08611
(609) 989-8888

Puerto Rican Education and
Cultural Center
444 Hopkinson Ave.
Brooklyn, NY 11212
(718) 345-4775

Puerto Rican Family Institute
116 West 14th St
New York, NY 10011
(212) 924-6820

Puerto Rican Organization for
Community Education and
Economic Development, Inc.
815 Elizabeth Ave.
Elizabeth, NJ 07201
(201) 351-7727

Puerto Rican Unity for Progress
427 Broadway
Camden, NJ 08103
(609) 541-1418

QUEST International Center
537 Jones Road
Granville, OH 43023

Spanish Action Council
629 South Main St.
Waterbury, CT 06706
(203) 756-2220

Spanish Community Center
303 Summer St.
Landsville, NJ 08326
(609) 697-2967

Spanish-Speaking Community of
Maryland, Inc.
8519 Piney Branch Road
Silver Spring, MD 20901
(301) 587-7217

State of Michigan Commission
on Spanish-Speaking Affairs
611 W. Ottawa, North Tower
P.O. Box 30026
Lansing, MI 48909
(517)373-8339

State of Minnesota Spanish
Speaking Affairs Council
506 Rice Street
St. Paul, MN 55103
(612) 296-9587

State of Nebraska Mexican
American Commission
P.O. Box 94965
Lincoln, NE 68509-4965
(402) 471-2791

State of Utah Governor's Office
on Hispanic Affairs
Department of Community and
Economic Development
Room 6234
Salt Lake City, UT 84114
(801) 538-3045

State of Wisconsin Governor's
Council on Hispanic Affairs
Governor's Office
819 N. 6th Street, Room 270
Milwaukee, WI 53203
(414) 227-4344

The Family Resource Coalition
(FRC)
230 N. Michigan Ave.
Suite 1625
Chicago, IL 60601

The Youth Project
1000 Wisconsin Avenue, NW
Washington, D. C. 20007
(202) 865-1596

Washington Commission on
Hispanic Affairs
1515 S. Cherry Street
Olympia, WA 98504
(206) 753-3159

Welfare Rights Network
514 54th St.
Brooklyn, NY 11220
(718) 492-5719

Education

American Association for Higher
Education (AAHE) Hispanic
Caucus
University of Texas
San Antonio, TX 782885
(512) 691-4110

Arizona Association of Chicanos
for Higher Education (AACHE)
P. O. Box 24261
Tempe, AZ 85285
(602) 423-6163

Asociacion Politica de Habla
Espanola/Spanish
Speaking/Surnamed Political
Association, Inc.
1461 Valencia Street
San Francisco, CA 94110
(415) 648-3686

Association of Hispanic Affairs
in Private Colleges and
Universities
817 W. 34th Street
Los Angeles, CA 90089-2991
(213) 743-5374

Association of Mexican-
American Educators (AMAE)
P. O. Box 1155
Pico Rivera, CA 90660
(213) 942-1500

AVANCE
1226 NW 18th Street
San Antonio, Texas, 78207

Bilingual Private Schools
Association (BIPRISA)
2660 S. W. 17th Street
Miami, Fl 33145
(305) 643-3507

Caribbean Cultural Center
408 W. 58 St.
New York, NY 10019
(212) 307-7420

Center for Prevention and
Recovery of Dropouts;
Intercultural
Development Research
Association
5835 Callaghan, Suite 350
San Antonio, Texas 78228
(512) 684-8180

Centro de Estudios
Puertorriquenos
Hunter College/CUNY
695 Park Ave.
New York, NY 10021
(212) 772-5695

Colorado Institute for Hispanic
Education and Economic
Development
1006-11th Street, Box 220
Denver, CO 80204
(303) 556-4436

Committee for a Multilingual
New York
c/o Puerto Rican Legal Defense
and Education Fund
99 Hudson Street, 14th Floor
New York, NY 10013
(212) 365-5361

Congreso Nacional de Asuntos
Colegiales (CONAC)
2717 Ontario Road, NW,
Suite 200
Washington, DC 20009
(202) 387-3300

El Concilio de El Paso
English-Plus Task Force
1220 N. Stanton
El Paso, TX 79902
(915) 544-4421

ERIC Clearinghouse on
Language and Linguistics, Center
for Applied Linguistics
1118 22nd Street, NW
Washington, DC 20034
(202) 687-6045

Hispanic Association of Colleges
and Universities (HACU)
411 S.W. 24th Street
San Antonio, TX 78207
(512) 433-1501

Hispanic Higher Education
Coalition (HHEC)
20 F Street, NW, Suite 108
Washington, DC 20001
(202) 638-7339

Inter-University Program for
Latino Research
Hunter College
695 Park Avenue
New York, NY 10021
(212) 772-5695

Iowa Spanish-Speaking Peoples
Commission
Lucas State Office Building
Des Moines, IA 50319
(515) 281-4080

Joint National Committee for
Languages
20 F Street, N.W., Fourth Floor
Washington, DC 20001
(202) 783-2211

Latin American Educational
Foundation (LAEF)
303 W. Colfax Avenue,
Suite 825
Denver, CO 80204
(303) 893-0656

Los Ninos
1330 Continental Street
San Ysidro, CA 92073
(619) 661-6912

Mexican-American Legal
Defense and Educational Fund
(MALDEF)
1430 K Street, N.W., #700
Washington, DC 20005
(202) 628-4074

Multicultural Education,
Training, and Advocacy (META)
50 Broadway, Suite 401
Somerville, MA 02145
(617) 628-2226

Museo del Barrio
1230 Fifth Avenue (at 104th
Street)
New York, NY 10029
(212) 831-7272

National Association for Chicano
Studies (NACS)
History Department
Santa Clara University
Santa Clara, CA 95053
(408) 554-4782

National Clearinghouse for
Bilingual Education
1118 22nd Street NW
Washington, DC 20035
(1-800) 321 NCBE

National Coalition of Advocates
for Students
100 Boylston Street, #737
Boston, MA 02116
(617) 357-8507

National Hispanic Psychological
Association (NHPA)
P.O. Box 451
Brookline, MA 02146
(617) 266-6336

National Hispanic Scholarship
Fund (NHSF)
P.O. Box 748
San Francisco, CA 94101
(415) 892-9971

National Institute for Resources
in Science and Engineering
(RISE)
4302 Star Lane
Rockville, MD 20852
(301) 770-1437

National Institute for Multi-
Cultural Education (NIME)
844 Grecian Avenue, NW
Albuquerque, NM 87107
(505) 344-6898

Nevada Association of Latin
Americans (NALA)
323 N. Maryland Parkway
Las Vegas, NV 89101-3134
(702) 382-6252

Office of Bilingual Education
and Minority Language Affairs
(OBEMLA)
US Department of Education
Washington, DC 20208
(202) 732-5075

Puerto Rican Latino Round-Table
c/o Centro de Estudios
Puertorriquenos
Hunter College
695 Park Avenue
New York, NY 10021
(212) 772-5691

Puerto Rican Organization to
Motivate, Enlighten and Serve
Addicts, Inc.
1776 Clay Ave.
Bronx, NY 10457
(212) 299-1100

REFORMA: The National
Association to Promote Library
Services to the Spanish-Speaking
American Library Association
50 E. Huron Street
Chicago, IL 60611
(312) 323-4400

Segundo Ruiz Belvis Neighbor
FCC
545 East 142nd St.
Bronx, NY 10454
(212) 579-4000

Solidaridad Humana
107 Suffolk St.
New York, NY 10022
(212) 260-4080
(212) 505-2262

Stop English Only
Hostos Community College
500 Grand Concourse
Bronx, NY 10451
(212) 960-1338

Texas Dropout Informational
Clearinghouse
609 Shoal Creek Boulevard,
Suite 200
Austin, Texas 78701

United Bronx Parents
773 Prospect Ave.
Bronx, NY 10455
(212) 991-7100

Health

Chicano Mental Health
Associates
P.O. Box 90428
San Jose, CA 95109

Community United for the
Rehabilitation of the Addicted,
Inc.
61 Lincoln Park
Newark, NJ 07102
(201) 622-3570

Crossroads, Inc.
48 Howe Street
New Haven, Connecticut 06511
(203) 865-3541

Field Orientation Center for
Underprivileged Spanish
443 Broad St.
Newark, NJ 07102
(201) 624-2528

Hispanic Counseling Center
80 North Franklin St.
Hempstead, NY 11550

Hispanic Health Council
98 Cedar St.
Hartford, Connecticut 06106
(203) 527-0856

Hispanics AIDS Forum
140 West 22nd St., Suite 301
New York, NY 10011
(212) 463-8264

Hot Line Cares, Inc.
2037 Third Ave.
New York, NY 10029
(212) 831-7050

Inter American College of
Physicians and Surgeons
1511 K Street, NW, Suite 311
Washington, DC 20005
(202) 628-0834

La Clinica Hispana
690 Howard Ave.
New Haven, Connecticut 06519

La Raza AIDS/SIDA Center
810 First Street, N.E, Suite 300
Washington, D. C. 20002-4205

Latino Caucus of the American
Health Association
KFF, 2400 Sand Hill Road
Menlo Park, CA 94025
(415) 854-9400

Latino Caucus of the American
Health Association
Department of Sociology
Pan American University
Edinburgh, TX 78539

LUZ Social Services, Inc.
2717 Ontario Road, NW,
Suite 200
Washington, DC 20009
(202) 232-7373

Mobilization for Youth Health
Services, Inc.
199 Avenue B
New York, NY 10009
(212) 254-1456

National Association of Hispanic
Nurses (NAHN)
2300 W. Commerce Street,
Suite 304
San Antonio, TX 78207
(512) 226-9743

National Hispanic Council on
Aging (NHCOA)
2713 Ontario Road, NW
Washington, DC 20009
(202) 265-1288

SER-Jobs for Progress National,
Inc.
1355 River Bend Drive,
Suite 240
Dallas, TX 75247
(214) 631-3999

Society of Spanish Engineers,
Planners and Architects (SSEPA)
P. O. Box 75
Church Street Station
New York, NY 10007
(212) 292-0970

South Bronx Mental Health
Council, Inc.
781 East 142nd St.
Bronx, NY 10454
(212) 993-1400

Immigration

Central American Refugee
Committee (CRECEN)
6020 Dashroad
Houston, TX
(713) 661-3937

Immigration Counseling Center,
Inc.
6001 Gulf Freeway
Building C-6 Suite 164
Houston, TX 77023
(713) 924-6045

Migrant Education Council
Education Commission of the
States
1860 Lincoln Street, Suite 300
Denver, CO 80295

Migrant Legal Action Program,
Inc. (MLAP)
2001 S Street, NW, Suite 310
Washington, DC 20009
(202) 462-7744

National Immigration, Refugee
and Citizenship Forum
227 Massachusetts Avenue, N.E.,
Suite #120
Washington, DC 20002
(202) 544-0004

National Migrant Referral Project
(NMRP)

2512 S. IH-35, Suite 220
Austin, TX 78704
(512) 447-0770

Refugee Service Center
CAL, 1118 22nd Street, NW
Washington, DC 20037
(202) 429-9292

Youth Labor

United Farmworkers of America
(UFW)
P.O. Box 62
Keene, CA 93531
(805) 822-5571

Tomas Rivera Center (TRC)
710 N. College Avenue
Claremont, CA 91711
(714) 625-6607

Society of Spanish Engineers,
Planners and Architects (SSEPA)
P.O. Box 75
Church Street Station
New York, NY 10007
(212) 292-0970

Hispanic Labor Committee
200 East 116th St.
New York, NY 10029
(212) 996-9222

Comite de Apoyo Trabajadores
Agricolas
P.O. Box 458
Glassboro, NJ 08028
(609) 881-2507

CAFE de California (Chicano
Advocates for Employment)
1012 J Street, 2nd. Floor
Sacramento, CA 95814
(916) 448-9016

Consumer Action Program of
Bedford Stuyvesant
815 Broadway
(718) 388-1601

East Harlem Community
Corporation
103 East 106th St.
New York, NY 10029
(212) 427-0500

Greater Washington Ibero
American Chamber of Commerce
1000 T. Jefferson Street, NW
Washington, DC 20007
(202) 737-2676

Hispanic American Career
Education Resources
611 Broadway, Room 812
New York, NY 10012
(212) 254-1444

Hispanic Business Alliance
(HBA)
P. O. Box 32043
Detroit, MI 48232
(313) 256-5104

Latin American Educational
Foundation (LAEF)
303 W. Colfax Avenue,
Suite 825
Denver, CO 80204
(303) 893-0656

Latin American Manufacturers
Association (LAMA)
419 New Jersey Avenue, SE
Washington, DC 20003
(202) 546-3803

Latin Business Association
(LBA)
5400 E. Olympic Boulevard,
Suite 237
Los Angeles, CA 90022
(213) 721-4000

Latin Chamber of Commerce of
U.S.A. (CAMACOL)
1417 W. Flager Street
Miami, Fl 33135
(305) 642-3870

Mexican-American Unity
Council (MAUC)
2300 W. Commerce Street,
Suite 300
San Antonio, TX 78207
(512) 226-3335

National Hispanic Business
Group (PAC)
67 Wall Street, Suite 2509
New York, NY 10005
(212) 238-9803

National Hispanic Coalition of
Federal Aviation Employees
14324 Lemoli Avenue, #13
Hawthorne, CA 90250
(213) 297-1830

National Hispanic Corporate
Council (NHCC)
P.O. Box 52085
Phoenix, AZ 85072-2085
(602) 9527747

Society of Hispanic Professional
Engineers (SHPE)
5400 E. Olympic Boulevard,
Suite 225
Los Angeles, CA 90022
(213) 725-3970

TELACU-The East Los Angeles
Community Union
5400 E. Olympic Boulevard,
Suite 300
Los Angeles, CA 90022
(213) 721-1655

U.S. Hispanic Chamber of
Commerce (USHCC)
4900 Main Street, Suite 700
Kansas City, MO 64112
(816) 531-6363

REFERENCES

Alatis, J. E. (1987). The early history of TESOL. *TESOL Newsletter, 21* (2), 4–6.

American Council on Education (1985). *Minorities in higher education.*Washington, D.C.: American Council on Education.

American Council on Education (1989). *Minorities in higher education.* Washington, D.C.: American Council on Education.

American Medical Association (1987). TB among Hispanics—leads from the MMWR. *Journal of the American Medical Association, 258* (12), 1583.

Anderson, N., & Rodriguez, O. (1984). Conceptual issues in the study of Hispanic delinquency. *Fordham University Hispanic Research Center Bulletin, 7* , 1–2, 2–5.

Anderson, R.E. (1986). Access of Hispanics to health and cut in services: A state of the art overview. *Public Health Reports, 10*(3), 238–252.

Andrade, S. J. (1983). *Latino families in the United States: A resource book for family life education.* New York: Planned Parenthood Federation of America Inc.

Applehome, P. (1987). Educators alarmed by growing rate of dropouts among Hispanic youth. *New York Times*, pp. B1, B3.

Arfa, F. (1981). Intestinal parasites among Indochinese refugees and Mexican immigrants resettled in Costa Contra County California. *Journal of Family Practice, 12*(2), 223–226.

Arias, B. M. (1986). The context of education for Hispanic students: An overview. *American Journal of Education, Special Issue, 95*(1), 26–57.

Aspira of New York. (August 29, 1974). *Decision accompanying Consent Decree.* 72 Civ. 4002 S.D.N.Y.

Astin, A. W. (1982). *Minorities in American higher education.* San Francisco, CA.: Jessey-Bass Publishers.

Astin, A. W. (1984). *The American freshman: National norms for Fall 1984.* Washington, D.C.: American Council on Education.

Astin, H. S., & Burciaga, C. P. (1981). Chicanos in higher education: Progress and attainment. Los Angeles: Higher Education Research Institute.

Avom, J. O. (1987). Latino families and health. *Family Resource Coalition Report, 6*(2)1.

Baca, L.M. & Cervantes, H.T. (1989). *The bilingual special education interface.* Columbus, Ohio: Merrill Publishing Company.

Banks, J. A. (1982). Educating minority youth: An inventory of current theory. *Education and Urban Society, 15*, 88–103.

Baratz-Snowden, J., & Duran, R. (1987). *The educational progress of language minority students: Findings from the 1983–84 NAEP reading survey.* Princeton, New Jersey: Educational Testing Services.

Barrera, M. (1979). *Race and class in the southwest.* Notre Dame, Ind.: University of Notre Dame.

Barrios, E. E., Mullay, K., Goldstein, J.C. D., & Munoz, E. (1987). Hypertension in the Hispanic and black community in New York City. *Journal of the National Medical Association, 79*(7), 740–752.

Becerra, R. M., Kamo, M., & Escobar, J. I. (1982). *Mental health and Hispanic Americans: Clinical perspectives.* New York: Green & Stratton, Inc.

Bennett, W. J. (1988). *The condition of bilingual education in the nation: 1988.* Washington, D.C.: Government Printing Office.

Bilingual Education Act. (1968). 20, U.S.C. 880(b) (1968) Washington, D. C.

Binkin, N. J., Rust K. R., & Williams, R. L. (1988). Racial differences in neonatal mortality: What causes of death explain the gap. *American Journal of Diseases of Children, 142*(4), 434–440.

Bonilla, F., & Campos, R. (1986). *Industry and idleness.* New York: Centro de Estudios Puertorriquenos, City University of New York.

Bray, D. (1984). Economic development: The middle class and international migration in the Dominican Republic. *International Migration Review, 18,* 217–236.

Brown v. Board of Education of Topeka (1954). 347 U.S. 483,745. Ct.686, 91 Led .8.

Brown, D. (1980). *Principles of language learning and teaching.* Englewood Cliffs, New Jersey: Prentice-Hall.

Brown, G. H., Rosen, N. L., Hill, S. T., & Olivas, M. H. (1985). *The condition of education for Hispanic Americans.* Washington, D.C.: Government Printing Office.

Bryant, C. A. (1982). Impact of kin, friend and neighbor networks on infant feeding practices—Cubans, Puerto Rican and anglo families in Florida. *Social Science and Medicine, 16,* 1757–1765.

Caban-Ramos, R.N. (1984). Attitudes of Puerto Rican college students towards seeking professional help for psychological difficulties. Unpublished doctoral dissertation, Ohio State University, Ohio.

Caetano, C. (1984). Acculturation and drinking patterns in northern California: Abstract. In United States Department of Health and Human Services, *Report of the Secretary's Task Force on black and minority health issues* (Volume 8, p. 62). Washington, D.C.: Government Printing Office.

Caetano, C. (1987). Acculturation and drinking patterns among United States Hispanics. *British Journal of Addiction, 82* (7),789–799.

Calabrese, R. L. (1988).The structure of schooling and minority dropout rates. *The Clearing House, 61* (7), 325–328.

California State Department on Education (1984). *Studies on immersion education: A collection for United States educators.* Sacramento, CA: State Department of Education.

Canino, I. A. (1982). The Hispanic child: Treatment considerations. In R. M. Becerra, M. Karno, & J. L. Escobar (Eds.), *Mental health and Hispanic Americans: Clinical perspectives* (pp. 159–168). New York: Grune and Stratton.

Canino, I. A. E. (1982). *The Puerto Rican child in New York City: Stress and mental health.* New York: Fordham University Hispanic Research Center.

Cardenas, J.A., Robledo M., & Waggoner, D. (1988). *The undereducation of America youth.* San Antonio, TX: Intercultural Development Research Association.

Cardoso, L.A. (1980). *Mexican emigration to the United States, 1897– 1931: Socio-economic patterns.* Tuscon: University of Arizona Press.

Carrasquillo, A., & Carrasquillo, C. (1979). *The Neorican: Unwelcomed in two worlds.* New York: Ediciones Puerto Rico de Autores Nuevos.

Castro, A. L. (1980). Bilingual programming: A viable alternative in corrections. In United States Department of Justice, *National Hispanic conference on law enforcement and criminal justice* (pp. 87–108). Washington, D.C.: Inter American Research Associates Inc.

Center for Disease Control. (1987). Child bearing patterns among Puerto Rican Hispanics in New York City and Puerto Rico. *Mortality and Morbidity Weekly Reports, 36* (3), 34–41.

Center for Disease Control. (1989). *AIDS weekly surveillance report.* Washington, D. C.: Government Printing Office.

Chaney, E. M. (1985). *Migration from the Caribbean region: Determinants and effects of current movements.* Washington, D.C.: Georgetown University, Center for Immigrants Policy and Refugee Assistance.

Chomsky, N. (1965). *Aspects of a theory of syntax.* Cambridge, MA: The MIT Press.

Coleman, J. S., Campbell, E. O., Hobson, C. J., Weinfield, F. S., & York, R.L. (1966). *Equality of educational opportunity.* Washington, D.C.: United States Office of Education.

Comas-Diaz, L. (1982). Mental health needs of Puerto Rican women in the United States. In R.E. Zambrana (Ed.), *Work, family and health: Latina women in transition* (pp. 1–10). New York: Fordham University Hispanic Research Center.

Crawford, J. (1989). *Bilingual education: History, politics, theory and practice.* Trenton, NJ: Crane Publishing Co.

Croipps, J.D. (1980). *The relationship between family life satisfaction and job satisfaction for employed Hispanic and anglo women.* Lubbock, TX: Texas Technical University.

Cummins, J. (1989). Empowering minority students. Sacramento, California: California Association for Bilingual Education.

Cummins, J. (1984). *Bilingualism and special education: Issues in assessment and pedagogy.* San Diego, CA: College-Hill Press.

Davis, C., Haub, C., & Willette, J. (1983). *U.S. Hispanics: Changing the face of America.* Washington, D. C.: Government Printing Office.

De la Torre, A. (1988). Bilingual education in the United States: Issues and resources. Unpublished manuscript, National Education Association, Washington, D. C.

De la Zerda, N., & Hooper, R. (1979). Employment interviewers' reactions to Mexican American speech. *Communication Monograph, 46,* 126–134.

Delson, L.C. (1985). Intra-ethnic, intra-cultural variations and similarities among Hispanics in the USA: Implications for patient compliance and health care provider education. Unpublished doctoral dissertation, University of Massachusetts, Amherst, Massachusetts.

Diaz, R. F. (1983). Thought and two languages: The impact of bilingualism on cognitive development. In E. W. Gordon (Ed.), *Review on Research in Education* (vol. 10, pp. 23–54). Washington, D.C.: American Educational Research Association.

Diaz-Briquets, D. (1986). *Conflict in Central America: The demographic dimension.* Washington, D. C.: Popular Reference Bureau.

Divoky, D. (1988). The model minority goes to school. *Phi Delta Kappan, 70* (3), 219–222.

Dolbeare, C. N., & Canales, J. A. (1988). *Hispanic housing crisis.* Washington, D.C.: National Council of La Raza.

Duran, R.P. (1983). *Hispanics' education and background: Predictions of college achievement.* New York: College Entrance Examination Board.

Edelman, M. (1984). Exploratory study on delinquency and delinquency avoidance in the South Bronx. *Fordham University Hispanic Research Center Bulletin* (7),10–13.

Elias-Olivares, L. (1983). *Spanish in the United States setting*. Rosslyn, VA: Inter America Research Associates.

Escobedo, L. G., & Remington, P. L. (1989). Birth control analysis of the prevalence of cigarette smoking among Hispanics in the United States. *Journal of the American Medical Association, 26*(1), 66–69.

Escutia, M. M., & Prieto, M. (1986). Hispanics in the workforce, Par. 1. Unpublished manuscript, National Council of La Raza, Washington, D. C.

Family Court Act, Section 712A-751.

Farber, A., & Rogler, H. L. (1981). *Unitas: Hispanic and black children in a healing community*. New York: Fordham University Hispanic Research Center.

Fernandez, R.R., & Velez, W. (1989). Who stays? Who leaves?: Findings from the Aspira five cities high school dropout study. Washington, D.C.: The Aspira Institute for Policy Research.

Finn, J. D. (1989). Withdrawing from school. *Review of Educational Research, 59* (2), 117–1421.

Fitzpatrick, J. (1982). Transition to the mainland. In E. Cordasco & E. Buchioni (Eds.), *The Puerto Rican community and its children on the mainland* (pp. 59–57). Metuchen, NJ: The Scarecrow Press, Inc.

Foner, N. (Ed.). (1987). *New immigrants in New York*. New York: Columbia University Press.

Ford Foundation (1982). *Not working: Unskilled youth and displaced adults*. New York: Ford Foundation, Office of Reports.

Ford Foundation (1983). *Child survival/Fair start*. New York: Ford Foundation, Office of Reports.

Ford Foundation (1984). *Hispanics: Challenges and opportunities. A working paper for the Ford Foundation.* New York: Ford Foundation, Office of Reports.

Ford Foundation (1989). *The common good: Social welfare and the American future.* New York: Ford Foundation, Office of Reports.

Frank, B. (1983). *Drug use among tenants of single room occupancy (SRO) hotels in New York City.* New York: New York State Division of Substance Abuse Services.

Gallagher, P. (1980). *The Cuban exile.* New York: Academic Press.

Gandara, P. (1986). Chicanos in higher education: The politics of self interest. *American Journal of Education, 9* (1), 256–272.

Garcia, J. A. (1981). *Hispanic job search effort in the United States.* (Final Report to the U.S. Department of Labor. Employment and Training Administration). Madison, WI: University of Wisconsin, Department of Rural Sociology.

Garcia, R. (1985). *Access to health care and other social indicators for Latinos in Chicago.* Chicago, IL.: Latino Institute.

Gayle, H. D. (1987). Malnutrition in the first two years of life: The contributions of low birth weight to population estimates. *American Journal of Diseases of Children, 141*(5),531–534.

Gould, W., MacManus, W., & Welch, F. (1982). *Hispanic earnings differentials: The role of English language proficiency.* Santa Monica, CA: Union Research Corporation.

Grassmuck, S. (1985). The consequences of Dominican urban outmigration for national development: The case of Santiago. In S. Sanderson (Ed.), *The Americans in the new international division* (pp. 145–176). New York: Holmes and Meier.

Gross, J. (1987a, August 27). The most tragic victims of AIDS: Thousands of victims. *New York Times,* Sec. 2, p. 5:1.

Gross, J. (1987b, July 17). Women who carry the virus for AIDS: Poor, isolated and often unaware. *The New York Times*, Sec 2, p. 4:1.

Grossman, H. (1984). *Educating Hispanic students*. Springfield, IL: Charles C. Thomas.

Guendelman, S., & Schwalbe, J. (1986). Medical care utilization by Hispanic children: How does it differ from black and white peers. *Medical Care*, 24(10), 925–940.

Gurak, D., & Kritz, M. (1982). Settlement and immigration processes of Dominicans and Colombians in New York City. Paper presented at the annual meeting of the American Sociological Association, San Francisco, California.

Gurak, D.T., Smith, D. A., & Goldson, M. F. (1982). *The minority foster child: A comparative study of Hispanic black and white children*. New York: Fordham University Hispanic Research Center.

Hall, E. T. (1976). *Beyond culture*. New York: Anchor Press.

Havighurst, R. J. (1978). Structural aspects of education and cultural pluralism. *Educational Research Quarterly*, 2(4), 5–19.

Hayes-Bautista, D. E., Schink, D. E., Werner, O., & Chapa, J. (1984). The growing Latino population in an aging American society: Policy issues in the emergence of an age-race stratified society. *Social Policy*, 15, 1.

Hazuda, H. P. (1986). Differences in socioeconomic status and acculturation among Mexican Americans and risk of cardiovascular disease. In United States Department of Health and Human Services, *Report of the Secretary's Task Force on black and minority health* (Vol. 4 pt. 2, pp. 367–390). Washington, D.C.: Government Printing Office.

Hendricks, G. (1977). *The Dominican diaspora*. New York: Teachers College Press.

Institute for Puerto Rican Policy (1989). *Towards a Puerto-Rican-Latino agenda for New York City.* New York City: Institute for Puerto Rican Policy.

Irigoyen, M., & Zambrana, R. C. (1982). The utilization of pediatric health services by Hispanic mothers. In R. E. Zambrana (Ed.), *Work, family and health: Latina women in transition* (pp. 63–73). New York: Fordham University Hispanic Research Center.

Jaffe, A. J., Cullen, R. M., & Boswell, T. D. (1980). *The changing democracy of Spanish Americans.* New York: Academic Press.

Jenkins, S., Sauber, M., & Friedlander, E. (1985). *Ethnic associations and services to new immigrants in New York City.* New York: Community Council of Greater New York.

Johnson, C. (1985). *Direct federal job creation: Key issues.* Washington, D.C.: Government Printing Office.

Johnston, W.B., & Parker, A. E. (1987). *Workforce 2000: Work and workers in the 21st century.* Indianapolis, IN: Hudson Institute.

Kraley, E.P. (1987). U. S. immigration policy and the immigrant populations of New York. In N. Foner (Ed.), *New immigrants in New York* (pp. 35–78). New York: Columbia University Press.

Krashen, S., & Biber, D. (1988). *On course: Bilingual education's success in California.* Sacramento, California: California Association for Bilingual Education.

Kumanyika, S. K. (1986). Ischemic heart disease risk factors in Hispanic Americans. In United States Department of Health and Human Services, *Report of the Secretary's Task Force on black and minority health.* (Vol. 4. Pt. 2, *Cardiovascular disease*, pp. 393–412). Washington, D.C.: Government Printing Office.

Lau vs. Nichols (1974). 414 U. S. 563.

Leavitt, J., & Kritz, M. (1989). *Three immigrant groups in NYC and human services: Dominicans, Haitians and Colombians.* New York: Community Council of New York.

Lee, V. (1985). *Access to higher education: The experience of blacks, Hispanics and low socioeconomic whites.* Washington, D.C.: American Council on Education.

Lyons, J. (1989). *Legal responsibilities in education agencies serving national origin language minority students.* Washington, D. C.: The American University.

Macias, R. R., & The Tomas Rivera Center. (1989). Bilingual teacher supply and demand in the U.S. Unpublished manuscript. University of Southern California. Center for Multicultural Research, California.

Maldonado, E. (1979). Contract labor and the origin of Puerto Rican communities in the United States. *International Migration Review, 13,* 103–121.

Maldonado, L.A. (1985). Altered states: Chicanos in the labor force. In W. A. Van Hornme, & T. V. Tonnessen (Eds.), *Ethnicity and the labor force* (pp. 145–166). Madison, WI: University of Wisconsin Systems.

Marcos, L. R., Murray, A., Urcuyo, L.K., & Kessdman, M. (1973). The effect of interview language on the evaluation of psychopathology in Spanish-American schizophrenic patients. *American Journal of Psychiatry, 133,* 549–553.

Marshall, R., Brings V. M., Jr., & King, A. V. (1984). *Labor economics.* Homewood, Ill.: Richard D. Irwin.

Mascola, L. (1984). Congenial syphilis: Why is still occurring? *Journal of the American Medical Association, 252* (13), 1719–1722.

Mass, L. (1985). *Medical answers about AIDS.* New York: Gay Men's Health Crisis.

Massachusetts Institute of Technology (1990). *Education that works: An action plan for the education of minorities.* Cambridge, MA: Quality Education for Minority Project.

Matute-Bianchi, M. E. (1986). Ethnic identities and patterns of school success and failure among Mexican-descendent and Japanese-American students in a California high school: An ethnographic analysis. *American Journal of Education, 1,* 233–255.

McCormick, M. C. (1985). The contribution of low birth weight to infant mortality and childhood morbidity. *New England Journal of Medicine, 312,* 82–90.

McGee, E. A. (1982). *Too Little, too late: Series for teenage parents. A working paper.* New York: Ford Foundation, Office of Reports.

Melendez, E., & Rodriguez, C. (1988). Puerto Ricans in the northeast and the changing economy: A summary of research issues. *Dialogo, 5,* 1–8.

Melville, M. (1988). Hispanics, class or ethnicity. *The Journal of Ethnic Studies, 16*(1), 67–83.

Mercado, A. L. (1986). The awareness and identification of socio-cultural factors in the initial assessment of the Puerto Rican family in child welfare. Unpublished doctoral dissertation, Fordham University, Graduate School of Social Work, New York.

Mercer, J. J. (1973). *Labelling the mentally retarded.* Los Angeles, CA: University of California Press.

Miranda v. Arizona (1976). U.S. 436 at 467.

Molina, R. M. (1987). Body size, fatness and leanness of Mexican-American children in Brownsville, Texas: Changes from 1973–1983. *American Journal of Public Health, 77*(5), 573–557.

Moore, J. L., & Pachon, H. (1985). *Hispanics in the United States.* Englewood Cliffs, New Jersey: Prentice-Hall, Inc.

Munoz, E., Lecca, P. J., & Goldstein, J. D. (1988). *A profile of Puerto Rican health in the United States: Data from the Hispanic Health and Nutrition Examination Survey.* Arlington, Texas: Health Services Research.

National Advisory and Coordinating Council on Bilingual Education. (1988). *Bilingual education: Twelfth annual report.* Washington, D.C.: Government Printing Office.

National Assessment of Educational Progress (1986). *The writing report card: Writing achievement in American Schools* (Report 15-W- 02). Washington, D. C.: Government Printing Office.

National Clearinghouse for Bilingual Education. (1989a). Educating refugees. *NCBE Forum, 12*(3), 1–4.

National Clearinghouse for Bilingual Education. (1989b). Reducing school dropouts among LEP students. *NCBE Forum, 12*(5), 1 & 3.

National Coalition of Hispanic Health and Human Services Organization. (1989). *AIDS: A guide for Hispanic leadership.* Washington, D. C.: National Coalition of Hispanic Health and Human Services Organization.

National Commission for Employment Policy (1982). *Hispanics and jobs: Barriers to progress.* Washington, D. C.: National Commission on Employment Policy.

National Commission on Secondary Schooling for Hispanics (1984). *Make something happen: Hispanics and urban high school reform* (Vol.1). Washington, D. C.: Hispanic Policy Development Project.

National Council of La Raza (1986a). *Beyond Ellis Island: Hispanics— immigrants and Americans.* Washington, D. C.: National Council of La Raza.

National Council of La Raza (1986b). *Hispanic youth employment: Establishing a knowledge base.* Washington, D.C.: U.S. Department of Labor.

National Council of La Raza (1987). *The Hispanic elderly: A demographic profile.* Washington, D.C.: National Council of La Raza.

National Council of La Raza (1989a). *Falling through the cracks: Hispanic underrepresentation in the Job Training Partnership Act.* Washington, D. C.: National Council of La Raza.

National Council of La Raza (1989b). *Getting started: Becoming part of the AIDS solution.* Washington, D. C.: National Council of La Raza.

National Employment of Fall Employment. (November, 1987). Focus on Hispanic Youth. *Jobs Impact, 7*(8), 1–3.

National Hispanic Center for Advanced Studies and Policy Analysis (1982). *The state of Hispanic America.* Oakland, CA: The National Hispanic Center.

New York City Department of Health (1986). *Summary of vital statistics—1984.* New York: New York City Department of Health.

New York State Education Department (1988a). *Evaluation of the implementation of the Regents Action Plan, Second Annual Report.* New York: State Education Department.

New York State Education Department (1988b). *Racial/ethnic distribution of public school students and staff.* New York: Information Center on Education.

New York State Education Department (1988c). *Successful schooling for the at-risk student.* New York: State Education Department.

New York State Education Department (1988d). *The New York Report: A blueprint for learning and teaching.* New York: New York State Education Department.

O'Hare, W. (1987). *America's welfare population: Who gets what.* Washington, D. C.: Population Reference Bureau.

Office of Assistant Secretary of Defense (1982). *Profile of American youth: 1980 Nationwide Administration of the Armed Services Vocational Aptitude Battery.* Washington, D.C.: Government Printing Office.

Office of Educational Research and Improvement (1987). *Dealing with dropouts: The urban superintendent call to action.* Washington, D.C.: Government Printing Office.

Olfield, G. (1983). *Public school desegration in the United States, 1960–1980.* Washington, D. C.: Center for Political Studies.

Olivas, M. A. (1981). *Research on Hispanic education: Students, finance and governance* (Program Report No. 81-B11). Stanford, CA: Institute for Research on Educational Finance and Governance Stanford University.

Olivas, M. A. (Fall, 1982). Federal education policy: The case of Hispanics. *Educational Evaluation and Policy Analysis, 4,* 305.

Olivas, M. A. (1986). *Latin college students.* New York: Teacher College Press.

Olivas, M. A., Crown, G. H., Rosen, N., & Hill, S. (1980). *The condition of education for Hispanic Americans.* Washington, D.C.: National Center for Education Statistics.

Ortiz, A. A. (1988). Evaluating educational contexts in which language minority students are served. *Bilingual Special Education Newsletter, 7,* 1, 3, 7.

Ortiz, A. A., & Polizoi, E. (1988). Language assessment of Hispanic learning disabled and speech and language handicapped students: Research in Progress. In A. Ortiz and B. Ramirez (Eds.), *Schools and the culturally diverse exceptional student: Promising practices and future directions* (pp. 3–44). Reston, VA: The Council for Exceptional Children.

Orum, L. (1986). *The education of Hispanics: Status and implications.* Washington, D.C.: National Council of La Raza.

Orum, L.S. (1988). *Making education work for Hispanic Americans: Some promising community-based practices,* Mimeographed manuscript, National Council of La Raza. Washington, D. C.

Orum, L., & Vincent A. (1984). *Selected statistics in the education of Hispanics.* Mimeographed, Washington, D. C.: National Council of La Raza.

Ovando, C. O., & Collier, V. P. (1985). *Bilingual and ESL classrooms: Teaching in multicultural contexts.* New York: McGraw-Hill Book Company.

Oxford-Carpenter, R., Pol, L., Lopez D., Stupp, P., Gendell, M., & Peng, S. (1984). *Demographic projections of non-English language background and limited English proficient persons in the United States to the year 2000 by state, age, and language group.* Rosslyn, VA: National Clearinghouse for Bilingual Education.

Padilla, E. R., Padilla, A. M., & Morales A. (1979). Inhalant marijuana, and alcohol abuse among barrio children and adolescents. *International Journal of Addiction, 14,* 945–964.

Payan, R., Flores, V., Paterson, R., Romero, I., & Warren, J. (1982). *Hispanics in higher education in the southwest: A three part program on research on attitudes, access, and achievement: Research prospectives.* Berkeley, CA: Educational Testing Services.

Peal, E., & Lambert, W. E. (1962). The relationship of bilingualism to intelligence. *Psychological Monographs, 76,* 1–23.

Perez-Stable, E. (1987). Issues in Latino health care. *West Journal of Medicine, 146,* 213–218.

Pessar, P. (1987). The Dominicans: Women in the household and the garment industry. In N. Foner (Ed.), *New immigrants in New York* (pp. 104–129). New York: Columbia University Press.

Pifer, A. (1979). *Bilingual education and the Hispanic challenge.* New York: The Carnegie Corporation.

Plisko, V.W., & Stern, J.D. (1985). *The condition of education. 1985 edition*. Washington, D.C.: National Center for Educational Statistics.

Poma, P. A. (1987). Pregnancy in Hispanic women. *Journal of the National Medical Association, 79*(9), 929–935.

Portes, A., & Bach, R.L. (1985). *Latin journey: Cuban and Mexican immigrants in the United States*. Berkely: CA: University of California Press.

Pottinger, S. J. (1970, May 25). *Memorandum to school districts with more than five percent national-origin minority group children regarding identification of discrimination and denial of services as the basis of national origin*. Washington, D. C.: Office of Civil Rights.

Powell, K. E. (1984). Recent trends in TB in children. *Journal of the American Medical Association, 251*(10),1289–1292.

Preyo, A. M. (1980). Family headship and drug addicts among the male Puerto Rican youths: An investigation of quality of family life. Unpublished doctoral dissertation, Fordham University, New York.

Quest International (1987). *Celebrating differences: Approaches to Hispanic youth development*. Grenville, OH: Quest International.

Ramirez, A.A. (1985). *Bilingualism through schooling: Cross-cultural education for minority and majority students*. Albany, New York: SUNY Press.

Ramist, L., & Albeiter, S. (1984). *Profiles, college bound seniors*. New York: College Entrance Examination Board.

Rodriguez-Fraticelli, C. (Summer, 1989). Puerto Ricans and CUNY: Twenty years after open admissions. *Centro de Estudios Puertorriquenos Bulletin* (6), 22–31.

Rogers, M. F., Thomas, P. A., Staicher, T. E., Noa, M. C., Rush, T. J., & Jaffe H. W. (1987). Acquired immune deficiency syndrome in children: Report of the Center for Disease Control National Surveillance, 1982 to 1985. *Pediatrics, 79*(6), 1008–1014.

Rogler, L., Schweitzaer, A., Schroeden, E., & Early, B. (1982). A new conceptual framework for mental health clinical service research on Hispanic populations. *Fordham University Hispanic Research Center Bulletin,* 4–5(1), 1–11.

Rosenwaike, I. (1987). Mortality differentials among persons born in Cuba, Mexico, and Puerto Rico residing in the United States. *American Journal of Public Health, 77*(5), 603–606.

Roth, D. (1984). *Hispanics in the United States: A brief examination.* Washington, D.C.: Government Printing Office.

San Juan Star (1988, December 15). Broad bilingual aid program settles segregation suit, p. 22.

San Miguel, J. G. (1987). Bilingual education policy development: The Reagan years, 1980–87. *NABE Journal, 12*(2), 97–109.

San Miguel, J. G. (June, 1984). Conflict and controversy in the evolution of bilingual education policy in the United States: An interpretation. *Social Science Quarterly, 65,* 505–518.

Sanderfur, G. D., & Tienda, M. (1988). *Divided opportunities: Minorities, poverty and social policy.* New York: Plenum Press.

Santiago, R. (1985). Understanding bilingual education—or the sheep in wolf's clothing. *Educational Leadership, 43 (1),* 79–83.

Santiago-Santiago, I. (1986). Aspira vs. Board of Education revisited. *American Journal of Education, 95*(1),149–199.

Santos, R. (1977). An analysis in earnings among persons of Spanish origin in the Mid-West. Unpublished doctoral dissertation, Michigan State University.

Santos, R. (1985). *Hispanic youth: Emerging workers.* New York: Praeger.

Sapir, E. (1921). *Language: An introduction to the study of speech.* New York: Harcourt Brace Co.

Seda Bonilla, E. (1975). Qué somos? *The Rican, 2,* 81–107.

Sherman, J., Celebuski, C., Fink, L., Levine, A., & St. John, E. (1987). *Dropouts in America: Enough is known for action.* Washington, D. C.: The Institute for Educational Leadership.

Shiono, P. H., Klebanoff, M.A., Graubard, B. I., Berendes, H. W., & Rhodas, G. G. (1986). Birth weight among women of different ethnic groups. *Journal of the American Medical Association, 255*(1), 48–52.

Sissons, P. L. (1979). *The Hispanic experience of criminal justice.* New York: Fordham University Hispanic Research Center.

Smith, P., & Wait, P.B. (1986). Adolescent fertility rates and childbearing trends among Hispanics in Texas. *Texas Medicine, 82,* (11), 29–32.

Spolsky, B. (1978). Language and bicultural education. *Educational Research Quarterly, 2*(4), 20–25.

Steinberg, L., Blende, N., & Chan, K. (1984). Dropping out among language minority youth. *Review of Educational Research, 54*(1), 113–132.

Stolzenberg, R.M. (1982). *Occupational differences between Hispanics and non-Hispanics.* Santa Monica, CA: The Rand Corporation.

Strother, D. (1986). Dropping Out. *Phi Delta Kappan, 67,* 325–328.

Suarez-Orozco, M. (1989). *Central American refugees and U.S. high schools.* Stanford, CA: Stanford University Press.

Sutton, C. R., & Chaney, E. M. (1987). *Caribbean life in New York City: Sociocultural dimensions.* New York: Center for Migration Studies of New York, Inc.

Texas Education Agency. (1989). *Report on 1987-88 public school dropouts.* Austin, TX: Texas Education Agency.

Thomas, P. (1974). When I was a little muchacho. *Civil Rights Digest,* 6(2), 13–14.

Time Magazine (October 16, 1978). *Hispanic Americans, soon the biggest minority,* 112(16), 48, 61.

Torres-Saillant, S., & Hernandez, R. (1989). Dominicans in Puerto Rico and the United States: Points of Review. *A Journal of Marginal Discourse 2,* (1).

Trevino, F. (1986). National statistical data systems and the Hispanic community. In United States Department of Health and Human Services, *Report of the Secretary's Task Force on Black and Minority health.* (Hispanic Health Issues, Vol. 8, pp. 45–52). Washington, D. C.: Government Printing Office.

Trevino, F., & Moss, A. J. (1984). *Health indicators in Hispanic, black, and white Americans.* Hyattsville, MD: U. S. Dept. of Health and Human Services, Public Health Service; National Center for Health Statistics.

Tucker, G. R., & Gray, T. C. (1980). The pursuit of equal opportunity. *Language and Society, 2,* 5–8.

Ugalde, A., Bean, F., & Cardenas, G. (1979). International migration from the Dominican Republic: Findings from a national survey. *International Migration Review, 18,* 1021–1044.

United States Bureau of the Census (1980). *Percentage of households owner occupied, 1980.* Washington, D. C.: Government Printing Office.

United States Bureau of the Census (1982). *U.S. Census of the population, 1980: Persons of Spanish origin by state* (Supplementary Report no. PC 30-SI). Washington, D. C.: Government Printing Office.

United States Bureau of the Census (1984). *Conditions of Hispanics in America today.* Washington, D. C.: Government Printing Office.

United States Bureau of the Census (March, 1985). *Persons of Spanish origin in the United States.* (Series P-20 No. 405). Washington, D. C.: Government Printing Office.

United States Bureau of the Census (November, 1986). *Projections of the Hispanic population: 1983–2000.* (Series P-25). Washington, D.C.: Government Printing Office.

United States Bureau of the Census (1988a). *Fertility of American women: June 1987* (Current Population Reports, Series p-20, No. 427). Washington, D. C.: Government Printing Office.

United States Bureau of the Census (September 7, 1988b). *Hispanic educational attainment highest ever.* United States Department of Commerce News.

United States Bureau of the Census (1988c). *Money and poverty status in the United States: 1987* (Current Population Reports, Series p-60, no. 161). Washington, D. C.: Government Printing Office.

United States Bureau of the Census (1988d). *The Hispanic population in the United States: March 1988.* (Advance Report, Series P-20, No. 431). Washington, D.C.: Government Printing Office.

United States Department of Education (1980). *High schools and beyond.* Washington, D.C.: Government Printing Office.

United States Department of Education, National Center for Education Statistics (1982). *Fall enrollment in colleges and universities.* Washington, D. C.: Government Printing Office.

United States Department of Education (1984). *The condition of education: A statistical report, 1984 edition.* Washington, D.C.: Government Printing Office.

United States Department of Education (1988). *The Condition of bilingual education in the nation.* Washington, D.C.: Government Printing Office.

United States Department of Health and Human Services (1984). *Health indicators for Hispanic, black and white Americans* (DHHS Pub. No. PHS 84-1576). Hyattsville, MD: National Center for Health Statistics.

United States Department of Health and Human Services (1985a). *Health status of minorities and low income groups* (DHHS, Pub No. HRS-P-DV 85-1). Hyattsville, MD: Government Printing Office.

United States Department of Health and Human Services (1985b). *Report of the Secretary's Task Force on black and minority health: Executive summary* (Vol. 1). Washington, D. C.: Government Printing Office.

United States Department of Health and Human Services (1986a). *Health status of the disadvantaged chartbook* (DHHS, Pub. No. HRS-P-DV86-2). Washington, D. C.: Government Printing Office.

United States Department of Health and Human Services (1986b). *Prevention of disease disability and death in blacks and other minority groups.* Washington, D. C.: United States Government Printing Office.

United States Department of Health and Human Services (1989). *Arthropometric data and prevalence of overweight Hispanics: 1982-84* (DHHS, Pub. No. 89-1689). (Series 11, No. 1989). Washington, D. C.: Government Printing Office.

United States Department of Justice (October, 1988). *1987 Statistical yearbook of the Immigration and Naturalization Service.* Washington, D.C.: Government Printing Office.

United States Department of Labor (1981). *Employment and training report of the President*. Washington, D. C.: U.S. Government Printing Office.

United States General Accounting Office (1987a). *Bilingual education: A new look at the research evidence*. Washington, D. C.: Government Printing Office.

United States General Accounting Office (1987b). *Bilingual education: Information on limited English proficient students*. Washington, D. C.: Government Printing Office.

United States House of Representatives (1983). *Hearings before the Subcommittee on Postsecondary Education on the Committee on Education and Labor, 98th Congress, First session*. Washington, D. C.: Government Printing Office.

Valadez, C. (1986). Effective teachers for language minority students, national needs. In *Compendium of papers on the topic of bilingual education* (Report of the Committee on Education and Labor, Serial no. 99-R. 99th Cong., 2nd session, pp. 82–105). Washington, D.C.: Population Reference Bureau.

Valdivieso, R., & Davis, C. (1988). *U.S. Hispanics: Challenging issues for the 1990s*. Washington, D. C.: Government Printing Office.

Vega, W. A., Kalody B., & Warkeit, G. (1985). Psychoneuroses among Mexican Americans and other whites: Prevalence and caseness. *American Journal of Public Health, 75*(5), 523–527.

Velez, C. N. (1981). Drug use among Puerto Rican youth: An exploration of generational status differences. Unpublished doctoral dissertation, Columbia University, New York.

Veltman, J. C. (1988). *The future of the Spanish language in the United States*. Washington, D.C.: Hispanic Policy Development Project.

Vernon, S. W., & Roberts, E. R. (1982). Prevalence of treated and untreated psychiatric disorders in three ethnic groups. *Social Science and Medicine, 16*(17), 1575–1582.

Villarreal, S. F. (1986). Current issues in Hispanic health. In United States Department of Health and Human Services, *Report of the Secretary's Task Force on Black and Minority health* (pp. 11–42). Washington, D.C.: Government Printing Office.

Wagenheim, K. (1970). *Puerto Rico: A Profile.* New York: Praeger.

Waggoner, D., & O' Mally J. (1984). Teachers of limited English proficient children in the U.S. *NABE Journal, 9*(3), 25–42.

Washington, V., & Harvey, W. (1989). Affirmative rhetoric, negative action: African-American and Hispanic faculty at predominantly white institutions. *Clearinghouse on Higher Education, 2,* 1–2.

Washington, V., & La Point, V. (1988). *Black children and American institutions: An ecological review and resource guide*: New York: Garland Publishing, Inc.

Weller, S.C., & Clairborne, C.I. (1986). Personal preferences and ethnic variations among anglo and Hispanic breast and bottle feeders. *Social Science and Medicine, 23*(6), 539–548.

Weyer, T. (1988). *Hispanic U.S.A.: Breaking the melting pot.* New York: Harper & Row.

Wilson, W. (1987). *The truly disadvantaged: The inner city underclass and public policy.* Chicago: Chicago University Press.

Wong-Fillmore, L. & Valadez, C. (1986). Teaching bilingual learners. In M. C. Wittrock, *Handbook of research in training* (pp. 648–685). New York: MacMillan Publishing Co.

Wright, A. L., Holberg, C., Taussig, L.M., & Group Health Medical Associates Pediatricians. (1988). Infant feeding practices among middle class Anglos and Hispanics. *Pediatrics, 82* (3 pt 2), 496–503.

Zambrana, R. E. (Ed.) (1987). W*ork, family and health: Latina women in transition.* New York: Fordham University Hispanic Rsearch Center.

ANNOTATED BIBLIOGRAPHY

American Council on Education (1989). *Minorities in higher education.* Washington, D.C.: American Council on Education.

An annual report on the progress of African Americans, Hispanics, Asian Americans and Indians in post-secondary education. Despite the efforts of some institutions and a number of states to expand access to higher education for underrepresented racial and ethnic groups, very little progress is presented in available statistical data.

Arias, M. B. (1986). The education of Hispanic Americans: A Challenge for the future. *American Journal of Education,* 95 (1).

This issue provides a picture of Hispanic children in schools. It summarizes national statistics of particular sub-groups, includes studies of individual regions and contains an in-depth examination of individual schools.

Aspira Association, Inc., Institute for Policy Research (1989). *Facing the facts: Hispanic dropouts in ten urban communities.* Washington, D.C.: Aspira Association, Inc.

Latino students continue to lag behind academically, obtaining lower grade point averages and dropping out of school at higher rates than any other major ethnic group.

Bean, F. D., & Tienda, M. (1987). *The Hispanic population in the United States.* New York: Russell SAGE Foundation.

This book uses the statistical yield of the 1980 census to analyze major changes and trends in American life. It describes significant social, economic, and demographic developments revealed by the decennial censuses.

Becerra, R. M., Kamo, M., & Escobar, J. (1982). *Mental health and Hispanic Americans: Clinical perspectives.* New York: Green & Stratton, Inc.

Addresses distinct Hispanic population groups as well as specific diagnostic categories on the mental health process of diagnosis, treatment and rehabilitation of Hispanic populations. The book emphasizes the continuing need to translate practical experience into practical policies, programs and resource allocations to insure that public activities enhance and promote the life of Hispanics.

Blea, I. (1988). *Toward a Chicano social science.* New York: Praeger Publishers.

Presents an overview of the nature and character of Mexican Americans in United States. It surveys their culture, their values, and their major social institutions and how they function in a minority relationship to the dominant Anglo society.

Borjas, G. L., & Tienda M. (1985). *Hispanics in the U. S. economy.* New York: Academic Press.

The studies in this volume provide insights into areas where appropriate policy could improve the status of Hispanics in the United States . For example, limited education rather than discrimination in the labor market is a chief cause of low wages. Why do Hispanic youth have so little schooling? The book addresses several policies to address the problem.

Cardenas, J. A., Robledo, M., & Waggoner, D. (1988). *The undereducation of America youth.* San Antonio, TX: Intercultural Development Research Association.

This booklet provides information on young people ages 6–12, from the 1980 census in the context of trend data through 1985. Examination of risk and other factors which may be related to the differences between the state rates of members of the same minority groups suggests more effective interventions to keep youth in school.

Carrasquillo, A., & Carrasquillo, C. (1979). *The Neorican: Unwelcomed in two worlds*. New York: Ediciones Puerto Rico de Autores Nuevos.

Social and educational agencies in both Puerto Rico and in the United States have inadequately dealt with Puerto Rican youth. Education, language and employment are the greatest handicaps to the adjustment of mainland Puerto Ricans in Puerto Rico.

Carrasquillo, A., & Sandis, E.E. (1984). *Schooling, job opportunities and ethnic mobility among Caribbean youth in the United States*. New York: Equitable Life Assurance Society.

A collection of papers concentrating on the interplay of schooling and job opportunities for Caribbean youth. The concentration on the interplay of schooling and job opportunities is a radical departure from the conventional focus on the role of education as the primary vehicle of class mobility.

Chicano Mental Health Association. (October, 1988). *An alarming state of affairs*. San Jose, CA: ESO Printing and Graphics.

It describes the over representation of Latino youth in the Juvenile Justice System and the lack of essential bilingual/bicultural staff in critical positions within the Probation Department. The study calls for several actions to address the problems experienced by Latino youth.

Collier, V. P., & Wayne P. T. (Fall, 1989). How quickly can immigrants become proficient in school English. *The Journal of Educational Issues of Language Minority Students, 5*, 26–38.

Acquisition of cognitive-academic second language proficiency does not occur quickly but is a developmental process that takes a significant number of years. How many years depends on the student's level of cognitive maturity in the first language and subject mastery in first language schooling.

Cuban American National Council, Inc. (1989). *The elusive decade of Hispanics.* Miami, Florida: Cuban American National Council, Inc.

The Cuban American National Council feels that addressing the question of whether the 1980's were or were not "the decade of Hispanics" serves a useful purpose and should be done suscinctly for the benefit of the general reader.

Cummins, J. (1989). *Empowering minority students. California.* Sacramento: California Association for Bilingual Education.

Programs that succeed in promoting minority students' academic growth develop in students a strong sense of confidence in who they are and in their ability to learn. These programs empower students.

Dolbeare, C. N., & Canales, J. A. (1988). *Hispanic housing crisis.* Washington, D.C.: National Council of La Raza.

It examines the housing characteristics and needs of Hispanic households in the United States, drawing on information contained in the 1980 Census and the 1983 annual housing survey. Housing quality is poor in one out of six Hispanic families.

Escutia, M.M., & Prieto, M. (1986). Hispanics in the workforce. Part I. Unpublished Manuscript. National Council of La Raza, Washington, D. C.

It reviews and summarizes Hispanic demographies and employment status, and assesses the extent to which federal employment and training programs past and present have helped to increase Hispanic employability.

Fernandez, R., Henn-Reinke, K., & Petrovich, J. (1989). *Five cities high school dropout study.* Washington, D.C.: Aspira Association Inc.

The analysis of five cities school dropout study yield 24 common characteristics for four groups of Hispanic ninth grade students enrolled in predominantly minority high schools in major U.S. cities during the 1986–1987 school year.

Fernandez, R. R., & Velez, W. (1989). *Who stays? Who leaves? Findings from the Aspira five cities high school dropout study.* Washington, D.C.: The Aspira Institute for Policy Research.

The major findings of this study suggest that the most important factors in predicting who stays in school among Latino ninth graders are age, grade, school attendance/absence and presence of father.

Finn, J. D. (1989). Withdrawing from school. *Review of Educational Research*, 59, (2), 117–142.

The likelihood that a youngster will successfully complete 12 years of schooling is maximized if he or she maintains multiple, expanding forms of participation in school-relevant activities. The failure of a youngster to participate in school and class activities, or to develop a sense of identification with school, may have significant deteriorative consequences.

Fitzpatrick, J. (1982). Transition to the mainland. In E. Cordasco & E. Buchioni (Eds.), *The Puerto Rican community and its children on the mainland* (pp. 57–59). Metuchen, NJ: The Scarecrow Press, Inc.

This article describes family patterns of transition in the mainland. It discusses transitional patterns in types of ceremonies, marriages and changes in values.

Foner, N. (Ed.). (1987). *New immigrants in New York.* New York: Columbia University Press.

This is a collection of ethnographic essays describing New York City largest groups of immigrants: Dominicans, Jamaicans, Chinese, Haitians, Vincentians, Grenadians, Koreans, and Soviet Jews. In a case study format the author examines the move to New York from the immigrants' perspective, analyzing its effects New York has had on their social and cultural worlds.

Ford Foundation (1982). *Not Working: Unskilled youth and displaced adults*. New York: Ford Foundation, Office of Reports.

A look at the demographic, technological and educational causes of youth and adult unemployment.

Ford Foundation (1983). *Child survival/Fair start*. New York: Ford Foundation, Office of Reports.

A look at the factors threatening the survival, health, and cognitive development of the world's disadvantaged children. It also describes the Ford Foundation's program to help these children get a fair start in life.

Ford Foundation (1984). *Hispanics: Challenges and opportunities: A working paper of the Ford Foundation*. New York: Ford Foundation, Office of Reports.

A look at the demographic, economic, social and political situation of Hispanics in the United States in the 1980's.

Gallagher, P. (1980). *The Cuban exile*. New York: Academic Press.

There are two groups of refugees: the purely political exiles and the upper bourgeoisie. The Cuban boat refugees are described as a separate wave of Cuban refugees, different from the 1960's.

Grossman, H. (1984). *Educating Hispanic students*. Springfield, IL: Charles C. Thomas.

It describes cultural factors which tend to characterize Hispanics living in the United States and the specific ways in which counselors, educators, psychologists and others should modify their techniques when working with Hispanic students and their parents who demonstrate these cultural traits. The authors conclude that: (a) there is a common denominator of Hispanic culture in the United States, (b) Hispanics believe that there is a Hispanic culture in the United States, (c) professional such as counselors, educators and psychologists should be trained to understand the Hispanics' cultural characteristics.

Hakuta, K., Ferdman, B. M., & Diaz, R. M. (1986). *Bilingualism and cognitive development: Three perspectives and methodological implications.* Los Angeles, CA: Center for Language Education and Research, University of California.

A historical perspective shows that many of the apparently contradictory findings about the effects of bilingualism on mental development have stemmed from failure to distinguish between different levels of bilingualism as defined by the different orientations.

Hayes-Bautista, D. E., Schink, D. E., Werner, O., & Chapa, J. (1984). The growing Latino population in an aging American society: Policy issues in the emergence of an age-stratified society. *Social Policy,* 15(1).

A position paper providing a philosophical basis for ways of providing better educational opportunities to Hispanic youth involving their families in their education.

Institute for Puerto Rican Policy. (1989). *Towards a Puerto Rican-Latino agenda for New York City.* New York: Institute for Puerto Rican Policy.

The number of Puerto Ricans and other Latinos in New York City has increased dramatically in the 1980's. Yet, it is apparent that the responsiveness of public policy has continued to lag significantly behind in terms of these communities' growing problems and aspirations.

Johnston, W. B., & Parker, A. E. (1987). *Workforce 2000: Work and workers in the 21st century.* Indianapolis, IN: Hudson Institute.

The book documents labor market trends that have been ongoing for some time—the shift from manufacturing to service employment. It illustrates how the confluence of these trends in the year 2000 poses a serious problem—and opportunities for policy makers.

Krashen, S., & Biber, D. (1988). *On course: Bilingual education success in California*. Sacramento, California: California Association for Bilingual Education.

It includes discussions of theoretical rationale and characteristics of successful programs as well as descriptions of seven schools districts in California.

Lee, V. (1985). *Access to higher education: The experience of blacks, Hispanics and low socioeconomic whites*. Washington, D.C.: American Council on Education.

The decision to attend college continues to be influenced by a student's socioeconomic circumstances.

Lyons, J. J. (1989). *Legal responsibilities in education agencies serving national origin language minority students*. Washington, D.C.: The American University.

This monograph written primarily for school officials and parents is a summary of federal laws establishing the rights of language minority students and defining the responsibilities of school districts serving them.

McGee, E. A. (1982). *Too Little, too late: Series for teenage parents. A working paper*. New York: Ford Foundation Office of Reports.

An examination of some major programs operating in the United States to serve teenage parents and their children, including a look at the range and quality of available services and comments by service providers.

Massachusetts Institute of Technology (1990). *Education that works: An action plan for the education of minorities*. Cambridge, MA: Quality Education for Minority Project.

This plan emphasizes the vital importance of reflecting a minority perspective in the national debate on educational needs and interests of Alaskan native, American Indian, African American, Mexican American and Puerto Rican people in the United States.

Moore, J. L., & Pachon, H. (1985). *Hispanics in the United States.* Englewood Cliffs, New Jersey: Prentice-Hall, Inc.

Offers an analysis of the history and prospects of a fast-growing segment of American society—the Hispanics. The authors point out that a surge of immigration and a high birth rate are contributing to their dominant position among American minorities.

National Association of Latino Elected and Appointed Officials. (1987). *First national conference on Latino children in poverty.* Washington, D.C.: National Association of Latino Elected and Appointed Officials.

This pamphlet summarizes the unique needs of Hispanic children in poverty. Their needs are still being overlooked by the nation's federal policy makers, civic affairs researchers and the media. The Conference proceedings clearly demonstrate that poverty is no longer a biracial issue.

National Association of Latino Elected and Appointed Officials. (1989). English only: The threat of language restrictions. *NALEO Background Paper 10.* Washington, D.C.: NALEO Education Fund.

This report provides information to refute accusations made by language restrictionists. A well-informed public tends to reject efforts to declare English an official language.

National Coalition of Hispanic Health and Human Service Organization (1989). *AIDS: A guide for Hispanic leadership.* Washington, D. C.: National Coalition of Hispanic Health and Human Services Organization.

AIDS has significantly affected the Hispanic community since 1981 when the disease was first detected. The cumulative incidence of AIDS is 2.7 times higher among Hispanics than among non-Hispanics.

National Council of La Raza (1989). *Getting started. Becoming part of the AIDS solution.* Washington, D. C. : National Council of La Raza.

It is a step-by-step guide to help Hispanic community-based organizations get started in AIDS education and prevention activities.

National Council of La Raza (1986). *Beyond Ellis Island: Hispanics Immigrants and Americans.* Washington, D.C.: National Council of La Raza.

Describes the role of Hispanics in American history, including their immigration patterns and experience and recounting their contributions to the United States.

National Hispanic Center for Advanced Studies and Policy Analysis. (1982). *The state of Hispanic America.* (Vol. 1, 2, & 3). Oakland, CA: The National Hispanic Center.

These are three compendiums of essays on issues affecting Hispanics in the United States: census data, economy, education, elderly, immigration, international trade and media.

National Commission for Employment Policy. (1982). *Hispanics and jobs: Barriers to progress.* Washington, D. C.: NCEP.

Hispanic Americans face three barriers to success in the job market: lack of proficiency in English, low levels of formal schooling and discrimination.

National School Boards Association. (1988). *Alcohol and drugs in the public schools: Implications for school leaders.* Alexandria, VA: National School Boards Association.

This monograph presents an update of the facts surrounding adolescent alcohol and drug abuse and provides extensive resources to assist school boards in developing effective school policies addressing the problem.

New York State Education Department (1988). *The New York Report: A blueprint for learning and teaching.* New York: New York State Education Department.

A task force report examining conditions of teaching, teacher preparation and teacher recruitment in New York State. It is reported that the present teaching system is working well for only a small percentage of students.

New York City Inter Agency Task Force on AIDS. (1987). *AIDS in New York City.* New York: City of New York.

The consequences of the AIDS epidemic are catastrophic in terms of loss of life and human suffering. AIDS has surpassed homicide as the leading cause of death among young men, and heart disease among men age 40–44.

O'Hare, W. (1987). *America's welfare population: who gets what.* Washington, D.C.: Population Reference Bureau.

In 1986, the welfare population of the United States consisted of 48 million of people or one fifth of the entire United States population, making welfare reform one of the most volatile issues facing United States policy makers.

Olivas, M. A. (Fall, 1982). Federal education policy: The case of Hispanics. *Educational Evaluation and Policy Analysis, 4,* 305.

It is an analysis of the history and prospects of the Hispanic population in the United States. The author indicates that a surge of immigration and a high birth rate are contributing factors to the dominant position of Hispanics among American minorities. It includes material on the impact of American institutions on Hispanics—the educational, health and mental health care systems, welfare services, criminal justice and immigration.

Ortiz, A. A., & Ramirez, B. A. (1988). *Schools and the culturally diverse exceptional student: Promising practices and future directions*. Reston, VA: The Council for Exceptional Children.

Provides a summary of current research literature on assessment and instruction for language minority handicapped students.

Orum, L. (1986). *The education of Hispanics: Status and implications*. Washington, D.C.: National Council of La Raza.

Provides an overview of the educational status of Hispanics and notes the implications of the data. It includes sections on each of the following: the history of Hispanics in the United States; demographics; school enrollment; educational conditions; literacy and educational conditions of Hispanic adults; postsecondary education and the composition of the teaching force.

Oxford-Carpenter, R., Pol, L., López, D., Stupp, P., Gendell, M., & Peng, S. (1984). *Demographic projections of non-English language background and limited English proficient persons in the United States to the year 2000 by state, age and language group*. Rosslyn, VA: National Clearinghouse in Bilingual Education.

It reports on predictions for non-English-language-background population in the United States across all ages: 28 million persons in 1976 to 30 million in 1980, 34.7 million in 1990 and 39.5 million in the year 2000.

Poma P. A. (1987). Pregnancy in Hispanic women. *Journal of the National Medical Association*, 79, 9, 929–935.

Physicians should be aware of the cultural differences and beliefs when treating pregnant Hispanic women. If these differences are understood and respected, the patient, in turn, will better respect the physicians opinion and advice.

San Miguel, G. (1987). The status of historical research on Chicano education. *Review of Educational Research, 57*, 4, 467–480.

In the mid 1960's, researchers began conducting studies that explored the historical dimensions of the Chicano educational experience in the Southwest. The purpose was to provide a historical description and interpretation of the quality of public school opportunities for children of Mexican descent. This field of professional study is still in its infancy.

Sherman, J., Celebuski, C., Fink, L., Levine, A., & St. John, E. (1987). *Dropouts in America: Enough is known for action.* Washington, D.C.: The Institute for Educational Leadership.

Various strategies designed to keep students in school are discussed in this report. The authors recommend that these strategies begin in the early grades of elementary school and continue through high school. Also discussed are major risk factors associated with the decision to leave school.

Sissons, P. L. (1979). *The Hispanic experience of criminal justice.* New York: Fordham University Hispanic Research Center.

The Hispanic experience of criminal justice system has been a sadly neglected one. The monograph considers the question of whether or not the Hispanic offenders' collective experience is different from that of offenders of other origins while being processed through the criminal justice system.

Stolzenberg, R. M. (1982). *Occupational differences between Hispanics and non-Hispanics.* Santa Monica, California: Rand Corporation.

It focused on occupational attainment of Hispanic male workers. Ethnic differences among Hispanics per sector do not seem to play an important role in Hispanic occupational achievement in the United States. But, schooling, knowledge of English affect occupational achievement.

Suarez-Orozco, M. (1989). *Central American refugees and U.S. high schools.* Stanford, CA: Stanford University Press.

Presents a psychological study of the experience of a group of Central American youth recently arrived to the United States.

Torres-Saillant, S., & Hernandez, R. (Eds.) (1989). Dominicans in Puerto Rico and the United States. *Punto 7 Review: A Journal of Marginal Discourse, 2* (1).

A compilation of essays, poems, and short stories on Dominican migration.

United Way of Tri-State (1988). *Outlook: The growing Latino presence in the Tri-State Region.* New York: United Way of Tri-State.

Latinos have comprised a distinct community in the tri-state region (Connecticut, New Jersey and New York). The rapid growth of the Latino community and the increasing role it will play in the tri-state region's future development must be helped with further human care services.

United States Department of Health and Human Services (1984). *Health indicators for Hispanics, black and white Americans.* (DHHS Pub. No. PHS 84-1576). Washington, D. C.: National Center for Health Statistics.

Data from the Health Interview Survey, the principal source of information on the health of similar, non-institutionalized population of the United States, were compiled for three years to present reliable data on various important health parameters for Hispanics.

United States Department of Health and Human Services. (1986). *Health status of the disadvantaged chartbook.* (DHSS Pub. No HRS-PDV86-2). Washington, D. C.: Government Printing Office.

This book utilizes colored charts and graphs to present extensive data from various sources on the health of various minority groups in the United States including African Americans, Hispanics and Native

Americans. The book's intent is to present the data, and readers can draw their own conclusions.

United States Department of Health and Human Services. (1986). *Report of the Secretary's Task Force on Black and minority health: Hispanic health issues* (Vol. 8). Washington, D. C.: Government Printing Office.

This document begins with several essays on various important topics of Hispanic health. It has an extensive list of abstracts of articles, published in the medical literature dealing with a wide array of Hispanic health issues. At the end, a list of agencies providing health care is included.

United States General Accounting Office (1987). *Bilingual education: A new look at the research evidence*. Washington, D. C.: Government Printing Office.

There is sufficient evidence to support the Bilingual Education Act requirement of the use of the native language to the extent necessary to help language minority students learn English.

Valdivieso, R., & Davis, C. (1988). *U.S. Hispanics. Challenging issues for the 1990s*. Washington, D.C.: U.S. Government Printing Office.

It discusses demographic issues on Hispanics in the United States. The monograph summarizes facts in the areas of Hispanic population groups, education, labor force and political force. According to the authors, the 1990's Census will tell a great deal about the changes that have occurred among Hispanics during the 1980's.

Zambrana, R. E. (1987). *Latina women in transition*. New York: Fordham University Hispanic Research Center.

The anthology provides a critique of the past work on Latina women, particularly Puerto Ricans. It addresses the issues of the special needs of Hispanic families and the changing roles of women within the family.

AUTHOR INDEX

SUBJECT INDEX